Real-Time Relationships

Real-Time Relationships
THE LOGIC OF LOVE

Stefan Molyneux

© 2017 Stefan Molyneux
All rights reserved.

ISBN-13: 9781975653095
ISBN-10: 1975653092

Contents

Real-Time Relationships: The Logic of Love ·1

Culture· ·4

Philosophy and Intimacy ·5

Religious "Reality"· ·7
          Positioning ·9

The Arc of a Relationship ·11
          Caution ·11
          Sex ·13
          The Love Bomb· ·13
          The Plateau ·14
          The Hiccup ·14
          The Descent ·14
          Lying ·15
          Entombment· ·16
          The Aftermath· ·18

Win/Lose ·21

Trust· ·24
          Closure and Self–Trust ·25
          Hedging ·26

- Baggage · · · 27

- Love · · · 29
    - Love and Objectivity · · · 29
    - Love – Compared to What? · · · 30
    - Internal State, or External Fact? · · · 31
    - Love and Pleasure · · · 32
    - Love: A Tentative Definition · · · 32
    - Love as a Response · · · 34

- Love and Virtue · · · 36
    - Love and Honesty · · · 36
    - Love and Courage · · · 37
    - Love and Sustainability · · · 40
    - Love and Security · · · 41
    - Security and Values · · · 42

- Objective Integrity · · · 44

- Why did you choose me if you don't even *like* me? · · · 47
    - "Fixing" the Painting… · · · 48
    - But – we can't change people at all? · · · 49
    - Acceptance and Rejection · · · 53

- Reversing Virtue and Vice · · · 55
    - Virtue and Honesty · · · 56
    - Virtue and Obedience · · · 56
    - The Inevitable Counterattack… · · · 59

- Counterfeiting Virtue · · · 61

- Polarization · · · 62
    - Projection · · · 63

- Zooming Out… · · · 65

- Changing Others · · · 67

Why We Succumb... · 69
    Enabling and the Vengeance of the Slave · · · · · · · · · · · · · · 69
    It's not entirely in the past... · 70
    "You Lack Empathy" · 75
    The horror of chores... · 75
    Nagging and Humiliation · 77
    The Abuse of Assumptions · 78
    You are in fact lazy and selfish..? · 78

The War of Narrative · 82
    Love and Mythology · 82

Feel the Burn! · 85
    Eliminating Responsibility · 86
    No Idea? · 87

Common Stories · 89
    You never support me... · 89
    Assuming you can... · 90
    Lacking Knowledge? · 91
    What on Earth? · 93

The Boxer · 94
    The Relief of Self-Control · 95
    Fleeing the future for the past... · 97

The Sadist · 100
    Child Abuse · 101
    The Child Unafraid... · 104
    The Escalation... · 107
    The Evil At The Core... · 108
    Controlling the Bed · 109

Why is this so important? · 110
    Self–Mythology · 110
    The Crossroads · 111
    Religion and Mythology · 112

The parable of the apple, or how to control a human soul............114

Virtue and Love···**139**

Honesty is the First Virtue ·····································141
    "Not Even Wrong" ··142

Relatedness···144
    Intimacy and Value ······································145
    Reciprocity ··145

Intimacy···147

I Want!···149

Love is a Verb...··152

Social Lies: Love, Power and Manipulation ·············154
    Religion and Anxiety·····································154
    The Pitfalls of Mythology ······························155
    Mythology and the Appearance of Control ·······156
    Statism and Anxiety ····································156
    The State and Society··································157
    The False Answers of Statism ·······················157

Love and Anxiety···159
    Trial by Fire ···159
    False Knowledge and Crime·························161

New York, 2001 ··162
    Empathizing with Vengeance ·······················163
    Hellish Reciprocity·······································165
    Backup Lies···167

Love and Ego Identification ·································168
    The "Stockholm Syndrome"··························169
    Sympathy and Integrity·······························170

- Democracy? ... 172
  - Morality and Victimhood ... 174
  - The Knowledge We Avoid ... 176
- Implosion ... 177
- The Humiliation of Knowledge ... 179
- Anxiety Avoidance and Relationships ... 181
- The Principles of Intimacy ... 183
  - Realities ... 183
- Virtue as "Objective Opinion" ... 186
  - God is Good? ... 187
- Ethics in the Service of Evil ... 190
- Ethical Attacks ... 192
  - Warning Signs ... 193
  - Ethical Mythologies ... 194
  - Cultural Programming and Predictability ... 195
  - Slave-on-Slave Violence ... 196
- Culture and Objectivity ... 198
  - Culture and Science ... 198
  - Culture and Objectivity ... 199
  - What Slaves Really Fear ... 200
- Why We Are Talking About Culture… ... 202
- The Costs of the Truth ... 205
- So – Why Speak? ... 207
- The Goal ... 209

Real-Time Relationships: The Theory · · · · · · · · · · · · · · · · · · · **213**

Thoughts Precede Emotions ·216

Emotions and Control ·218
        Expectations: An Example ·218

Thoughts and Frustration ·222

Choose Your Thoughts, Choose Your Feelings… · · · · · · · · · · · · · · · ·224

The Impossibility of Control… ·226

My Best Friend and My New Girlfriend · · · · · · · · · · · · · · · · ·227

Control versus Curiosity ·229

Using Others ·231
        Catastrophes ·231
        The Truth I Am Avoiding… ·232
        Introducing Myself to Myself… · · · · · · · · · · · · · · · · · · ·235

Anxiety and Control ·237
        The Subtle Tyranny of Inconsistency · · · · · · · · · · · · · · ·238
        The Vengeance of the Slave ·239
        The Dangers of Vengeance ·240

The Slavery of Childhood ·242
        Holding Our Own Chains… ·243

Power and Liberty ·246
        Remaining Vulnerable ·247

Power and Family ·249
        Choice and Quality ·251
        Family and History ·251

The Empiricism of Emotions ·256
    The Propaganda of Regret ·256
    The Facts of Your Feelings ·257

Propaganda and Motivation ·260
    Power Versus Pleasure ·260

Follow the Benefit... ·263

Culture, Propaganda and Exploitation · · · · · · · · · · · · · · · · · · ·265

Becoming Free: Real-Time Relationships In Action · · · · · · · · · · · · 267

The Alternative to Grudging Compliance... · · · · · · · · · · · · · · · ·269
    The Real-Time Relationship (RTR) · · · · · · · · · · · · · · · · · ·270
    The Core of Fear ·272
    Slavery and Freedom ·273

The Hypocrisy of "Consideration"... ·275
    The Key to the Cell ·276
    Testable Hypocrisy? ·277
    The Impossibility of Adult Reciprocity · · · · · · · · · · · · · ·278
    Following the Maternal Benefit ·281

RTR and Empiricism ·282
    Diagnosis ·282
    Paranoia? ·284
    Exploring the Facts ·286

Barriers to the Truth ·288
    Working with the Facts... ·289
    Criminal Slaves ·290

Speak the Truth ·291
    Integrity in Honesty ·292

Conclusions and Facts · · · 295
    Avoiding "Story Time" · · · 296

Post Hoc Ergo Propter Hoc · · · 299

Avoiding Mythology · · · 301

"Inflicting" Emotions · · · 303

Quality of Service · · · 305
    Consultation · · · 306

Identification and Self-Expression · · · 308
    Depth Right at the Surface · · · 308

Feeling Your Feelings · · · 310

Your First Feeling… · · · 312
    Slowing Down… · · · 313
    The Truth We Repress · · · 315

Emotions and Exploitation · · · 317
    Even Deeper · · · 318
    Even Deeper! · · · 319
    The Truth Within · · · 321

Dodging Defenses · · · 324
    Flying from Flight… · · · 324
    Evil and Lying · · · 326
    Honesty and Proof · · · 327

Typical Defenses · · · 328
    Minimization · · · 329
    Self-Pity · · · 329
    Denial · · · 330
    Counter Attack · · · 331

    Genial Blankness····································332
    Framing··332
    Aggressive Appeals to "Compassion" ··················333
    Aggressive Appeal to "Self-Respect"·················333

The Conversation ··334
    The Principles at Work ······························338
    What Next?···340
    The Endgame ······································342
    Dead Souls ··342
    On the Other Hand…································344

Your beautiful world awaits – but not forever… ···············345

    Conclusion ··347

Real-Time Relationships: The Logic of Love

Some of the greatest movies of the past ten years explored what it is like to live in an illusion. "The Sixth Sense," "Fight Club" – and, greatest of all, "The Matrix."

Let's start with a spoiler or two, shall we?

In "The Matrix," a young man is awakened from a computer-generated imaginary world to find that he is enslaved by robots who are paralyzing him with the illusion of life in order to harvest his electrical energy.

This is a wonderful metaphor on many levels, and tells us an enormous amount about our "relationship" with truth and reality.

In the movie, the robots that were originally invented to serve mankind end up ruling mankind and spinning an illusory "reality" which keeps their former masters entombed in the mere appearance of a life.

My take on this metaphor is that it is really describing *propaganda*.

For instance, the *government* is an institution that was originally designed to serve citizens – "government by and for the people."

However, as we have seen countless times, what we create to *serve* us ends up *ruling* us.

Governments that were supposedly created to keep our property safe from thieves now steal upwards of 50% of our income under the guise of "taxation."

Governments were supposedly created to give us participation in the "democratic process" – yet if we do not agree with whatever those in the government decree, we are threatened with violence and imprisonment.

Through the endless infliction of pro-state propaganda in government schools, we grow up believing in mad illusions such as "countries," "virtuous violence," "participative democracy," "voluntary taxation," "moral murder" in the form of "armies" and so on.

In our churches, we are taught as children to believe that deranged fairy tales represent objective and absolute truth. We are expected to believe with all seriousness that we are evil because a woman made from the rib of a man listened to a talking snake. We are asked to swallow the proposition that an invisible being who drowned almost everyone in the world is the very paragon of virtue.

In our families, we are taught that our relations are virtuous and have value simply because they share some of our DNA – while at the same time being told that racism is evil.

In our relationships, we are taught that "love" can be willed, that others owe us affection, obedience and respect, and that bullying is the same as being assertive.

Standing at the border of a country, we see that the land does not change color, as indicated on maps. Gravity does not change as we step across this imaginary line; reason, physics and morality remain utterly constant.

We believe – or rather, the belief is inflicted upon us – that we owe allegiance to imaginary lines, imaginary gods, and the imaginary virtue of our tribe.

Awakening from these mad dreams is a disorienting, frightening and wonderful experience.

Philosophy is the tool that we use to undo our illusions.

Philosophy reveals to us the simple truths that are self-evident to toddlers, yearned for by teenagers – and attacked and dismissed by most adults.

Philosophy is in its essence about *relationships* – the relationship between a statement and its truth-value; the relationship between logic and empiricism, "self" and "other," choice and virtue, integrity and happiness – the mind and reality.

However, most importantly, philosophy is about our relationships with each other.

Philosophy – like all knowledge – is a communal endeavour, since it cannot exist without the collective and accumulated values of language, prior thought – and our shared capacity to process sensory reality.

A man born alone on a desert island cannot practice medicine, or science – or philosophy.

Philosophy reveals the truth to us about our relations with each other, with reality, and with truth itself.

If we are free, philosophy will strengthen our wings.

If we are enslaved, philosophy will weaken our chains.

Culture

ost books about relationships will talk about your spouse, your parents, your siblings, your friends, your children and so on.

We will address all these in this book, but I have also included an analysis of your relationship to your *society* in terms of religion, politics and culture.

I don't believe that it's possible to effectively analyze and improve our interactions with others without taking into account the larger social or philosophical context that we inhabit. If we are to achieve our goals of honesty, integrity and true personal freedom, the values that were inflicted upon us as children by culture must be rigorously examined.

The directions that a passerby gives us will do us little good if our overall map is wrong.

Thus, this book will touch on your social, cultural and political relationships and the impact they have on your personal relationships. Since your emotional reactions to these issues can be as strong as anything you feel about your personal relationships, excluding them from a book designed to give you happiness and peace of mind would leave the world at best half unexamined.

Philosophy and Intimacy

As I discussed in my two previous books – "On Truth: The Tyranny of Illusion," and "Universally Preferable Behaviour: A Rational Proof of Secular Ethics," mythology is the opposite of truth, since it provides the *illusion* of truth and so prevents further exploration.

In this book I will argue that truth is a necessary prerequisite for intimacy.

"On Truth" was primarily about our relationship with our parents in the past. "Universally Preferable Behaviour" was primarily about our relationship with truth, reality and virtue in the present.

This book is primarily about our relationship with ourselves and others in the *future*.

It is a book about honesty of the most challenging and rewarding kind: honesty with – and about – yourself.

Most times in life, we do not even know that we are lying. We do not know that we are failing to process reality – both inner and outer – correctly because we are addicted to mythology, or making up stories which drug us with the *illusion* of truth, rather than humbly pursuing truth in reality.

In our collective past, mythology dominated our thinking – particularly in the realms of ethics, society and reality. In the realm of ethics, we constructed vast imaginary entities such as gods, nations, states, classes and so on, all of which inevitably caused us to surrender our autonomy and sense of personal control to the tall tales of madmen.

With regards to society – particularly family – we substituted blood and accidental proximity for virtue. We were – and are – trained by those who accidentally rule us biologically to submit to those who accidentally rule us geographically.

With regards to reality, we imagined that lurid, corrupt and insane tales about gods, devils and talking snakes could provide us some sort of truth about the material world.

The humility required to subject our wild and narcissistic imaginings to the twin disciplines of logic and evidence has been sorely lacking throughout human history, and it is not hard to see the effects of this lack of humility in the realms of science in the past and ethics in the present.

In the realm of our *relationships*, however, we remain positively medieval.

In the Middle Ages, when an eclipse was observed a myth was invented to "explain" the event. God was angry, a witch is among us, sinners abound and so on. Some senseless and brutal sacrifice was made, some hellish amalgam of torture and murder was inflicted on some hapless epileptic or imbecile, and "order" was restored – and anxiety reduced – to the temporary relief of all.

In the same way, in our personal relationships, when discomforts arise, we create stories to "explain away" our emotions.

If a man causes us anxiety, then he is "aggressive." If a woman rejects us, then she is "cold." If our child criticizes us, then he is "ungrateful." If we get fired, our boss is "vindictive." If our wife leaves us, women are "selfish."

Religious "Reality"

In the religious approach to "truth," the priest makes a prediction – "worship my God and your harvest will be good" – and then invents "sinners" to take the blame if his prediction fails to materialize. In this way, the possibility of disproof – of personal responsibility for the priest – is eliminated.

All too often this is our default position in relationships as well.

We enter into relationships based on our predictions of how they will turn out. Who but a masochist would continue dating a woman if he knew *for certain* she would break his heart within six months? Would you marry a woman and have children with her if you knew that she would divorce you and take you for everything you had?

Of course not.

We make predictions about relationships – and then, when those predictions fail to come true, we invent "sinners" to take the blame.

We embark upon our relationships with the highest hopes and ambitions and then, when they crash in flames or peter out into nothing, we begin mythologizing the reasons why.

Compared to medieval priests, we are often more sophisticated in our defenses nowadays. We provide quasi-enlightened reasons as to why our relationships fail, which on the surface seem to contain some aspects of personal responsibility, but which are really the same old mythologies dressed up in new psychological garb.

For instance, if my marriage fails because I work too hard and ignore my wife and children, I may openly confess that I worked too hard – but then, inevitably, self-pitying justifications will creep into my explanation…

"My wife left me because I worked most Saturdays and spent two or three days a week on the road. I definitely should have spent more time at home, but then of course she really *liked* the vacations on the French Riviera, and the children apparently really *needed* their ski lessons, and she *did* install that kiln in our basement for her pottery. I should have put my foot down earlier and forced her to make a decision, and not just let her desire for more and more stuff keep driving me back to the office!"

Implicit in this kind of mealy-mouthed "explanation" is the basic premise that, "My wife is a greedy materialist who wanted to have her cake and eat it too. She wanted all this great stuff, she wanted all the status that came with the big house and a nice car, but she also wanted me to be home to take care of her as well!"

You often hear the same complaint with regards to sex. For instance, a man may say:

"I'm not allowed to have an affair, because I am married – yet my wife refuses to have sex with me, so I'm totally stuck. She holds a monopoly veto on our sex life, which she uses *constantly* – yet I am not allowed to look outside the marriage for sex!"

Wives have similar complaints about their husbands:

"He says that he wants to help me around the house, but then he does everything so badly that I am forced to run around fixing everything up after him, so that it turns out to be more work than it's worth!"

Or:

"He always complains that I nag him too much, but I wouldn't have to repeat myself if he only listened to me in the first place! If he just took the garbage out when I asked him to, I wouldn't have to keep asking him!"

Or:

"He thinks that having sex will make us close. I keep telling him that I can only have sex with him if I feel close *already*. That just makes him angry – and then he expects me to want to have sex with him because he'll get pouty if I *don't!*"

Positioning

As we can see, conflicts in relationships so often escalate into subtle put-down exercises, wherein a frantic and insistent kind of *positioning* occurs: "I am right and you are wrong" – or, more accurately: "I am good and you are bad."

How many times do we hear people complain about their relationships, basically saying, "If my partner only did the right thing, everything would be great!"

This is a mad kind of mythological fantasy – not to mention completely paralyzing.

When things go wrong we have a great tendency to avoid the pain of responsibility by making up stories that blame others, or circumstances, or fate, or God and so on.

Responsibility can be very painful, and mythology provides an instant relief for this pain. In particular, *blame* is a very addictive form of self-medication which helps us avoid the pain of responsibility – but also traps us in negative, difficult or even dangerous situations.

The Arc of a Relationship

typical dysfunctional romantic relationship tends to have distinct phases.

Caution
When two people meet and are romantically interested in each other, there tends to be a phase of initial caution in which they examine each other for potential compatibility.

We will call this man "Bruce," and this woman "Sheila."

The more functional the individuals, the longer this phase lasts. If an insecure woman is looking for an insecure man, this phase tends to be very short. When they first meet, she looks for "markers" indicating low levels of self-esteem. These can include a lack of eye contact, a nervous laugh, tattoos, drug use, compulsive joke-telling, underachievement, pomposity, or a kind of baseless arrogance.

Once Sheila establishes that Bruce's self-esteem is either genuinely low or artificially "high," she immediately feels more comfortable with him.

Sheila has low self-esteem because she believes things that are not true about herself and others. She remains insecure because she is actively preferring short-term gains to long-term gains. For instance, if she has an abusive father, but stays in touch with him, then she is choosing continued abuse (long-term pain) in order to avoid the anxiety of confrontation (short-term pain).

Since Sheila has developed an "avoidance mechanism" for dealing with her anxiety, inviting a man of true moral courage and integrity into her life would be a disaster for her illusions. Such a man would immediately see that she was being abused by her father and would care enough about her to encourage her to either improve her relationship with her father or get him out of her life. (A wiser and more experienced man would know that she cannot improve her "relationship" with her abusive father, which would be even more anxiety provoking for her.)

If Sheila chose to continue her relationship with her father, a moral man would realize that she is habitually sacrificing ethics, virtue, integrity and self-esteem for the sake of immediate anxiety avoidance. This means that throughout her life, abusive people will forever control her behaviour, and she will continually sacrifice the good people around her for the sake of appeasing the evil or corrupt people.

None of us can sustain any moral decision in the absence of at least the appearance of an ethical justification. If a man of self-esteem confronts a woman who enables abusers, she will be inevitably drawn to defend her appeasement on "moral" grounds. "Family is an innate value." "I think it's important to be a good daughter." "Forgiveness is a virtue."

In other words, the woman is not just amoral, but rather *anti*-moral, because she just makes up "moral" justifications for her cowardly actions.

No man of genuine self-esteem could stay in a relationship with such a corrupt woman, since she uses virtuous definitions to enable her own subjugation to evil. In particular, no moral man would ever have children with such a woman, who would inevitably raise them as frightened and obedient or rebellious slaves.

Since all of this is well-known unconsciously, a woman of low self-esteem is inevitably bound to end up dating a man of low self-esteem. We can think of this relationship as essentially a mutual covenant to maintain corrupt falsehoods. "Let me believe my lies, and I'll let you believe yours."

Of course, like all corrupt falsehoods, it cannot last.

Sex
After the self-esteem issue has been established, the dating aspect of the relationship can begin.

In the case of insecure individuals, sexuality always makes a premature entrance. Since a woman of low self-esteem does not have any genuine virtues to offer a man, such as courage, integrity, nobility and so on, she must *create* value in some other manner.

Typically, the "value" that this type of woman brings to the early part of a relationship is sexual availability.

The Love Bomb
In many cults, such as Christianity, potential recruits are subjected to what is often called a "love bomb," wherein massive amounts of artificial affection are injected into a mostly-empty soul. This tends to wash away any lingering sense of personal boundaries and judgment, triggering what psychologists call "fusion," or the uncritical elevation of an individual to a status of near-deific perfection.

The introduction of a highly-sexualized interaction produces a biochemical form of euphoria, which typically lasts from three to six months. During this time, ego boundaries tend to dissolve, there are few if any difficult decisions to be made, there tends to be an isolation from both friends and family – and the cycle of sexual tension, desire and release tends to consume the mind and body.

The Plateau
At the highest point of this interaction, the couple tends to make decisions about their long-term futures.

This is akin to deciding whether or not you can fly while high on PCP.

This is when couples decide to commit in some significant manner, such as moving in together, or getting engaged, or simply planning a permanent future.

The Hiccup
Shortly after the commitment is made, the couple begins to re-enter the world, and the sexual euphoria begins to wear off. At the same time, they begin to deal with the mundane practicalities of negotiating their living arrangements and/or potential nuptials, as well as entering as a couple into a more complex social world.

As they begin to re-enter the world, interactions with friends and family begin to influence the couple. Bruce begins to see what Sheila is *really* like around her mother. Sheila begins to notice that Bruce's brother drinks to excess, and Bruce says nothing. He sees how shrill she becomes around her friends; she sees how susceptible he is to peer pressure.

The Descent
As Sheila and Bruce begin to make decisions about their lives together, they notice that their lack of boundaries is beginning to cause real friction in their negotiations. Also, since they have spent so much time having sex instead of learning how to actually communicate with each other, they find that their level of commitment is far ahead of their ability to negotiate. They have bonded out of euphoria, neediness, relief and hyper-sexuality, rather than mutual respect and regard for one another.

At this point, the woman generally becomes less sexually available.

The reason for this is the underlying low self-esteem that caused the hyper-sexuality in the first place.

Since she had little intrinsic value to offer Bruce initially, Sheila substituted sex for self-worth.

As their relationship progresses, however, and the sexual euphoria wears off, she begins to feel resentment towards sex.

One way to understand this transition is to picture a rich and insecure man who dazzles his dates with extravagant outings. He flies them to Paris, takes them out on his yacht, buys them jewellery, and drapes them in fur. Naturally, they respond with "devotion" and "ardour."

As the relationship develops, however, he begins to resent the need for constant extravagance. "Would she really love me if I didn't buy her things?" he wonders. In order to find this out, he becomes increasingly irritable towards her desire for gifts. When she suggests a weekend away on the French Riviera, he rolls his eyes and snaps at her.

The same insecurity about his own intrinsic value that caused him to lavish gifts on her now causes him to withdraw his "generosity." The same insecurity that prevented him from offering himself to her without "extras" now causes him to withdraw those extras, in the mad hope that she will find him valuable without gifts.

In other words, after buying her, he hopes that she is not in it for the money.

This is how it works with female sexuality after the initial phase of euphoria.

Lots of sex in the beginning means a whole lot less sex later on.

Lying

As negotiations about mutual living arrangements, sexuality and social life become more and more difficult, it also becomes more and more difficult for Sheila and Bruce to retrace their steps and figure out where they went wrong at the beginning.

For instance, as Sheila's resentment towards sex begins to rise, she will tend to make up excuses as to why she doesn't want sex – and those excuses are not designed to fool Bruce, but rather to fool *herself*.

She will claim that she is tired, or that she has to get up early. She will snap that he is only ever interested in "one thing," or that she doesn't feel "close enough" to have sex, or that he is doing a million and one things wrong, which is killing her sexual desire, and so on.

The truth of the matter is that she is making up stories – inventing "sinners" – in order to avoid the truth about her own growing repugnance towards sex.

If Sheila were to speak with total honesty, she would say something like this:

"Bruce, I had a lot of sex with you early on because I don't feel like I'm worth much of anything. The fact that you were willing to have sex with me despite the fact that I was manipulating you tells me everything that I need to know about your level of integrity, and capacity to love. If you really loved me, you would not pressure me to have sex when I feel depressed. If I were really lovable, I would not have used sex to create artificial value."

The end result of this kind of conversation, of course, is the termination of the relationship – which is why it is so studiously avoided, and a million distractions are invented in order to avoid that core reality.

Entombment
As conflicts begin to rise, Bruce and Sheila enter the phase of "slow entombment."

In this phase, conflicts which cannot be resolved generally start to be avoided. If Bruce does not like Sheila's parents, and it upsets her when he talks about them, the "solution" becomes to simply *not talk about her parents*.

Similarly, if Sheila dislikes Bruce's drinking, and it upsets him when she brings it up, they "solve" the problem either by her refraining from bringing it up, or by him beginning to drink in secret.

This process continues unabated. Bit by bit, unresolved conflicts create localized minefields that prohibit free movement and spontaneity. "Don't go there" becomes a near-constant mantra.

Since the solution to anxiety is to control the other person's behaviour which "causes" the anxiety, the relationship turns into a kind of "soft tyranny." Since it is considered "wrong" to cause the other person anxiety, any behaviour which results in anxiety must be banned as immoral.

Over the next few months or years a creeping paralysis enters into the relationship, as more and more topics become "off limits."

As spontaneity and authenticity become less and less possible and the endless regulations of behaviour pile up, inevitable resentments begin to creep in. Both Sheila and Bruce feel over-controlled, and their interactions become more and more rigid and empty. The cowardice that lies at the root of controlling each other in order to manage their own anxiety becomes more and more evident as time goes on.

Generally, there are two possibilities for this kind of endless increase in the bureaucratic hyper-regulation of the relationship. If neither party takes a "stand," then the abusive "rules" continue to pile up until one or both parties wake up one day completely unable to breathe. An overwhelming rush of frustration – or perhaps a full-fledged panic attack – takes hold, and there is a sudden and savage breakup.

The second possibility is for the "fronts" in this subterranean war to harden. This is analogous to a guerrilla conflict turning into the frozen hell of First World War trench warfare.

In this second scenario, each party picks one or a few fixed positions and just continues to pound their partner on the basis of those. For Bruce, it might be the lack of sex. For Sheila, it might be the lack of emotional participation in the relationship, or help around the house, or some such topic.

Unconsciously, this represents a desperate attempt to stop the endless proliferation of petty rules, since both Sheila and Bruce instinctively understand the inevitable result of *that* process. Rather than moving on from each prior conflict, thus generating new conflicts which must be avoided by the creation of new "rules," Sheila and Bruce start to repetitively attack each other on the grounds of just a few particular issues. This prevents the creation of new rules – thus staving off the end of the relationship – at the price of remaining trapped in endless circling conflicts.

In fact, Sheila and Bruce remain drawn to these few particular conflicts and cannot leave them alone. An unconscious "contract" is created, wherein any frustration about new problems is channeled into a replay of some agreed-upon existing conflict. This is just another way of avoiding the inevitable end of the relationship that would result from "dealing" with new problems.

This second scenario is the route most often taken by couples with children. Since the stakes of ending a relationship are far higher for parents, they tend to revert to this "broken record" form of problem avoidance rather than allow the escalation of new problems to destroy their relationship.

The Aftermath
Earlier, we talked about how the religious approach to "truth" is to make predictions, and then invent "sinners" to take the blame when those predictions fail to come true.

REAL-TIME RELATIONSHIPS

After Bruce and Sheila break up, they will invariably begin the process of inventing scapegoats or "sinners" to take the blame for the failure of their relationship.

This failure was not primarily the relationship itself, but rather *their own predictions about the relationship.*

They entered into a relationship with each other based on the prediction that they would stay together and be happy. Early on, they openly praised each other to the skies, to themselves and their friends and family.

How, then, can they explain the dismal failure of the relationship and eventual distaste for each other?

Well, there is really only one way to explain it – see if this seems familiar.

Sheila will say: "He just ended up being a real bastard – and there was no way to predict that at the beginning."

Bruce will say: "She seemed like a really nice girl, at first – but as it turns out, she had some real issues that she wasn't willing to address."

This is the "one-two" punch that is designed to bring down the truth. "I was correct when I praised her early on, and I am now also correct when I condemn her at the end."

This mythology provides relief from anxiety in the short-term ("How could I have been so careless with my heart?") while creating far greater anxiety in the long-term.

If a group of villagers live at the base of a volcano, and they ascribe the eruption of the volcano to the anger of the fire god, they will inevitably end up performing various rituals to "appease" this anger. Since these rituals have in fact nothing to do with the eruptions, the villagers end up staying near the mountain, imagining that they are creating some form of safety or predictability.

Imaginary answers create perpetual danger.

The moment that the villagers accept that they cannot predict or control the eruption of the volcano, they will move, thus creating real safety and predictability.

When our predictions fail to come true, we can either attempt to determine why we made such a mistake, or we can make up an imaginary answer – thus guaranteeing a repetition of the mistake.

When a relationship fails, we can either attempt to understand the dangerous clues that were embedded in our interactions from the very beginning – which doubtless existed – or we can just blame the other person for mysteriously "changing."

If we take the route of blaming the other person, we certainly let ourselves off the hook – but we also guarantee that we will remain blind to cues that we really need to see in the future. By blaming the other person, all we do essentially is say that there is no way to predict the outcome of a relationship based on early interactions. In other words, when it comes to relationships, all we can do is cross our fingers and hope for the best.

This is why it keeps happening.

Win/Lose

Why do these conflicts continually escalate in this manner?

One central tragedy of our lives is that we are so often raised in win/lose relationships. If our parents get offended, we are punished. If our teacher gets angry, we get detention. If we want something, someone else must give up something.

This same pattern repeats itself in all of our adult relationships.

Most lovers only know how to "get their way" through either overt aggression, or passive aggression (in general, the male and female tools, respectively).

Men say: "If I don't get what I want, I will be angry."

Women say: "If I don't get what I want, I will be sad."

These strategies generally result from a fundamentally narcissistic approach to the world. The possibility of a win-win negotiation is never considered, because it has never been taught or demonstrated.

Let's take a more concrete example.

My wife Christina really enjoys watching a television show called "Dancing with the Stars." I do like watching the dance routines, but have a tough time making it through all the filler and commercials. Last night, I went upstairs to get a DVD for us to watch and then when I came downstairs saw that Christina had found the show on TV and was settling in to watch it.

I would have preferred it if she had not found the show – so that we could watch the DVD – but that was sort of out of my hands at this point.

Many couples would look upon this as a win/lose situation – that Christina would watch the show and I would suffer through the filler and commercials, or that Christina would not get to watch her show, and watch the DVD I chose instead. Or, perhaps, that Christina would tape the show and watch it on her own, or some other solution.

However, although I would have preferred to watch the DVD, I sat down and happily watched the dancing show.

How is that possible?

Well, quite simply it is possible because I take an enormous amount of pleasure in my wife's pleasure. (Shoe shopping excepted, of course – I am only a mortal man!)

I love watching the play of delight on my wife's face and the intensity of her enjoyment. To take pleasure in the pleasure of another human being is foundational to a loving relationship. It certainly is true that I would have received 100% pleasure from watching the DVD, and 90% pleasure from watching my wife's enjoyment of the dancing show, but I can scarcely claim to be hard done by because I had to choose between 100% pleasure and 90% pleasure!

If you cannot take pleasure in your partner's pleasure, then win-win negotiations become impossible. If I got +100% pleasure from watching my DVD, and -100% pleasure from watching the dancing show – and if my wife faced the reverse proposition – then one of us would have to win, and the other would have to lose.

This concept of the "minor sacrifice" is something that every couple should openly discuss and work on. I very much want my wife to be happy in our marriage, because if she is not happy then I cannot be happy either. If I get exactly what I want every single time, no matter what her preferences, then it is impossible – according to the principles of Universally Preferable Behaviour – for her to remain happy.

Since my happiness depends on remaining married to her, my happiness can never in general exceed hers in the long run.

Trust
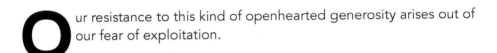

Our resistance to this kind of openhearted generosity arises out of our fear of exploitation.

We say to ourselves: "If I give her what she wants every single time, I will never get what I want. She will take advantage of my generosity, and I will end up a slave to her every whim, and never get my needs met!"

My response to this is:

If that is true, then you should know it <u>before</u> you get involved!

When I was younger, I went out with a woman who openly said that she expected me to pay for our outings. "A man's generosity is financial; a woman's generosity is composed of… other things," she said seductively.

I was somewhat alarmed by her perspective, but I decided to give it a shot. I did pay for our outings, without complaint, and then waited for reciprocity.

It never came, and the relationship ended. I was sad, but never looked back.

Closure and Self-Trust

To achieve true happiness and peace of mind, we must come to a *resolution* about each relationship in our lives – what is commonly called "closure."

"Closure" is the achievement of *self-trust in our own judgment*. Fundamentally, we never really trust others, but rather only ourselves. It was not this woman that I needed to trust, but my own judgment about her proposition.

When we doubt, generosity always provides certainty.

In my 20s, I was involved in a long-term relationship with a woman who wanted to get into the filmmaking business. After watching her struggle for some time, I decided to write and fund a movie for her. We did end up making the movie, which did quite well.

A month or two after we had finished making the movie, I asked her to reread an unpublished novel of mine that she had criticized, and give me suggestions for improvements. She half-heartedly agreed to do so, but week after week went by and she never picked up the manuscript.

Eventually I confronted her on this, and explained my hurt feelings and mistrust of her capacity for reciprocity. She replied that the reason she had not read my novel was because I had not "motivated" her to do so. Naturally, I responded that she had not "motivated" me to spend a small fortune making a film to further her career, but rather I had done so out of a desire to help her!

This relationship also did not last for very long after this interaction.

I am by nature more cautious than generous, and I do find trusting others a challenge. In the above cases, though, generosity was the most liberating approach I could have conceivably taken. If I had hedged my bets in either of these relationships, and given 1% more while waiting for 1% more reciprocity, I would never have achieved certainty.

In relationships – particularly romantic relationships – *generosity creates certainty*. Giving 150% of yourself – even beyond your own "comfort zone" – quickly highlights any deficiencies in reciprocity from your partner.

When I first met my wife Christina, her capacity for love and devotion far outstripped my own. I had been somewhat scarred in the romantic trenches of my youth, and it took some time for my own heart to open up to match her generosity. I did openly talk about my difficulties in this area with her, however, which helped alleviate her concerns. "I am trying to open my heart as quickly as possible," I said, "because you certainly deserve my full affections, but I am having trouble matching your openness."

In the same way, if I owe monetary debt, but am temporarily unable to pay it, I am morally bound to inform my creditor of the situation, reaffirm my commitment to pay, and work like hell to get hold of the money.

Hedging
Couples get continually stuck in the tug-of-war of conditional reciprocity – "I gave you a back rub, now you owe me sex!" – which always creates more and more resentment. Not only is such "generosity" totally undercut through the expectation of reciprocity ("I'll take out the garbage if you do the dishes") but the degree of mistrust that is communicated by this sort of "grudging giving" is overwhelmingly insulting at its root.

If I told you that you were my best friend, and you asked me to lend you $5,000, and I said to you: "Let's just start with $5, and see where it goes from there," would you feel elevated by my response?

Of course not. You would be insulted. "How can you call me your best friend, and not trust me with any sum larger than five dollars?"

"Well," I might reply, "some people in my past never paid me back."

Here we run into a fundamental problem, which is at the root of countless relationship discords.

Baggage

We all arrive with scars, and that is not a bad thing. A boxer without scars has never fought an equal, and a lover without baggage has never risked his heart. To some degree we do learn through pain, and being on the receiving end of falsehoods and betrayal can do wonders to sharpen our criteria for trustworthiness.

However, we do run into a fundamental problem when we mistrust our lover.

Either she really *is* untrustworthy – in which case we chose to enter into an intimate and lengthy relationship with an untrustworthy woman – or, she *is* trustworthy, but we have a hard time trusting because we have been betrayed in the past.

If we have been betrayed in the past, though, we have either learned who to trust or we have not. If we *have* learned who to trust – primarily ourselves – then we cannot reasonably call our current partner untrustworthy.

If we have *not* learned to trust, then we cannot *blame* our current partner for being untrustworthy.

To explain what I mean by this, let us return to our "loan" example.

First I tell you that you are my best friend, and then I refuse to lend you any money because I have lent and lost money in the past.

"Well," you say, "are you still 'best friends' with those who ran off with your money?"

"Of course not!" I reply indignantly.

"Thus you find untrustworthiness to be a trait unworthy of someone you call a best friend?"

"Yes."

"Thus anyone you call your best friend must be the opposite of the people who harmed you in the past."

"Yes."

"Thus if you tell me that you are afraid that I will not pay you back, then you are telling me that I am untrustworthy. However, since you have rejected those who failed to pay you back in the past *because* they were untrustworthy, but you claim that I am your best friend, then you are in the illogical position of claiming that I am both trustworthy and untrustworthy at the same time. If I am trustworthy, then I surely have earned the title 'best friend,' and you should lend the money to me. If I am untrustworthy, then it is unjust to call me your 'best friend,' since you find untrustworthiness such a vile character trait."

Thus keeping people in our lives who exhibit traits we call negative utterly prohibits us from blaming them for exhibiting those traits. If we act in opposition to our beliefs, we cannot reasonably blame other people for the results.

In the same way, when the fateful words "I love you" escape our lips, they cannot be reasonably construed as a recipe, but rather as a fully digested meal. We cannot reasonably say, "I love you, but I do not trust you." We cannot reasonably say, "I love you, but I expect you to think and act completely differently in the future."

But of course we use the words "I love you" for almost every purpose except what they actually mean.

Love

"Love" is a word that is subjected to such fantastical delusions that reclaiming its right meaning seems a near-impossible task. The word is flung around to mean anything from fetishistic attachment to co-dependency to "loyalty" towards rabid delusions such as gods and countries.

There are some things, however, that we must be able to agree on if we are to come to some reasonable understanding about how to improve the quality of our relationships.

Love and Objectivity

First of all, love must be a state that has at least some objective qualities. If love is a completely subjective state, then the concept of "quality" does not exist at all – and thus neither does "improvement."

Furthermore, saying to someone "I love you" is a meaningless statement if the phrase merely represents purely internal or subjective preferences. We can say "I love jazz," but jazz is not a conscious entity and can flow from a CD. To proclaim love for another human being, however, is to say that our *internal state is elicited by another person.* In other words, the "you" in "I love you" involves objectivity, since we experience each other through the medium of empirical reality.

If another person elicits our internal state, then some objectivity must be accepted.

Secondly, we must also accept that the word "love" represents something other than a merely *chosen* preference. We cannot pick a woman out of a crowd and command ourselves to love her. In other words, love must be somehow related to the actions of another person, and not simply willed. None of us would feel particularly flattered if someone told us they "loved" us while knowing nothing about us.

Thus "love" must be in its essence a reaction to the objective actions of another human being.

Thirdly, the feelings of affection that are elicited by the actions of another person cannot be entirely contradictory. My wife cannot tell me that she loves me because I am honest, and that she also loves my brother because he is dishonest. I cannot love a person because of his loyalty, and then claim to love another person equally because of her disloyalty.

Love – Compared to What?
One of the most fundamental questions in philosophy – and psychology – is the question: "Compared to what?" When I say that a proposition is "true," then I mean that it is true compared to something else – falsehood, or inconsistency with internal logic or empirical validation.

Similarly, when we look at the question of love, clearly love is an expression of a preference. Naturally, we must then ask, "A *preference – compared to what?*"

If I say that I love honesty, then clearly I love it compared to dishonesty. If I say that I love virtue, then clearly I love virtue compared to vice or corruption.

Now, since we can only determine the traits of another human being through empirical observation, our experience of "love" must involve the actions of another (said actions can include words, of course). Just as our conception of "tall" is derived from the objective (i.e. measurable) characteristics of a man – and "tall" is valid relative to the average height of a human male – just so is our experience of "love" derived from the objective characteristics (words and actions) of another human being.

Thus "love" must be valid relative to an objective and external standard, which we shall work to define shortly.

Internal State, or External Fact?
The question then arises: to what degree is love valid relative to an objective and external standard?

Love cannot be completely and utterly defined by an objective and external standard, since that would mean that everyone must love the *one person in the world* who most completely conforms to that standard, which would be absurd. If we said that love was valid relative to height, then everyone in the world must love the tallest person, which flies in the face of the obvious variety of personal preferences the world over.

If I say that I like ice cream, then clearly I *prefer* ice cream to other foods that I relatively dislike. This is a largely subjective matter.

On the other hand, if I say that I prefer good health, then clearly I am expressing a desire for something that can be measured at least to some degree objectively. I cannot reasonably say that I prefer good health, and that I also prefer dying of cancer.

It is also important to differentiate between standards that can be achieved, and standards that cannot be achieved. If I say that I love good health, and then define "good health" as never getting a cold, sleeping lightly or having a headache, then clearly what I love is unattainable, and my "love" can only be measured relative to varying degrees of disappointment.

Love and Pleasure

It scarcely seems required, but it is worth noting that love *must be considered a pleasurable experience*. This does not mean that love always entails pleasure – any more than physical health means never experiencing any pain at all – but it must be a positive experience in general.

In other words, the positive aspects of "love" must vastly outweigh the negative aspects, just as the positive aspects of "health" must vastly outweigh the negative aspects, such as eating well and exercising.

A decent rule of thumb is to expect a positive relationship to be composed of 9/10 good things, to 1/10 bad things.

To put this together, we can say that love has the following characteristics:

1. It has elements of objectivity.
2. It is elicited by the behaviour of another person.
3. It is a favouring of certain characteristics relative to their opposites, or deficiencies thereof.
4. It is pleasurable.

Love: A Tentative Definition

I'm going to put forward a tentative definition of love, which conforms to the above requirements. We shall examine this proposition in more detail below.

> **Love is our involuntary response to virtue.**

Science has elements of objectivity, insofar as it relies to some degree on personal inspiration, but must be validated through reason and evidence.

Love also has elements of objectivity, insofar as it relies to some degree on personal preferences, but must be validated through reason and evidence.

Of course, the idea of "validating" love offends our sensibilities to some degree, since love is so often considered to be a form of divine madness or inspiration. What, then, is meant by "validating love"?

Well, in the realm of romantic relationships, we are motivated to a considerable degree by biological attraction, or raw sexual desire. In the same way, we may feel an irrational exuberance of greed when we see an overturned Brinks truck spilling banknotes into the wind. We may even seize some of these banknotes, before shaking our heads and returning our ill-gotten gains.

Philosophy is required because our instincts can lead us astray, as in the case of eating and certain phobias. We may be sexually attracted to certain characteristics such as large breasts or bald heads, but those desires lie squarely in the realm of animal reproduction, rather than what would properly be called "love." Teenagers may get a fairly strenuous degree of sexual satisfaction from their hand, but this would scarcely be called love.

The world looks flat, but in truth it is round. Some people are sexually attractive, but that does not mean they are lovable.

Since love has elements of objectivity, the objective elements of love must be tied to universal values, the existence of which I proved in my previous book on Universally Preferable Behaviour.

Again, this does not mean that all love is identical. The concept of "health" has elements of objectivity, but is also measurable relative to a variety of standards. A "healthy" AIDS patient is quite different from a healthy athlete. The "healthiest" person in a cancer ward is not healthy relative to the majority of people.

In the same way, we can assume that there is one person in the world who is the very best person for you to be with. Does that mean that you could never be happy with anyone else?

Of course not.

As with all disciplines, we have to weigh the pros and cons of perfection versus attainability. There is also only one "perfect" job in the world for us as well, but we can quite easily starve to death looking for it.

If we look at something like "honesty" as a behavioural trait that elicits admiration, it is true that everyone has differing degrees of commitment to – and execution of – honesty, but there is still an objective difference between honesty and dishonesty.

If I value honesty – and I am honest myself – then I will value somebody who is honest 99% of the time more than somebody who is honest 90% of the time. (100% honesty can be considered an unrealistic goal, like 100% health, or being "perfectly reasonable.")

Naturally, I would prefer to be with someone who is as honest as possible, but I will likely have to "settle" for the most honest person that I can find. The fact that I am willing to compromise my standards with regards to honesty – partly borne of a reasonable humility regarding my own capacity for honesty – does not mean that I will value a liar. If I am a mathematician, some of my proofs will doubtless fail – but that does not mean that failing to achieve perfect consistency is exactly the same as starting out to commit a fraud.

Love as a Response

If I stand in front of a mirror weighing 300 pounds and smoking my 40th cigarette of the morning and say "I am healthy," have I affected my health in any objective manner?

Of course not. I have merely chosen to say the words "I am healthy" rather than achieve actual health through consistent actions.

My words have not affected reality at all. I have merely put the cart before the horse. If I lose weight and quit smoking, I can reasonably stand in front of the mirror and say "I am healthy" (or at least "I am healthier"). My words thus become an accurate identification of an objective state – a state which has *preceded* my words and in a sense *provokes* them.

My words are thus a *response* to my empirical behaviour, measured in objective terms (weight loss, smoking cessation).

Similarly, if I stand in front of you and say "I love you," this statement only has validity if it is a *response* to your behaviour. I can stand in front of the most evil and hateful human being on the planet and also say the words "I love you," but my preference does not make that person any more lovable – any more than telling myself that I am healthy unclogs my arteries.

As I talked about in my book "On Truth," people in general prefer – or find it far easier in the short term – to do whatever they please in the moment, and then redefine their actions as "universally virtuous."

It is equally true that people in general prefer – or find it far easier in the short run – to date whomever they desire, and then redefine their partner as "lovable."

Ask most young women what they are looking for in a man and you will hear various variations on the theme of tall, dark and handsome – or, if they are slightly younger, "cute and funny."

I have asked this question of many people, and I have never heard the word "virtue" mentioned once.

Love and Virtue

Does love have anything to do with virtue?

Yes, yes and *yes!*

Love and Honesty
It is impossible to imagine genuine love in the absence of honesty. For love to be genuine, it must be an accurate assessment of particular traits within another human being. If the person that we claim to "love" constantly lies to us or falsifies his actions, then whatever perception we have of that person that causes us to love him are incorrect.

Since that which causes us to love is incorrect, our "love" must thus be invalid.

To analogize this, imagine that you work for me and I pay you in cash. However, when you try to spend your earnings, you discover that I have paid you with counterfeit bills. As a result, I have received value through your work, but you have not received value through my payment. My dishonesty has thus generated a false value for you, because if you knew that I was going to pay you with counterfeit money, you would not have worked for me to begin with.

Since the truth would have produced an opposite action in you – a rejection of employment, rather than an acceptance of it – your diligent behaviour was as unjustified as your interpretation of my honesty.

In the same way, if I tell you that I am courageous, and virtuous, yet hide sordid aspects of my life from you, drink in secret and so on – and you believe me – then you will feel more positive towards me than if I told you the truth.

Since our emotions are so directly dependent upon our perceptions and are so foundational to our experience of the world, someone who lies to us is fundamentally manipulating our experience of the world.

Since our emotions also alter our bodies biochemically, a liar who gets close to us manipulates our biochemistry as surely as if he were drugging us directly.

Thus our own emotional stability, which is a key part of a peaceful and happy life, requires as a bare minimum general honesty from those around us.

Love and Courage
Fundamentally, courage is not bravery with regards to another human being, but rather with regards to moral ideals.

My wife, though wonderfully courageous in many areas, has a certain weakness when it comes to social gatherings.

For instance, she has an ex-friend who is involved in a highly dysfunctional relationship. Recently, when we were at a party, we were told that this woman had gotten married to her boyfriend. Christina exclaimed: "Oh, that's *great!*"

I was somewhat surprised, to say the least, and really put my foot in it by saying to her in front of everyone: "Really? I didn't think you were such a big fan of their relationship."

(It's always good to have something to talk about during the drive home.)

Of course, I was not particularly concerned with Christina's disavowal of her true feelings in company – particularly since the woman in question showed up at the party later on. I was more concerned with the fact that she placed the perceptions of others above the truth of her own feelings – feelings which were accurate and valid. I was most concerned, however, with the fact that she did not seem *conscious* of her reversal of values. If she had expressed approval with her friend standing right behind her, I would have understood her caution – however, there was no compelling and immediate reason to express approval of something she did not in fact approve of.

The reason that this troubled me, of course, was that I really didn't like the idea that Christina could betray her values – even in this minor manner – for the sake of the possible disapproval of the people we were talking to, who we see maybe once every year or two.

This also made me feel insecure, since Christina and I both hold trusting our own feelings as a high value – as well as honesty of course. I really disliked the idea that the virtues we believed in and practiced were sort of a "private world" that had nothing to do with the "real world" of everyone else.

You know that feeling you get if you are dating a woman who never wants to introduce you to her friends? You get this uneasy sensation that you are kind of "below the radar," or something to be hidden relative to her life as a whole. You are, in fact, a sort of embarrassment, in that she obviously feels that she must be "slumming" in some manner. If she felt that you would enhance her status with her friends, she would drag you to see them against your will if she had to.

When I was 17, I worked in a day-care centre teaching a room full of kids. I became friends with a woman who was slightly older, and was just going through a divorce. Over dinner one evening, she told me about her psychic abilities. Because I was 17, my hormones and I listened attentively.

Over a departmental lunch the next day, I mentioned her psychic abilities as part of a more general conversation. She became completely red-faced, and chastised me afterwards for bringing that up.

REAL-TIME RELATIONSHIPS

So many of us have this kind of "private world" that we openly disavow, scorn and reject when we are in the company of others. This is a form of cowardice, since we abandon what is precious to us for fear of the disapproval or rejection of others.

In other words, we reject ourselves rather than be rejected by others.

This avoids the pain of humiliation, but also keeps us trapped in an underworld of people we know will humiliate us if we are honest.

The reason that this habit is so hard to respect or love is because it involves so many contradictions.

If a certain belief or habit is truly valuable, it does not lose its value in the presence of others. Real money does not lose its value in the presence of counterfeit currency – quite the opposite is true in fact.

Conversely, if the opinions of others is the best methodology for determining our values, then those values cannot exist except through the opinions of others – thus there should be nothing to hide in the presence of others, since no values have been accepted or practised without their prior approval.

It is hard to respect someone who wants to "have his cake and eat it too" by holding private virtues that he consistently disavows in public. We tend to shy away from these sorts of people not only because of their hypocrisy, but also because these sorts of contradictory values make raising children enormously difficult.

If you ask a woman to evaluate a particular situation and she openly says, "Oh, I have no idea, I'll have to check with all my friends," then there is no possibility of equality in her relationship with her friends. If all her friends hold the same values, then they will be empty echoes of endless cross-referencing, with no ideas or opinions being generated at all.

At least one of her friends must be able to generate opinions, which everyone else then references.

Thus she both prefers and dislikes opinions – she dislikes having her own for fear of disapproval, and so she must prefer that other people create her opinions for her.

Of course, you never *do* meet people who openly tell you that they have no opinions, but must always ask their friends – and that is why these cowardly evasions are so odious. People always claim that their opinions are both virtuous and true, that they have integrity and are willing to stand up for what they believe in, and then they generally fold at the slightest sign of pressure or disapproval.

The fact that they fold – as we all do at times – does not warn them that they are not actually living their values, and must more closely examine their companions. Since everyone has a general access to the self-medicating madness of instant mythology, all that people do when they act in a cowardly manner is redefine their actions as virtuous in some manner.

Thus a woman may say: "I know that I said that, but I didn't want to offend people (*I'm nice*), and besides, people don't change (*I'm practical*), and we were enjoying their hospitality (*I'm not ungrateful*), and the person in question was going to show up (*I'm prudent*) – and besides, yesterday you said X, Y and Z (*you're hypocritical*)."

This is why a lack of integrity tends to make us uneasy – because it always ends up being an attack on truth in general and our integrity in particular.

Not too relaxing…

Love and Sustainability

We do not call a tire "good" if it ruptures right after being installed. "Quality" has a lot to do with sustainability. A bridge is not of high quality if it collapses six minutes after being built.

In many ways, virtue is fundamentally about *sustainable behaviour*. Clearly, lying is not very sustainable behaviour – particularly in a long-term relationship — because reality is always opposing the words of the liar. As "intimacy" grows in a relationship and more and more people get involved in the couple's interactions, lies become less and less sustainable.

Similarly, cowardice is also unsustainable in a relationship, since cowardice is always supported by justifications (lies) which reframe cowardice as "courage." This creates an unstable situation where cowardly behaviour is both condemned and praised, resulting in highly inconsistent behaviour.

Integrity, of course, is all about sustainable behaviour — its opposite, conformity, is all about seeking the approval of others, which produces highly inconsistent behaviour. People inflict a need for conformity on us as children by attacking us for independent thought and evaluation, because any such thought reveals their hypocrisy. Thus conformist habits always stem from the desire of those who hold power over us to blind us to their inconsistent and hypocritical actions. This is why conformity and integrity are so fundamentally opposed.

If we love certain characteristics or virtues, then clearly our love will stabilize and increase to the degree to which those characteristics or virtues are stable, and increase.

Love and Security

Security is an essential ingredient for intimacy. Security results from a feeling of predictability and safety, which in turn arises from consistent benevolence on the part of others. If we are randomly attacked by our lover, we can never feel safe or secure. If we have to use a rickety old footbridge to cross a chasm, each wobbly step will be a fearful nightmare.

Why do we stay in relationships where we do not feel safe and secure? One central reason is that we have a habit of listening to people's *words*, rather than regarding their *actions*. The old adage "actions speak louder than words" has fallen out of favour in our modern age, but it is essential for evaluating potential relationships of any kind.

Abusive behaviour always results from a lack of integrity.

If, on a first date, a woman tells you openly that she will attack you whenever she feels insecure, angry or vulnerable – and promises to blame you when you get upset about being attacked – you would be very unlikely to continue dating her.

No, people always tell you that they are acting virtuously, even if their actions completely contradict their stated values. If a woman has a habit of attacking others when she feels anxious, that behaviour can only be maintained *if she redefines her abuse as virtuous in some manner*. She will say that she is only defending herself, or that she has been patient for a long time but "enough is enough," or that the other party started the conflict, and so on.

If her culpability can be proved beyond a shadow of a doubt, she then reverts to the secondary defense of abusers, which is to say that it is ignoble to point fingers and play "the blame game," that "forgiveness is a virtue," and "we need to move on now."

In other words, she will openly state that unjustly attacking others is wrong, and then will unjustly attack others.

This lack of integrity ensures that no one around her will ever feel a consistent sense of security or safety. (In fact, that is exactly what it is *designed* to do, since destabilizing people is an essential prerequisite for controlling them.)

Security and Values
If we accept that integrity to virtue creates security – and that security is a necessary prerequisite for love – then we can understand why it is so important to have *values in a relationship that both parties can refer to*.

If an agreement can be reached that raised voices and name-calling are inappropriate to a loving relationship, then if one person yells or name-calls, the other person can object to that behaviour based on values that both parties have accepted.

It is impossible to have security – or integrity – without shared and objective values.

If I hand you $1,000 and think it is a loan, but you see it as a gift, then I will not perceive you to be acting with integrity if you never pay the "loan" back – just as you will never perceive me to be acting with integrity if I demand my "gift" back.

Similarly, if a woman holds "keeping others happy" as a core "value," then she will view any emotional confrontation or uncomfortable honesty as "rude."

On the other hand, if she holds "honesty" as a core value, then she will view a consistent avoidance of necessary confrontations or honesty as "cowardice."

If a man believes that verbal abuse is "assertiveness," then asking him to refrain from verbal abuse is the same as asking him to be a coward – which will never happen, since few if any people will ever voluntarily pursue an action they define as immoral or ignoble.

If a woman believes that nagging is necessary to get what she wants, then asking her to give up nagging would be like asking her to give up having any needs or preferences, which will never happen.

Following our above methodology, when considering integrity, we must next ask: "Integrity *to what?*"

Objective Integrity

Having integrity is acting in accordance with rational values. This is an enormously hard thing to achieve, both because most of the "values" we were given – or rather which were *inflicted* upon us – are so ridiculously self-contradictory, and also because living with integrity actively eliminates a goodly number of people from your life.

Women often say that they dislike nagging, but don't know any other way to get their needs met.

This is a prime example of *not* living with integrity.

If my wife has to nag me to meet her needs, then she is basically telling me that I do not care about her, and that I will never lift a finger to meet her needs unless she constantly complains that I am not meeting her needs.

In the movie "The Breakup," Jennifer Aniston tells Vince Vaughn that she wants him to *want* to do the dishes with her.

What she means by this is that she wants him to want to help her, to make the job of entertaining easier, and to place her needs above his own, at least temporarily.

The reason that this kind of behaviour is so corrupt is that it is so fundamentally self-contradictory.

If Jennifer has to constantly nag Vince to meet her needs, then clearly she believes that he does not voluntarily want to meet her needs in the first place. He does not respect what she wants, or does not care that she wants it – either way, he is treating her entirely disrespectfully.

She feels frustrated because she does not feel *visible* to him – as women so often say: "If he only *knew* how important this was to me, he would not *hesitate* to provide it." Thus Jennifer gets stuck in a "broken record" loop of attempting to become visible to Vince, so that he will give her what she wants.

Fundamentally, then, she is nagging him because she feels invisible to him – because she feels that he is rejecting who she really is.

This is entirely hypocritical.

Obviously, what Vince wants is to *not be nagged*. Over and over, he complains that she keeps nagging him. He also does not seem to enjoy entertaining – and Jennifer's obsessive perfectionism appears particularly odious to him.

It is thus ridiculous for Jennifer to chastise him for not meeting her needs, when by that very chastisement *she* is failing to meet his need, which is *to not be chastised*.

The tragic irony is that Jennifer feels rejected, and so rejects the man *that she chose* because he is rejecting her.

This is exactly like saying: "I need a form of transportation," then spending years testing various makes of cars and researching all the alternatives, and then finally purchasing a car – and then, when you get it home, standing in front of it and exclaiming: "Excellent, now I'm going to turn this thing into a *boat!*"

Men always resist being turned into "boats" – while women experience men's resistance at being transformed into something they are not as a rejection of *themselves*. They will openly say to a man they have chosen: "Change!" and then feel genuinely rejected when he does not change.

Of course, asking someone to change is rejecting him, at least as he is. To choose a man, and then reject a man, and then complain that *you* feel rejected, is quite mad.

If the innocent car in the woman's garage could speak, surely it would say: **"If you wanted a boat, why on earth did you buy a car?"**

Why did you choose me if you don't even *like* me?

The reason that couples so strenuously avoid this elemental conversation is that if you have bought a car when you really want a boat, the point is not to nag the car into becoming a boat, but to take the car back and get a boat instead.

You cannot claim to love someone, and then want him to change.

If you're looking for a painting and spend years finding just the right one, you don't then bring it home and start painting *over* it – particularly if you're not even a painter!

Clearly, since no one is forcing you to go looking for a painting, you should just buy the *right* painting and be content with what you have.

If you are not a mental health professional or a well-versed philosopher, then when you try to change people, you are like someone who has no idea how to paint attempting to "improve" a painting.

If you *are* a mental health professional or a philosopher, then you are wise enough to know that people do not change, and so you will never buy a painting that you have to "paint over."

Most economists accept that any attempt by a coercive monopoly such as the state to interfere with the natural flow of voluntary trade will create ever-growing distortions in the marketplace.

In the same way, any attempt to interfere with a person's natural personality through any kind of aggression or rejection will create ever-growing distortions in his character. Nagging, for example, leads to an excess of fear, irritation and passive aggression, which in turn leads to increased nagging…

"Fixing" the Painting…

If we attempt to "correct" a painting because just a small part of it is "wrong," we will inexpertly daub a blob of paint and then stand back to review our handiwork.

Naturally, because we lack knowledge and skill, we will have inevitably made the painting *less* pleasing than it was before.

Logically, we should then sigh and say: "Well, since I am obviously not a painter, I will now stop trying to 'fix' this painting – and the fact that I have now made the painting *less* attractive will serve as my perpetual warning about trying to 'fix' paintings again in the future."

Surely, if the painting were sentient, we should also apologize to it for making it uglier.

Ahh, if only we were that logical!

Sadly, what people actually do is continue to try and "fix" the painting, making it uglier and uglier, and less and less suited to their purposes.

As things get worse and worse they get more and more angry, and throw more and more paint at the painting, and get more and more frustrated, and blame the painting, and blame the paint, and blame the paintbrush – everything but themselves!

And we all know where that leads in the end.

At some point, they stand back from the painting – now completely unrecognizable from what they originally bought – which lies buried and unrecoverable under mountains of ugly and clashing colors.

They stare at that mess and say to themselves: "I really can't believe that I ever liked this painting – it is the ugliest thing I have ever seen, and I'm going to throw it out!"

Then, they go shopping for a new painting that they can take home and "improve," and the whole cycle begins again.

The final tragedy is that if people genuinely accepted that they cannot "improve" a painting, they would be far more careful about the paintings they bought, and would not accept imperfections or ugliness, knowing that they cannot improve it after they get it home.

In other words, the final ugliness of the painting is actually brought about by believing that the painting can be made *less ugly*.

Without the fantasy that a painting can be made more beautiful, true beauty could in fact be achieved.

The belief that we can reshape the personalities of other people creates a deep and inescapable polarization within a relationship, which is captured for comic effect in the statement: "I love you, you're perfect, now change!"

But – we can't change people at all?
In our minds, we all generally know the basic principle that we cannot change others – but this does not seem to fit with the reality that we expect to improve within a relationship.

If two human beings do not change at all in proximity to each other, then what is the point of a relationship? When we go to university, we have a relationship of sorts with our professors, and we expect to change based on that relationship. We expect to grow in knowledge and wisdom, or technical skill, or mental agility, based on having them as professors.

In the same way, if we sign up at a dojo to learn jujitsu, we expect to change – to improve – based on our relationship with our instructor.

If love is our involuntary response to virtue, then if a relationship results in an increase in virtue, then surely it will result in an increase in love – something to be ardently desired, it would seem.

How can this seeming paradox be resolved – that we must not strive to change people, but that the best relationships result in improvements for both participants?

Let us return to our painting metaphor to see if we cannot unravel this knot.

Imagine that you and I are not *consumers* of art, but *creators* of art.

Both our paintings are accepted by a gallery, and when we show up to have a look at them, we are immediately drawn to the beauty of each other's work.

While conversing with each other, we find that we have very similar goals as artists – to ennoble people by drawing their attention to the beauty of the world they live in.

As reasonable artists, we know that objective feedback on our own work will help us achieve our goals. Thus the next time I am working on a painting, I call you when I am halfway through and ask you to have a look and let me know what you think.

You arrive, look over my painting with great attention, ask me what it is that I am trying to achieve, and then give me objective and valuable feedback on how to shape the light, colour and composition to more completely achieve my objective.

This process goes back and forth for several months — and then, since our mutual feedback is truly helping us achieve our artistic goals, and bringing us even greater joy as artists, we decide to rent a studio together and paint in the same room.

As we work together, our paintings become more and more beautiful and our trust in our own and each other's artistic judgment grows. I learn from your feedback and you learn from mine — we internalize the principles that we provide each other, and then as we improve, we help each other surmount the new obstacles that always arise from increased excellence.

We have our disagreements, of course — but sometimes it seems that we learn even more from our disagreements! Our conflicts are resolved patiently, positively and productively, thus affirming the strength of our relationship and allowing our mutual trust to grow even stronger.

We can all understand that this kind of relationship is mutually beneficial, and results in great improvements in both skill and joy for both parties.

How is this different from a desire to change someone?

Well, the difference is that we are both helping each other achieve noble goals that we arrived at the relationship *already committed to pursuing*.

I am not trying to turn you from a plumber into a painter, and you are not trying to turn me from a painter into an accountant. If you want to paint beautiful portraits, I am not trying to turn you into Jackson Pollock. If you enjoy dribbling paint in semi-random patterns, I am not trying to turn you into Jean Auguste Dominique Ingres. If you want to make a living as a painter, I do not try to downgrade your ambitions and turn you into a hobbyist.

The difference is that I am not setting your goals — which really means, in essence, that *I am not attempting to alter your values, but rather help you achieve them*.

In the above example of the conflict between Jennifer and Vince, we can see that Jennifer's fundamental error – the mistake that makes the relationship inevitably doomed – is that she is attempting to alter his values.

"I want you to *want* to help me do the dishes!" she exclaims in frustration – thus revealing that what she really wants is for his values to be the opposite of what they are. Clearly, he *doesn't* want to help her do the dishes – what she demands from him is the complete opposite of that existing desire.

This would be like me approaching you as you regard your painting in an art gallery, *and attempting to turn you into the opposite of a painter.*

We can surely picture the absurdity of an Olympic coach marching up to some overweight chain-smoking stranger lounging on a park bench and snarling at him to become more motivated, dammit, to get his ass off that park bench and start taking his training *seriously*!

The smoker would doubtless stare up in bewilderment, wondering what on earth could motivate someone to march up to him out of nowhere, and expect him to act in complete opposition to his clearly-expressed existing preferences.

On the other hand, if I desperately want to win an Olympic medal, and I have the ability and drive to train and diet endlessly, then a coach is essential to help me achieve my goal.

In the first example, the coach is not attempting to facilitate the goals of the chain-smoking stranger, but rather to set his goals *in direct opposition to all available evidence!* (Also known as: *imposing your own goals on others.*)

In the second example, the coach is not attempting to set goals for the motivated athlete, but rather facilitate the achievement of those goals *in accordance with all available evidence.*

When we treat people as *objects to be fixed* – like paintings we can paint over – it is not about them, but about us. When we attempt to "correct" a painting, we are fundamentally the only person in the room.

When we treat people not as objects, but as complementary souls – not as paintings, but *painters* – we can truly merge our lives in trust, love and beauty, because there are in fact two people in the room.

This is the difference between *changing* people and *helping* people.

This is the difference between control and love.

In relationships, this is the difference between dismal failure and joyous success.

Acceptance and Rejection

Acceptance is the opposite of rejection. It is logically impossible to both accept and reject something at the same time, just as it is impossible for a rock to fall both up and down at the same time.

Why, then, are we so drawn to attempt to "improve" the people that we claim to love?

Well, because it is far less uncomfortable to attempt to improve others than to actually improve *ourselves*.

How can we justify the fundamental contradiction that we both love someone and want her to change in significant ways?

The first thing to understand is that we don't actually want to change someone else.

This may sound startling, but it is easily provable.

If I spend years shopping for a home, and then finally buy a small condominium, and then demand that, in order to complete the sale, the condo must be converted into a four bedroom house, my real estate agent would regard me as largely insane.

"If you *want* a four bedroom house, then you should shop for a four bedroom house!" she would say – and quite rightly too!

If I buy the condominium, and move in, and then constantly complain to everyone that my condominium is *not* a four bedroom house, then clearly I have bought the condominium not because I want a four bedroom house, but rather because *I want to complain about not having a four bedroom house.*

This is a very important distinction, which Edward Albee writes about in "Who's Afraid of Virginia Woolf." George and Martha have a demonically abusive marriage, and George complains about it endlessly, until Martha finally screams at him that he married her *in order to be abused.*

Why on earth would somebody enter into a relationship in order to complain about that relationship?

It does seem rather counterintuitive, but it makes sense logically when you look at the root causes.

Reversing Virtue and Vice

If I act in a cowardly manner, but I redefine my cowardice as "courage," then I am turning morality completely upside down by converting a vice into a "virtue."

If I am a doctor, and redefine "cancer" as "health" (and vice versa), then everything that I do will be the opposite of good medicine. I will inject cancer cells into healthy people, tell them to smoke and refrain from using sunscreen, and I will attempt to hasten the progress of cancer in sick people.

By redefining that which is unhealthy as that which is healthy, I have reversed the cause and effect in everything I do.

I have in fact *become* a kind of cancer.

In the same way, if I redefine my cowardice as a virtue – a cowardly action in and of itself – *then I reverse the cause and effect of all my relationships.*

Let us say that I fear my parents because they are abusive, either overtly or covertly.

It is not cowardice to openly admit that I am afraid of my parents.

It is also not cowardice to submit to my parents' will as long as I openly admit my fear. If they want me to come to dinner and I go, I am not necessarily a coward.

How can that be possible – to submit to bullying without being cowardly?

Virtue and Honesty
The first prerequisite for virtue is honesty. With honesty comes at least the possibility of integrity, which can survive a temporary surrender to bullying, just as your liver can survive a glass of wine or two.

If I openly say to my wife: "We must go to my parents' house for Sunday dinner, although I hate and fear them, because I am too afraid to either confront or avoid them," then my wife has at least an accurate understanding of the reality of the situation.

She clearly understands that my true desire is *not* to go to my parents' house, and that my barrier is my fear of my parents.

Armed with that knowledge, my wife can then help me to get what I really want by talking me through the fear that blocks me from achieving it.

This is analogous to one painter helping another painter overcome his fear of submitting his work to a gallery – something that he desperately and openly desires.

On the other hand, if I claim that I "love" my parents when I really hate and fear them, then an inevitable and terrible sequence of events is set into motion.

Virtue and Obedience
If I say that I love my parents, then I must define obedience to their wishes as obedience to virtue.

This may sound confusing, so let us look at it in a little more detail.

If I say that I completely respect my doctor, then obedience to his instructions is obedience to the objective principles of health. If I say that I completely trust my financial advisor, then obedience to his wishes is obedience to sound principles of financial management.

In the same way, if I say that I love my parents, then they must be good and virtuous people, and so naturally it follows that they must also love me – since if I were not a good person, I would not be able to love them for their virtue.

If we love each other, then obviously we take pleasure in each other's company and have each other's best interests at heart, and contact can only enhance the pleasure, integrity and virtue of our lives.

If I trust my doctor, and contact with my doctor always enhances my health, then anyone who tells me to avoid my doctor must *ipso facto* have the goal of harming my health. If my financial advisor is always right, then only a corrupt con man would tell me to fire my financial advisor.

Thus if I reframe my fear and hatred of my parents as "love," anyone who tells me to avoid my parents must be an evil person who only wishes me harm.

Do you see the horrors that we set in motion when we lie about virtue?

Since obedience to my parents' wishes is also obedience to "virtue," when my parents ask me to come over for an intermittent Sunday dinner, refusing to attend is the equivalent of refusing to be virtuous – in fact, committing a moral crime.

This reversal of values creates endless catastrophes in our relationships.

If we have redefined our cowardice as a virtue, then we will inevitably perceive certain traits in those around us as dangerous and negative.

If I my stockbroker is corrupt and is busily robbing me blind, then any competent stockbroker who comes across me will see that immediately, and say:

"This stockbroker that you think is very good is actually corrupt, and is violating most if not all professional ethics, and is taking you to the cleaners, and will leave you penniless. For instance, the degree of 'churning' that he is performing on your account is utterly unsustainable – you would require returns of 20-30% to break even, given the commissions he is generating for himself by buying and selling stocks in your account…"

This competent stockbroker would then give you objective reasons as to why you should no longer trust your existing stockbroker, but rather fire him immediately.

Naturally, if you have defined obedience to your corrupt stockbroker as obedience to financial responsibility, having this obedience revealed as conformity to financial *irresponsibility* would create enormous anxiety within you.

If you claim that you want to be healthy – and genuinely *do* want to be healthy – and you take up chain-smoking as a result of the advice of a corrupt doctor, hearing your doctor debunked will make you very upset.

Realizing that we have conned ourselves puts us in a state of excruciating vulnerability, since it reveals so much about our own family histories, and how we were exploited and rendered "easy prey" by our parents.

Some people, of course, are able to handle this upset if they are in fact dedicated to being healthy. They will survive their own shame, humiliation and anxiety, fire their corrupt doctor, and reform their habits.

However, the majority of people will simply shoot the messenger.

Clearly, people who redefine their vices as virtues have already demonstrated their preference for avoiding their own anxiety by making up stories.

Since the best predictor of future behaviour is relevant past behaviour, what do you think that these people's response will be to a situation that increases their anxiety?

Why, they're just going to make up another angry story to "explain away" their "mistake."

The Inevitable Counterattack…
Health is not a *moral* attribute, and so the preceding medical analogies are far less emotionally charged than the reality of redefining vices as virtues.

If my parents are corrupt or evil, then obedience to their wishes is obedience to corruption or evil.

In essence, if I obey corrupt or evil principles, I am in fact corrupt or evil.

Nothing is more emotionally volatile than labeling someone "corrupt" or "evil."

"Evil" is obedience to evil principles or evil people.

"Corruption" is redefining that evil as "the good."

No sane human being can look in the mirror and say: "I am evil." Even a monster such as Hitler portrayed himself *to himself* as the saviour of Germany, the liberator of the Aryan race, and so on.

The moment that a human being looks in the mirror and says, "I am evil," he must change.

This is a central reason why people would rather redefine "evil" as "the good" – since if they cannot, they are revealed as evil and must immediately start to change.

Thus if I invert rational values and redefine my cowardice as courage, I must inevitably banish everyone from my life who has even a hint of the following characteristics:

- Genuine courage
- Moral perceptiveness
- Integrity
- Honesty
- Empathy
- A true capacity to love
- Curiosity
- …and so on.

Counterfeiting Virtue

If I am a counterfeiter, I need to keep people away from me who can easily detect false currency. If I am a drug dealer, I am unlikely to befriend "drug enforcement" agents. If I am a liar, people with a strong ability to detect falsehoods – and the courage to confront liars – will be anathema to me. If I am a con man, I must prey upon the weak and gullible. Strong and perceptive souls will always be safe from me, since I will avoid them like the plague.

In the same way, when I pervert rational values by redefining my vices as virtues, I am inevitably drawn to reject and revile strong and virtuous people – and inevitably drawn towards weak and corrupt people who will not challenge my own corruption.

In other words, reversing *virtue* reverses *love*. Instead of being drawn towards virtue for the sake of happiness, you are drawn towards vice for the sake of avoiding pain.

Claiming that you are virtuous when you are not inevitably draws you to "love" people who are unlovable.

If you "love" yourself for your vices, you will inevitably be drawn to "love" others for their vices – and, as inevitably, to hate and fear other people for their virtues, just as you hate and fear true virtue in yourself.

Polarization

In this way, we are drawn to bond with people that we fundamentally dislike. We are drawn to them by the inescapable logic of our own premises – however, the hypocritical falsehoods of those premises also causes us to recoil from those we desire.

This form of attachment is basically a kind of self-destructive addiction rather than any form of benevolent love. A man who has redefined his vices as virtues has the same relationship with those that he claims to "love" that a heroin addict has to his heroin in the later stages of his addiction. He needs it because it relieves his anxiety, but he hates it because it is destroying his life.

In the same way, my partner is a mirror of myself – her virtues are my virtues, her vices are my vices.

Her capacity for honesty is my capacity for honesty.

Her integrity is my integrity.

To take a minor example of how this looks in practice, imagine a woman who has gained a few pounds struggling into her clothing, which has just returned from the dry cleaners. A mature person will first go and weigh herself, to see if she has gained any weight. An immature person will blame the dry cleaners for shrinking her clothing, or, if she finds out that she has gained weight, will blame her boyfriend for buying potato chips, or not telling her that she has gained weight, or society as a whole for "demanding" that women remain thin.

Projection

Of course, if I know that I am a coward but redefine my cowardice as "courage," I do not eliminate my knowledge of my cowardice. If I am fat and redefine fat as "healthy," I do not eliminate my knowledge of my obesity. If I steal a car, I do not suddenly believe that I actually *bought* it.

How, then, can I evade or ignore my knowledge of my own cowardice?

Well, the most common mechanism is a devilish psychological defense called "projection."

Projection is the habit of ascribing our own negative qualities to other people.

The most common example of this is *passive aggression*.

Let us return to our troubled couple, Sheila and Bruce.

If Bruce is frustrated but does not, cannot or will not openly express his frustration, then he will begin to cause problems for other people: either through tangential complaints, snappy comments, stony silence, or surly stomping.

Sheila will then ask him: "What's wrong?"

Naturally, Bruce will reply: "Nothing!"

Of course, Sheila knows that this is not the case, and will ask him again. Again and again, Bruce will deny that anything is wrong, thus causing her intense frustration.

It is in this manner that the frustration passes from Bruce to Sheila.

As Sheila becomes increasingly frustrated by Bruce's provocation and subsequent stonewalling, Bruce begins to express increasing exasperation towards her.

He claims to be irritated by her persistent questioning – which allows him to unload his original frustration, but blame it on *her actions* instead of *his own thinking*.

Zooming Out...

To a far greater degree, we can see the same mechanism at work in the realm of geopolitics.

Let us take a little spin back to 2001.

George Bush wants to invade Iraq, but he cannot openly express that he wants to invade Iraq – so he must make up reasons that place the ownership for his decision squarely on the shoulders of Saddam Hussein. Thus he can "legitimately" turn from an initiator to a reactor, from an aggressor to a leader acting in "self-defense."

Thus he continually repeats the mantra that Saddam Hussein is an aggressor who wants to attack the United States – thus "legitimizing" his own aggression, which is the true source of the conflict.

In the same way, our parents will often tell us that we are "selfish" for not wanting to drop by for another boring or unsettling Sunday dinner. "You are selfish," they will say, "because you are ignoring the feelings and needs of other people, and only thinking of what *you* want!"

However, it is clear that they are failing their own definition of "virtue" by ignoring *our* desire not to attend Sunday dinner, and only thinking of what *they* want. They selfishly want us to be there despite the fact that it goes

65

against our desires – but then they get angry at us for not wanting to be there because it goes against *their* desires.

Madness!

Thus we can see that *projection* is a mechanism for self-avoidance, or for actively rejecting knowledge of our own motivations.

If we are angry at our wife, but provoke *her* into anger instead of expressing our own anger and then release our anger based on the fact that *she* is angry, all that we have done is set an elaborate trap which allows us to abusively "release" our feelings without ever learning their cause.

Of course, the reason that we do not want to learn the cause of our actions is that we know deep down that our actions are unjustified – and most likely cravenly aggressive.

If I buy a stereo from a guy in a van, I will be reluctant to ask for a receipt, since I will want to avoid the knowledge that it is stolen. It is not the receipt that I am avoiding, but rather the knowledge that I am profiting from crime, and thus enabling criminals.

Changing Others

It would almost seem that, as a species, we are utterly addicted to changing others' behaviour rather than examining our own.

There is something so elementally seductive about playing the "know it all" card and lecturing others on their deficiencies. When problems arise, for all too many people this is the default position.

If they have a near-miss in a car, their first impulse is to blame other drivers.

If they become irritated with someone, their starting position is always that the other person's deficiencies are *causing* that irritation. If their children misbehave or develop bad habits, it is always the selfishness of the child, the influence of the peer group, or the tyranny of the media that is to blame.

Why is it that we are so drawn to blaming others and inevitably and endlessly attempting to correct *them*, rather than examining our own motives and ideas for the causes of our problems?

The obvious answer is that we prefer the short-term gain of self-righteousness to the long-term gain of actual growth and improvement in our habits – yet that does not explain very much, since we diet, exercise, go to work and see our dentists, and do all other sorts of things which sacrifice short-term gains for long-term gains.

Thus we can see that human beings certainly *do* have the capacity to defer immediate gratification for the sake of long-term advantage. Why is this so rarely the case in one of the most important aspects of our lives – our personal relationships?

Why We Succumb…

First of all, other people can be manipulated in a way that, say, our teeth cannot. We can convince another person that he alone is to blame for the problems in our relationship, but we cannot "convince" a tooth that it is not infected when it is. We can bully another person into believing that he is responsible for our overeating; we cannot bully the fat off our bellies.

Secondly, the general lack of integrity in those around us positively enables the kind of "blame game" that goes on in relationships. People who are raised badly, who end up with weak wills, weak characters and manipulative habits, can be easily blamed and controlled.

If we could only achieve the kind of integrity that, say, a tooth has, we would do an enormous service to the mental health and happiness of the world.

Enabling and the Vengeance of the Slave

Allowing other people to treat us badly is a subtle form of aggression against them.

It arises from a fairly primitive time in our species, when slavery and hyper-control dominated our interactions.

If a slave hates his master – as deep down he surely does – but cannot retaliate against him in any violent or assertive manner, what are his options?

Well, when you want somebody dead, but you cannot kill him openly, *your best option is to exacerbate his unhealthy habits.*

In other words, a slave can eventually take vengeance on his master by continually bringing him a drink, sitting with him while he drinks, and endlessly offering to refill his glass.

On a psychological level, the slave can effectively re-create his own misery in the mind of his master by *both provoking and submitting to bullying.*

Every time the master beats the slave, the misery and self-loathing of the master increases. Every time the master screams at the slave, the soul of the master dies a little more. Every whip of the lash kills the master's capacity for love, contentment and peace of mind.

This, of course, is Nietzsche's "slave morality," in which the slave takes a form of masochistic satisfaction and dark glee in the spiritual destruction of his master. The passive-aggressive "moral superiority" of the slave is the only satisfaction that such a beaten-down creature can hope for.

The problem, however, is that by continually pursuing the insidious satisfaction of passive-aggressive masochism, the slave often becomes dangerously addicted to this form of vengeance.

In other words, *the slave becomes addicted to having a master* and finds life without this form of underhanded revenge entirely lacking in stimulation and satisfaction.

It's not entirely in the past…
Now, since most of us are raised as virtual slaves within our families and schools, it is all too common for us to become addicted to having masters

– and thus attempting to "master" our rulers through self-pitying moral superiority and the enabling, or supporting, of self-destructive behaviours on the part of those who command us.

If left unexamined, this drive to destroy those who control us inevitably leads us to seek out those who will control us, and then endlessly attempt to destroy them.

As mentioned earlier, the weapon of the slave is "moral superiority," or beatific self-righteousness. To *really* undo his master, the slave must set up a standard of "forgiveness," and "unconditional love," by which he tortures the infected conscience of his master.

The way that this paradigm translates itself into modern relationships – particularly romantic, but also parental – is that both parties intermittently take on the roles of master and slave, or persecutor and persecuted, or "unjust attacker" and "self-righteous victim." Since their lives are based on attack, condemnation, self-righteous vengeance and frustrated control, they remain in a continual state of provocation, attack, withdrawal and moral pomposity, creating an endless closed loop of ever-increasing frustration, bitterness, fear and resentment.

On a more overt level, we can see this kind of interaction occurring in the typical cycle of an abusive marriage. Let's be stereotypical and talk about the husband as the abuser.

Over a few weeks, Bruce becomes increasingly tense and snappy. In turn, Sheila responds to his growing aggression through provocation, either in the form of complete obsequience – which irritates him – or endless questions and nagging defiance, which inflames him. Bruce then asserts his dominance and releases his tension by attacking Sheila in a titanic blow-up either physical or verbal in nature.

However, since Bruce has asserted his dominance in such a hysterical and abusive manner, the power in the relationship now passes from Bruce to Sheila.

Since Bruce has acted so obviously unjustly, Sheila now gains control of the moral narrative of their relationship, and uses it to bully Bruce.

After his attack, she threatens to leave him. He comes crawling back, apologizing and begging for forgiveness – now playing the part of the slave instead of the master. Sheila withholds her "forgiveness," enjoying the new power that she has over him, and abusing him in turn, both by torturing him morally and staying in the relationship.

When we disapprove of someone morally but remain in an intimate and supporting relationship with him, we are acting entirely immorally ourselves.

If I work for a corrupt boss, and am fully aware that he is stealing from his customers but continue to work for him, I am enabling his corruption as surely as if I were performing it myself. I may attempt to assuage my conscience by nagging at my boss to be a "better" man, or tentatively bringing up my "objections" in meetings, but as time goes on, and I do not quit, everyone understands that my nagging is just a ritual designed to enable me to continue to take money from a corrupt person or organization while continuing to pretend to myself that I am moral.

By continuing to work for this corrupt man – while professing my own devotion to moral principles – I am clearly communicating to him that morality is simply a tool for self-deception, and that ethical exhortation is merely self-medicating hypocrisy. This "enables" his corruption even more so than the customers he steals from, who would doubtless flee his predation if they discovered it.

Thus remaining in relationships with immoral people while complaining that they are immoral is one of the most subtle forms of abuse in the world. It is revoltingly hypocritical, insofar as it uses ethics to enable and justify corruption.

This is the difference between the mugger who steals from you because he wants to buy a drink, and the socialist who steals from you because she wants to "help the poor."

When you look closely for this kind of interaction in the relationships of those around you – or your own relationships, for that matter – it becomes blindingly obvious and virtually omnipresent.

A man "persecutes" his wife for her lack of sexual desire, and then plays the victim when he is criticized for not helping around the house. When the woman is attacked for her lack of sexual interest, she responds with a passive aggressive "moral" argument: "I do not feel like having sex because you are not emotionally available, or we are not close enough, or you yelled at me yesterday, or I am worried about finances, or I am stressed out because I have too much housework, or you don't help enough with the kids etc etc etc."

If we break down the man's moral argument, he is basically saying: "I agreed to pursue a monogamous relationship with you, giving up sex with all other women. This creates an implicit obligation on your part to have sex with me since you hold a monopoly on sexual interactions. By continually refusing to have sex with me, you are setting a terrible and unjust trap wherein I will be tempted to pursue an affair, which will result in my personal and financial destruction. Since you are using sex to punish and control me in our relationship, but I am not allowed to pursue sex outside of this relationship, you are putting me up against the wall, which is a most hateful and unloving thing to do."

His wife, on the other hand, is saying something like: "I do not feel close to you, because you are not emotionally available, which is a failure of your duties as a husband. You also yelled at me yesterday, which is abusive, and also a failure on your part as a husband. I complain about finances because you do not make enough money. I'm stressed about housework because you do not help enough. The kids are driving me crazy because I always have to be the disciplinarian, while you get to be the 'fun' dad who just plays with them. Thus, you are cold, lazy, unambitious and abusive. In fact, asking for sex when you know that I feel this way is further evidence of your coldness and abusive tendencies!"

As we can see, if we look closely, what is really going on here is a not-too-subtle tug of war over the *moral narrative* of the relationship, which is essentially a revolving slave-to-master interaction.

Deep down, we all know that if we can get someone to admit that a certain behaviour is morally wrong, he can in no way continue to defend that behaviour, and must change.

As I have argued from the very beginning of my podcast series, morality is the most powerful tool in the arsenal of mankind.

Whoever controls "morality" controls the relationship.

We all understand this instinctively, and so continually use stories and mythologies to attempt to gain control of the moral narrative of a relationship.

The reason that we never fully succeed is that we are perpetually creating "rules" for our partner that we do not follow ourselves.

We are all perfectly aware of this kind of hypocrisy in others when we read about priests who molest children, anti-homosexual Congressman who solicit gay sex in bathroom stalls, or people like Oprah who continually talk about feminism and "woman power" while simultaneously presenting an endless cavalcade of fear-mongering stories about attacks on women. Dr. Phil is another example of this kind of phenomenon. He continually attacks those who use violence to resolve their problems while praising soldiers to the skies.

There are several common mythologies at work in romantic relationships, which we would be wise to learn by heart.

"You Lack Empathy"

The first and most common moral mythology – particularly for women – is the essential criticism: "You lack empathy."

The criticism of "selfishness" is so common that it can be hard to hear after a while.

Many, many women truly believe that if their husbands were genuinely empathetic, their marriages would be enormously improved, and their needs would be met.

The simple truth of the fact, though, is that most people are happy to talk about what they think and feel if they meet with genuine acceptance and respect.

What women are really saying when they complain that their husbands "lack empathy" is that their husbands are not thinking and feeling what their wives *want* them to think and feel.

Let's look at a common example.

The horror of chores…

A fairly constant complaint from women is that their husbands seem supernaturally resistant to initiating chores.

"Why oh why is it that I have to ask him a dozen times to take out the garbage? It's not like garbage day magically changes from week to week! Why can he not get it through his head that I don't want to have to manage him like some sort of mother? And if he's *not* going to take out the garbage, why doesn't he just *tell* me so I can do it *myself*, instead of just continually promising that he's going to do it 'in a few minutes'?"

This is a clear example of "moral positioning." Here is a translation of the subtext:

"You're sooo not going to get laid!"

Or, alternatively:

"He does not respect my needs, he is not pulling his weight in this household, he is just manipulating me by appeasing me in the moment, while having no intention of doing what I ask. He is passive-aggressively frustrating me – he is selfish and lazy, and is turning me into a nag, so that *I* end up looking like the bad person when *he's* the one who's not doing his chores!"

On the surface, this seems like a seductively appealing narrative. Who could fail to sympathize with such a hard done by and put upon woman, struggling to maintain a household while her husband lazes and obfuscates on the couch?

Sadly, it is all pure nonsense.

By attempting to control his behaviour through nagging repetition, this woman is bypassing the most important question she needs to ask about *why he is doing what he is doing* (or not doing).

In other words, she claims that he is not being empathetic towards *her* needs, while at the same time she is not being at all empathetic towards *his* needs.

Clearly, by not taking out the garbage, he is communicating to her that he does not want to take out the garbage.

By making up a story that portrays him as lazy and negligent, his wife is *creating a mythology about his motivation* rather than honestly attempting to understand it.

This is not science or logic or empiricism or common sense or intimacy, but *religion*.

Remember, when bad things happen in the world of religion, "sinners" are invented to take the blame.

In this case, the "sinner" is laziness – or the husband in general.

We may as well say, when striving to understand the cause of an illness, "Satan made me sick!" Sure, it's a comforting story with a protagonist and antagonist and a satisfyingly vindictive moral theme.

Sadly, it just has nothing to do with reality whatsoever.

If I am genuinely "lazy," I may possess that trait for any one of a myriad number of reasons. I may be depressed or lonely, or feel over-controlled, or sense that my life is going in the wrong direction, or have any variety of medical deficiencies or ailments, or I may believe that my life lacks meaning and purpose, or I may be worried about possible moral transgressions on my part, or I may feel that I am embedded in a corrupt or compromising work environment, or my children may be going through a certain phase that reminds me of sad times in my own childhood, or I may be worried that I no longer love my wife…

There can be 10,000 or more reasons underlying my "lack of motivation."

A wife who does not sit down with sensitivity and empathy to ask her husband why he is unmotivated is just a bully and has no moral right whatsoever to criticize her husband for *his* lack of sensitivity and empathy.

Nagging and Humiliation
She is also humiliating him in a way that can be hard to see.

If we are married to someone, we must certainly claim to love and respect him above all others. If we treat him, however, as if he is a "defective household chore robot," then we are implicitly denigrating him in truly terrible ways.

When a wife marches up to her husband, demands that he take out the garbage, and implies that he is lazy and selfish, she is clearly communicating the following:

"I know that I promised to love and respect you for all eternity, but right now getting the garbage outside the house is infinitely more important to me than understanding your soul. In fact, I'm perfectly willing to attack your nature, ethics and initiative in order to get you to take the trash out. On my scale of values, moving the trash is an infinite plus. Understanding your soul *is not even on my list!"*

To see that your true personality and being is not even on the list of your wife's priorities – and that you have been displaced by empty and trivial tasks – is unbearably humiliating.

If this humiliation were truly *felt* by all the spouses in the world, it would be like a neutron bomb in the world of marriage.

Marriages, like buildings, would be left standing – there would just be no people in them.

The Abuse of Assumptions
As I talked about in my book "On Truth," morality is almost always used as a weapon of control and dominance.

When your wife marches up to you and demands in a shrill and exasperated tone for you to "PLEASE take out the *garbage!*" – implying that you are lazy and selfish – there are really only two possibilities.

You are in fact lazy and selfish..?
Naturally, if you *are* lazy and selfish – and we assume that these pejorative terms accurately represent the entire sum of your personality – then attacking you for being lazy and selfish after voluntarily choosing you as a life partner is patently ridiculous.

If my wife could have married any man with any accent in the world, but chose me, it would seem rather strange for her to attack me for having a British accent, claiming that every man with a British accent – who is not currently residing in England – is a pretentious phony.

If I *am* a pretentious phony, then it is quite silly for my wife to attack me for *being* a pretentious phony. If I am not a pretentious phony, then my wife would only use that abusive term to hurt me – and she would only be able to hurt me with it if I was not in fact a pretentious phony, or disliked pretentious phonies myself.

If I were a pretentious phony, then clearly I would have developed that personality trait because I lacked self-esteem, and so felt a need to portray myself as wiser or smarter than I actually was in order to gain the good approval of others. (In other words, as a self-defensive "initial strike" against potential attacks.)

Now, I would only have developed this low self-esteem and dependence upon the approval of others if I had been persistently attacked and condemned by my parents when I was a child.

If, when expressing my authentic opinions, I had been dismissed as an ignorant philistine, I would then be sorely tempted to manufacture more "sophisticated" opinions in order to avoid being attacked.

In other words, I would be "pretentious" as an adult because I had been verbally abused as a child.

It is, then, *entirely abusive* for my wife to verbally abuse me for traits that have resulted from a history of having been verbally abused.

If you are "lazy," it is generally because you feel a significant disconnect between your choices, your actions, and the effect you can have on your environment.

In psychological studies, when chickens or rats are given random punishments and rewards, they tend to become inert, because they cannot create any sense of rational cause and effect between their choices, their actions and their environment.

Personal energy and initiative, in other words, generally arise from a feeling of *efficacy*.

Depressed or inert people feel that their "locus of control" resides somewhere outside themselves. A micromanaged child will not easily develop a sense of personal initiative since his entire being is dedicated towards satisfying the endless and contradictory demands of other people.

It's tough to plan your future when you're dodging bullets.

I knew a woman who, when making toast, had to suffer through her mother hovering over her and constantly correcting everything she was doing. She should have brushed the breadcrumbs off the bread before putting them into the toaster, the heat was on just a little bit too high, she should not turn away from the toaster while it was in operation, in case something caught fire – and when all was said and done, she did not clean the toaster nearly well enough!

The amount of stress involved in heating two slices of bread was ridiculous. This woman had virtually no chance to develop her own methodology of thinking, of testing cause and effect, of deciding *for herself* how even minor goals could be best achieved.

Inevitably, she found herself largely paralyzed in the realm of major life decisions, and tended to navigate from moment to moment, based on the approval or disapproval of those around her. She wanted to achieve great things with her career, but ended up working as a secretary despite a very good education, because she had simply not developed the capacity to identify and pursue goals on her own accord, and according to own judgment – and, of course, remained hypersensitive to criticism, which crippled her ability to negotiate, and so progress in any career.

Sadly, her paralysis also invited micromanagement from others. She would proclaim her desire to achieve a certain goal, but then would take no steps towards it, while continually complaining about the difficulties of achieving it. This would invite an endless stream of people into her life who would help her set up action plans, alternative approaches, proactive time management goals and so on.

I never did see anyone actually ask what she felt when she sat down to attempt to achieve her goals.

If that question had been asked, and an honest answer had been provided, real progress could have been made.

Unfortunately, by telling her how to achieve her goals, people were in fact stepping into the role of her mother, since when we tell people what to do, we automatically denigrate their existing abilities. If I met you on the street and explained to you in great detail how to put your left foot forward, and then your right foot forward in order to walk, you would scarcely feel elevated by my opinion of your existing ability to walk.

In the same way, when a wife denigrates her husband for failing to initiate and complete chores without instruction, she is actually abusing him, denigrating him, and re-creating exactly the same circumstances – and exactly the same abuse – that prompted his inertia to begin with.

And yet, if you listen to her surface story, you will likely walk away entirely convinced that *she* is the victim in the interaction with her husband.

On the other hand, if you are not lazy, but your wife tells you that you are, then clearly she is using the pejorative to manipulate you.

Keep your eyes peeled. Do not be fooled.

The War of Narrative

As mentioned earlier, most relationships are founded on a *war of narratives* in which competing mythologies jockey for the dominant position.

Love and Mythology
How many times in relationships do we have the following interaction:

- "Hey, that really hurt me, what you just said."
- "I had no desire to hurt you, you must be oversensitive, or must have misunderstood me. I'm sorry that you are so upset."

The first statement is a statement of fact, the second statement is a statement of *mythology*.

For about six months, Christina and I had lengthy conversations about what I called "zinging."

Christina would say something that hurt me, and I would express my surprise and upset. With total sincerity, she would apologize for the fact that I got hurt, claiming that she had no intention to hurt me, that she had no idea that it would be hurtful, and so on. To her endless credit, she did not say or imply that I was oversensitive or paranoid.

REAL-TIME RELATIONSHIPS

I replied that I completely believed that she did not consciously want to hurt me – since that would be sadistic, and thus would be a complete deal-breaker as far as the relationship went.

This was very confusing for her, of course, and was a great challenge to her sense of her own virtue and benevolence. As we continued to work on this problem of, "Stef gets hurt despite the fact that Christina has no desire to hurt him," we did slowly get to the point where Christina was willing to explore her own history, and how she was never really apologized to in her own childhood, after she was hurt.

Eventually, we got to the point where we understood that Christina had been treated callously or cruelly at times in her childhood, and then when she expressed hurt everyone told her that no one had any intention to hurt her, that she was oversensitive, and so must have misunderstood the intentions of those around her. If she continued to express her upset, she was punished. When she was spanked, her mother would snap: "Why are you crying?"

The ironic thing about this all-too-typical interaction is that Christina was in fact ignoring her *own* hurt feelings rather than mine – and those hurt feelings existed in *her* past, not in *my* present.

Human beings are in essence pattern-making machines. In her childhood, Christina's hurt feelings were endlessly minimized and ignored by others, and so a pattern was set up within her own mind, which was: "hurt = minimize."

When her parents hurt her, and she expressed pain, her parents then experienced pain themselves – since no one really wants to hurt someone they claim to love. (Certainly when Christina finally understood that she was in fact causing me pain through her stinging comments, it was very painful to her – both because she did not want to cause me pain in the present, and because she then re-experienced her own childhood pain.)

Since Christina's parents did not want to experience the pain and anxiety of having caused their child pain, they blamed *her* sensitivity and paranoia for causing her pain – and so, by extension, their pain.

In other words, it was fundamentally *their own pain* that they were minimizing – their dismissal of Christina's criticisms was an effect of their own self rejection.

They rejected Christina because they rejected themselves.

Feel the Burn!

ne of the problems that arises from this habitual interaction is the *lack of feedback* it creates.

In fact, it could be said that the entire point of this book is to convince you that you *need to feel pain*.

Pain is healthy, pain is good – pain is essential to the healthy functioning of mind and body.

If we could will away the agony of a toothache, we would become very ill and possibly die. If we did not walk gingerly on a sprained ankle, we could create chronic bone problems. If we did not reduce our use of a pulled muscle, we could tear it irretrievably.

We understand the value of pain in the physical sense – however, in the emotional realm we have access to a numbing drug called "blame" that seductively promises to eliminate our anxiety, guilt, shame and remorse in the moment.

If we understand our use of blame as a classic addiction, it becomes far easier to comprehend.

We can look at an addiction as any habit that reduces anxiety or pain in the moment at the cost of failing to address (and probably exacerbating) the underlying cause.

If I take a mood-enhancing drug because I feel sad, I am not dealing with my sadness, but just "nuking" the symptom. If I take sleeping pills because I am too stressed to sleep, I am only solving the problem of being awake, not of being stressed.

Of course, it can be highly beneficial to minimize discomfort while dealing with the real underlying issue – i.e. to use Novocain during a root canal, or take antidepressants while going to therapy – as long as the underlying issue is in fact being addressed.

In the same way, there are many ways that we can approach each other's irrationalities which minimize defensive reactions and upsets. What is not productive, however, is temporarily eliminating anxiety by permanently ignoring the problem.

The most common way of eliminating discomfort in the moment is to create a story which eliminates responsibility.

Eliminating Responsibility
One continual pattern in life is that people will drive around for years looking for a suitable cliff, take a running leap over the edge, and then spend decades complaining that they were unjustly pushed.

A woman will spend years dating and choosing a man, and then months or years in a relationship, and then months engaged, and then get married – and then with a completely straight face complain about her husband, saying with all sincerity that she had "no idea" about his true nature.

No Idea?

There are really only three possibilities when a woman says that she had "no idea" that her husband was X, Y or Z – despite having *years* to get to know him before marrying him.

If she is genuinely clueless about her husband, then either she is functionally retarded in her ability to judge people, or he is a truly cunning sociopath who can mask his true nature for years, with no clues whatsoever about his dangerous or dysfunctional nature – or she is lying about her ignorance of his nature.

In the first case, she may well complain about her husband, but it could be easily said that he has far more to complain about her, in that she has a negative ability to judge people and very likely needs help tying her shoes. She thought that her boyfriend was the best guy for her, and he turns out to be problematic in significant areas. That is not just a misjudgment, but rather an *anti*-judgment. It's not like taking a shortcut that doesn't work out as efficiently as you hoped: it is more like continually driving the completely wrong way while checking the map and stopping to ask for directions.

If the woman really is that foolish, then she would be too vapid to actually blame her husband for what he does, since her understanding of cause and effect would be so absent that she would be more likely to blame her unhappiness on the motion of the moon.

If she *can* correctly identify her husband's dysfunctional behaviour as the "cause" of her unhappiness, then she is intelligent enough to have perceived his true nature long before they even became boyfriend and girlfriend.

If she then says that her husband is truly a cunning sociopath who fooled everyone for years, then we know that she is lying. There is no possibility that a sociopath can be so cunning that he can fool everyone for years about his true nature. If this were possible, then there would never be such a diagnosis as "sociopathic," because such creatures would be able to avoid or mask their symptoms in all possible scenarios and tests.

Thus it can never be possible that a wife can complain first and foremost about the actions of her partner. This would be equivalent to a dermatologist blaming the sun for his sunburn.

Common Stories

Stories are characterized by a number of common traits. The first and most obvious is the use of the words "always" and "never."

For instance, a husband may say to his wife, "You *never* support me!"

His wife may retort: "You *always* accuse me of that!"

Other common stories include:

- "I have to do everything around here."
- "You never take responsibility for your actions."
- "Why don't you ever just sit down and really talk to me?"
- "You never lift a finger around here unless I tell you what to do."
- "You're just so passive."
- "You never take initiative."
- "You're just lazy."
- "You're so vain."
- "It's like you're *married* to that computer!" (Sorry, my voice recognition software was running when my wife came into the room...)

You never support me...
Let's take a look at this statement and see how we know that it is a story.

If I tell you that you never support me, then that is either true or it is abusive. In other words, any time I tell you something negative about yourself — particularly if it is an absolute statement — then either I am telling you the truth about yourself or I am lying to you in order to hurt you. (For more on this, see my book: "On Truth: The Tyranny of Illusion.")

If it is *true* that you have never supported me, then either you lack the capacity to support anyone, or you have the capacity to support others but choose not to support me.

If you lack the capacity to support anyone, ever, in any way whatsoever, then criticizing you for this lack is the direct equivalent of criticizing a man with no arms for his inability to play basketball, or calling a non-Greek speaker "stupid" for not being able to speak Greek.

Clearly, when we criticize someone, we can only do so with justice if he is capable of correcting his behaviour. This is why no person with any sensitivity calls a mentally retarded person "stupid," a woman in traction "lazy," or a man with Tourette's syndrome "rude."

If the behaviour cannot be corrected, then criticizing it is abusive.

Assuming you can…
Assuming that you are capable of supporting me, if I tell you that you never support me then either you *have* a desire to support me — but choose not to — or you do *not* have a desire to support me at all.

If you know *how* to support someone, but do not have a desire to support me at all, then clearly you believe that I am not worthy of being supported. In other words, there are people in your life that you *do* want to support — and do support — but I am not one of them. This must be because I am behaving poorly relative to those other people that you support, since supporting someone is an act of love.

If my bad behaviour is causing you to refrain from supporting me, even though you could, then if I attack you for your lack of support, this will only make you *less* likely to want to support me.

It is ridiculous for me to criticize your behaviour in such a way that I reinforce that behaviour. This is exactly like a woman giving her husband money to gamble, going with him to the casino and cheering him on, and then laying into him about his gambling habit. It certainly happens, of course, but it is quite ridiculous.

Furthermore, supporting someone must involve believing in his better nature or potential and helping him to achieve it in a positive manner. If I roundly criticize you for failing to support me, then I am saying that it would be better or nobler for you to support me. However, I am not at all helping you to achieve that "better" state in a positive manner, but rather just attacking you for failing to achieve it.

In other words, attacking you for failing to support me is the exact opposite of being supportive.

In this way, I am modeling the exact same behaviour that I condemn as unjust and unworthy in you.

Is it any wonder, then, that you hesitate to support me?

When I attack you for failing to support me, it is exactly the same as if I were a chronic liar proclaiming my honesty and demanding that you tell me the truth.

Yuck.

Lacking Knowledge?
On the other hand, if you have a desire to support me, but do not, then clearly what you lack is the *knowledge* of how to support me.

If the only thing that you lack is a knowledge of how to support me, then the only way that I can practically get you to support me is to give you that knowledge.

If I am Chinese, and I want you to be able to talk to my parents, who do not speak English, then I would respectfully ask that you learn Mandarin.

If you agree to learn Mandarin, then the question is whether I or someone else will teach you.

If I will teach you, then obviously I must be able to speak Mandarin in order to be able to teach you. If I do not speak Mandarin, then it would be highly hypocritical of me to criticize you for *your* inability to speak Mandarin.

Also, at a very practical level, I would be unable to teach you the language.

If I told you that it was of great value to be able to speak to my parents in Mandarin, but I did not speak Mandarin myself, then clearly the solution would be for both of us to take classes in Mandarin.

If I did speak Mandarin and I offered to teach you the language, it would only make sense to accept my offer if I was in fact a good teacher.

If my "courses" in Mandarin consisted of me yelling at you that you just aren't getting the language – in an incomprehensible foreign language no less – then clearly I in fact have no interest whatsoever in actually teaching you Mandarin.

Instead, I am using my knowledge of Mandarin to humiliate you, by setting up a standard called "learn Mandarin," and then making it completely impossible for you to learn that language.

If, at some point, you found out that the incomprehensible foreign language that I was yelling at you in was not in fact Mandarin, but some sort of gibberish, and that I did not know Mandarin at all, then you would very likely become completely enraged at my hypocrisy, condescension, and manipulation.

What are the odds that you would ever respect me as a teacher, friend or companion again?

Such are the perils of manipulative storytelling.

What on Earth?
What on earth could be the motivations for such a dysfunctional interaction? Why would I want to attack someone for not supporting me – distinctly unsupportive behaviour – when I actually *could* be supported if I modeled better behaviour, or chose a better partner?

In other words, if I so greatly fear being unsupported, why would I create conditions which will inevitably result in me being unsupported?

The Boxer

Why is it that we are so inevitably drawn to re-create that which we most fear?

To understand that, let us look at the parable of a boxer named Simon.

As a child, Simon is subjected to physical abuse. He is slapped, pushed, punched and beaten.

Since he is a child, he is helpless to resist these attacks. How, then, can he survive them?

Well, since clearly he cannot master his environment, or those who are abusing him, that leaves only one choice for poor Simon.

Simon must master *himself*.

He cannot master his attackers – or their attacks – he can only master his *reaction* to their attacks.

He has no control over the external world – he can only have control over his *internal world*.

All children take pleasure in exercising increasing levels of control over their environment. If control over their *external* environment is impossible, however, they have no choice but to start exercising increasing control over their *internal* environment: their thoughts and feelings.

This is all quite logical, and something that we would all wish for, as the best way to survive an impossible situation.

If we cannot get rid of the *source* of our pain, what we most desire is to get rid of the pain *itself*.

The Relief of Self-Control

Thus Simon grows up gaining a sense of efficacy and power *by controlling his own pain, fear and hatred*.

The pleasure that most children get out of mastering external tasks such as tying their shoelaces, catching a ball and learning to skate, Simon gets out of "rising above" and controlling his terrifying emotions.

Can we blame Simon for this? If anaesthetic is readily available, would we want to scream through an appendectomy without it?

When Simon is young, his self-control remains relatively stable. As he gets older, though, his parents slowly begin to reduce the amount of physical abuse they inflict on him. This is particularly true during and after puberty, when he is becoming old enough to tell others about the abuse, and also because his increasing size makes it less and less possible to dominate him physically.

How does Simon *feel* about these decreasing physical attacks?

Two words: *terrified* and *disoriented*.

Simon's entire sense of power and efficacy – his very *identity* even – has been defined by his ability to master and control his own emotions in the face of terrifying abuse.

In other words, in the absence of abuse, he has no sense of control, efficacy or power.

In addition to being taught all the *wrong* things, Simon has also been taught almost none of the *right* things. He does not know how to negotiate, he does not know how to express his emotions, he has not been taught empathy, he has not been taught sensitivity, he has not been taught win-win interactions – the words that are missing from Simon's social vocabulary could fill a shelf of dictionaries.

Thus, in the absence of violence, not only does Simon feel powerless – since his sense of "power" arose primarily as the result of his ability to *survive* violence – but he is also increasingly thrust into a world of *voluntarism*, where sophisticated skills of self-expression and negotiation are required for success.

As he enters into his teenage years, for the first time since he was very young Simon feels excruciatingly powerless – and *vulnerable*.

Since *vulnerability* was the original state he was in before he began to repress and control his emotional responses to those around him, he unconsciously feels that he is in enormous danger. (This arises from the reality that he *was* in enormous danger when he was a child, but he is only now feeling it for the first time.)

The reason that he disowned his emotions in the first place was because he felt fear and hatred in the face of physical attacks. It was the reality of his vulnerability that provoked the self-defense of dissociation and "self-mastery."

Thus for Simon, vulnerability is always followed by excruciating and self-annihilating attacks.

Having spent years mastering his responses to these attacks, he has not learned how to deal with vulnerability in a positive and self-expressed manner.

As he becomes an adult, however, Simon no longer needs to defend himself against attacks – thus undermining his sense of control – and he also moves faster and faster into a world of voluntary interactions for which he is utterly unprepared.

Simon also unconsciously knows that learning the skills necessary to flourish in this voluntary world – if that is even possible for him anymore – will take years of excruciating labour.

Fleeing the future for the past...
Simon has access to a drug that can instantly make all of his anxiety go away. This drug can restore his sense of control, eliminate his bottomless terror of voluntary interactions, and place him right back in familiar territory where he feels efficacious, powerful and in control.

That drug, of course, is violence.

Simon finds that when he leaves the world of voluntary interactions and re-enters the world of violence and abuse, his anxiety vanishes. His sense of efficacy and control returns, and he feels mastery over his own world again.

Like an army that does not want to be disbanded, in the absence of external enemies, Simon must create them.

After realizing the relative joy and serenity that he feels after getting involved in physical fights, Simon goes down to his local gym and puts on some boxing gloves.

He finds that he is very good in the ring, because where other people feel fear and caution, he, due to his years of self-mastery, feels power and control. When he is in the ring he does not feel anxious, he does not feel afraid – he does not even feel angry – he simply feels the satisfaction of being in a situation that he can control.

The endorphins released in Simon's system by violence quickly become addictive.

True addiction requires both a highly positive reaction from taking a drug and a highly negative reaction from abstaining from it. For Simon, boxing not only restores his sense of control, but it also eliminates the crippling anxiety he feels in the absence of violence.

Sadly, familiarity breeds content…

This is the psychological story of a boxer, of course, but it can equally apply to criminals, soldiers, policemen, and others drawn to dangerous situations.

Simon was utterly terrified of violence when he was a child, so how can we understand his pursuit of boxing as a career when he becomes an adult?

When we become addicted to controlling our fears, we can no longer live without either control or fear.

Simon became addicted to controlling his responses to abuse – *thus he can no longer function in the absence of abuse.*

Addiction also worsens when every step down the road of repetition makes it that much harder to turn around.

This applies to Simon in many, many terrible ways.

Every time he uses the defenses he developed in his childhood, he reinforces the value of violence in his adult life. Every time he avoids the anxiety of voluntary and positive interactions through the use of violence, he takes yet another step away from learning how to negotiate in a positive manner with kind and worthwhile people.

In other words, every time he "uses" the drug of violence, he makes the next "use" of violence that much more likely – and resisting the drug that much harder.

In this way, we can truly understand how a man can be drawn to endlessly repeat that which terrified him the most as a child.

In hopefully less extreme ways, Simon's story can also help us understand why we are so drawn to repeat that which we fear the most.

Were you rejected as a child? Beware your desire for rejection.

Were you verbally abused as a child? Watch out for verbally abusive people: they will inject you with addictive endorphins.

Were you sexually abused as a child? Watch out for predators: they will tempt you with the self-medication of surviving them.

The Sadist

The above analogy can help us understand how someone can end up spending his whole life attempting to "master" violence.

However, at least Simon is getting into the ring with an equal. How can we understand a parent who ends up abusing his or her child?

A basic fact of human nature is that it is impossible for anyone to do anything that involves a moral choice without moral justification. George Bush could not invade Iraq without claiming that it was an act of "self-defense," or "just punishment." When parents talk about screaming at or hitting their children, they always justify their actions by claiming that, "We have tried everything else and gotten nowhere." Or, they claim that their exasperated responses are generated by the misbehaviour of their children: "He just doesn't listen; he doesn't show us the proper respect," etc.

It is impossible to imagine a parent standing in front of a mirror and saying: "I am abusing my innocent child." Any parent capable of making such a statement would have recoiled in horror the first time that he yelled at or struck his child, and sought the necessary help.

Continued abuse requires continual *moral justifications*. In fact, the very worst aspects of the abuse that a child receives are not so much the physical fear and pain, but rather the *moral corruption* of the lies that are told to justify the abuse.

For a child, being beaten is terrible, but being repeatedly told that the beating is a *just response to his "bad" actions* is worse.

So – how could this possibly come about?

Child Abuse
For the sake of this example, let us assume that the parent was abused in her own childhood, as is so often the case.

We will take the example of a mother named Wendy, who ends up verbally abusing her daughter Sally.

Wendy was verbally abused when she was a child. She was told that she was bad, disrespectful, disobedient, ungrateful, selfish and so on.

From Wendy's childhood perspective, her own mother loomed like a titan in her little world. One of the amazing things about the differences in perspective between parent and child is that the parent screams and hits because the parent feels helpless. However, to the child, the parent seems virtually omnipotent.

We can assume that the Christian God destroyed Sodom and Gomorrah because He felt helpless to reform its inhabitants. However, from the standpoint of the city-dwellers burning alive in a sea of flames, God's complaint that He felt helpless would be utterly incomprehensible. If God is all-powerful, as He claims, how can he claim frustrated helplessness as his motivation? If an all-powerful deity cannot reform individuals, how can those individuals, with infinitely *less* power, be expected to reform themselves?

If parents knew how large they loomed in their child's world, they would use a far, far lighter touch in their discipline. When you are around somebody whose hearing is preternaturally sensitive, you only need to whisper; yelling is both unnecessary and abusive.

When Wendy was a child, her mother's verbal abuse was utterly overwhelming. The stress of having someone five times your size, who has complete and utter power over you, yelling at you, putting you down, denigrating you, or abusing you in some other manner causes a fundamental short-circuit in a child's neurological system. It is the equivalent of taking a man terrified of heights and constantly dangling him out the open door of an airplane. He may "acclimatize" himself to the repetitively awful stimulation, but only through extreme dissociation from his environment, which comes at a terrible personal cost. Victims of repetitive torture undergo the same "out of body" experience wherein they cease to feel, and in many ways cease to live, at least emotionally.

When a child is abused, she experiences her life as a series of fundamentally impossible situations. The capacity to abuse arises out of a lack of bonding, a lack of empathy, an absence of sensitivity towards the feelings of the child.

A child's only security is her *bond* with her parent. Abuse is a deliberate severing of that bond – a "strangling with the umbilical." Abusing a child requires that you eliminate your capacity to empathize with her. If a child perceives that she cannot rely on her bond with her mother – which is to say that her mother's capacity to empathize with her comes and goes at best – then the child feels fundamentally insecure, because positive and empathetic treatment cannot be relied on.

When you are under the total power of someone who can treat you badly whenever she feels like it, you are placed into an impossible situation because that person will inevitably command you to show "respect" and "love" towards her.

If your abusive mother detects that you fear her, for instance, she will generally react with aggression. If at a dinner party your mother raises her hand and you cower in fear and beg her not to hit you, she will get very angry.

Thus you must pretend on the outside the opposite of what you feel on the inside. You must show "love" and/or "respect" despite feeling fear and hatred.

Thus, when Wendy's mother verbally abused her, Wendy could not react with fear or hatred, because that would only increase her mother's attacks. ("I'll give you something to cry about!")

Thus Wendy had to disown and repress her own authentic emotional responses and mimic their exact opposite. All her fear and pain had to be "magically" transformed into "love" and "respect."

This form of the "Stockholm Syndrome" has disastrous effects on a child's long-term emotional development and integrity. Instead of learning how to interact in a rational manner with reality, the child ends up forced into a situation of eternal hyper-vigilance wherein she constantly scans the behaviour of those around her, endlessly alert for any signs of an impending attack.

If you are driving a car and suddenly notice a number of wasps in the car with you, it will become very hard to concentrate on the road. In addition, imagine that you had to keep driving under increasingly difficult conditions, while the number of buzzing wasps in your car kept multiplying – all the while knowing that you were allergic to wasp venom – this is the endless livid terror of all too many childhoods.

This kind of terrible "split focus" ("I must keep driving / I must not get stung") empties out the spontaneity and richness of the child's inner life. Just as we cannot daydream while being pushed out of a plane, we cannot develop an internal discourse with ourselves if we are in a constant state of hyper-vigilance with regards to our surroundings.

If a child in an abusive environment stops scanning for danger, the pain of being attacked is then combined with the shock of surprise, and the inevitable self-flagellation for lowering one's guard. Daydreaming, or self-conversation, thus becomes a form of "self abuse," insofar as it increases the risk and agony of being attacked – it becomes as dangerous as a tightrope-walker losing his concentration and risking falling to his death.

This terrible equation – "relaxation = danger" – keeps the child in a constant state of high alert, of hyper-vigilance, and effectively prevents her from ever coming to a true understanding of her situation.

In a nation, a state of war creates the panic, haste and hysteria that prevents people from effectively questioning their government. Just so does hyper-vigilance in childhood prevent children from rationally evaluating their parents' behaviour.

Thus, with all this in place, when Wendy becomes an adult and gives birth to Sally, an awful series of events is set into motion.

The Child Unafraid...
To understand how parental cruelty comes into being, the first and most important fact to remember is that *children enter this world in an unabused state*. They are not afraid, they are not hyper-vigilant, they are not twisted, they have not become enemies to themselves or others – they are curious, perceptive, engaged and benevolent.

Remember – as a child, Wendy learned that relaxation was danger. Thus when Sally is born, Sally is fundamentally *relaxed* in a way that Wendy has no conscious memory of.

Since for Wendy relaxation is followed by attack, Sally's relaxation creates great anxiety for her mother, because she associates it with an impending attack. In the same way, if Sally were crawling towards a set of steep stairs, Wendy would feel great anxiety and a compulsion to snatch Sally away from the impending danger – very aggressively if need be.

For Wendy, then, when Sally in all innocence engages in actions that in Wendy's world would have triggered a terrible attack, it reawakens all of the repressed pain, fear and hatred in Wendy's heart. When this occurs again and again, Wendy genuinely feels that Sally is *creating* or *causing* terrible attacks of pain, fear and hatred in her.

Now, the last time that someone else created pain and fear in Wendy, it was her own mother attacking her when she was a child. For Wendy, then, any sudden eruption of pain and fear is associated with a direct attack. Thus for Wendy, Sally's innocent anxiety-provoking behaviour *is the direct emotional equivalent of her parents' abusive attacks.*

Furthermore, the only way that Wendy could create any sense of security and control as a child was to brutally repress her own emotional responses. In other words, "that which causes anxiety must be brutally repressed" is the law of her emotional land.

Now, when Wendy was a child she could not brutally repress her own parents, because that created further attacks – thus she had to brutally repress her *own* anxieties.

The difference with her own child, however, is that she now has the power to repress Sally, which she did not have with her own parents when *she* was a child.

It is in this way that she makes the transformation from victim to abuser.

Since she experiences Sally's actions as attacks upon herself, Wendy feels justified in controlling Sally's behaviour so that these attacks do not occur.

If our child continually kicks us in the shins, we consider it good parenting to prevent this child from acting in such an abusive manner. We must do whatever it takes, we say to ourselves, to prevent our child from hurting others. *What will happen*, we think, *if we allow our child to act in such a horrible manner?* A life of brutality, loneliness and rejection seems inevitable, and we could scarcely call ourselves good parents if we allowed *that* to happen.

Many parents start off with relatively calm and patient lectures, but the absolute of *"thou shalt not"* remains determinedly hovering, in the not-too-distant background.

"It upsets Mommy when you act like that," we may say gently – however, like the initially polite letters from the IRS, a not too subtle threat is always visible between the lines. We talk about "politeness," "niceness" and "consideration for the feelings of others," and so on, but what we are really saying is: "It makes me angry when you make me anxious, so you'd better stop!"

Children, due to their amazingly perceptive natures, find it hard to take these lectures seriously, because they sense the contradiction and narcissism at the root of such speeches. Thus they generally tend to continue to do what comes naturally to them, despite the anxiety that their actions cause other people.

Since the children remain in an un-brutalized state, they do not themselves directly feel the anxiety that their actions provoke in their brutalized parents. In the same way, if I do not have a migraine, playing loud music will bring me pleasure. If I do have a migraine, obviously it will not.

Since children continue to do what comes naturally to them, and since their actions continue to provoke anxiety, pain and rage in their parents, their parents feel a growing sense of helplessness and frustration and an increasing loss of control over their own emotions.

The basic lesson that Wendy learned in her own terrible childhood was that when someone does something that makes you feel bad, the solution is to stop the other person from doing that thing.

Thus, when Sally's actions provoke awful feelings in Wendy, Wendy's inevitable reaction is to prevent Sally from performing those actions, so that Wendy does not have to feel those terrible emotions.

To be a "good" daughter, Sally must stop doing whatever causes Wendy anxiety.

If Sally continues to act in a way that causes her mother anxiety, Wendy will be inevitably driven to the "conclusion" that Sally *wants* to cause her pain – or, at best, is utterly indifferent to the pain that her actions cause.

In this way, Wendy can frame a perception of her daughter that includes the pejoratives "cruel" and "selfish."

Now, the battle lines are truly becoming drawn.

If we say to our child: "Stop doing 'X,' because it makes me feel bad," surely the solution is simply for the child to stop doing 'X,' right?

Sadly, no.

The Escalation...

The true nature of Sally's "offense" towards Wendy is that Sally is *unafraid*.

Remember that in Wendy's childhood, being unafraid always invited attack – or made the inevitable attack even worse. Thus Sally's state of calm or self-possession creates an overwhelming sense of "impending doom" for Wendy.

When Wendy was a child, spontaneous self-expression invited attack. Now that she is a mother, when Sally sits and sings to herself, this causes increasing anxiety in Wendy, and at some point she will express disapproval to Sally.

At this point, perhaps Sally stops singing. However, five minutes later, Sally states that she wants to go for a walk.

In Wendy's world, expressing an open desire always invited attack – thus when Sally says that she wants to go for a walk, Wendy also feels anxiety, and once more snaps at Sally.

As we can imagine, this process can go on and on virtually *ad infinitum*.

There is no end to the escalation of "little rules" that end up snaking around Sally, like an infinity of tiny spider webs that eventually leave her bound and immobile.

However, even if Sally were to obey every single one of her mother's "rules," she would *still* not be safe.

As Sally becomes more and more inhibited and more and more fearful, Wendy begins to feel guiltier and guiltier. Sadly, Wendy also interprets this as some sort of "manipulative aggression" on Sally's part and so is inevitably drawn to accuse Sally of "playing the victim" *in order to make Wendy feel bad.*

In this way, there is no possibility whatsoever that Sally can ever satisfy her mother.

If Sally acts in a natural, independent manner, she provokes an attack. If she acts in an unnatural, obedient manner, she provokes an attack. Since she can neither be spontaneous nor obedient, neither act nor refrain from acting, there is nothing that she can do to avoid being attacked or criticized in some manner.

The Evil At The Core...
The central problem is that Wendy is *attempting to manage her own anxiety by controlling Sally.*

However, since Sally is *not* the actual source of Wendy's anxiety, controlling Sally's behaviour will only temporarily alleviate Wendy's anxiety – while making it worse deep down, since she is acting unjustly and blaming Sally for her own feelings.

Controlling the Bed

To understand this madness more fully, imagine that you are bedridden in a hospital and I am standing by the controls of the bed.

"Can you raise the head of my bed so that I can eat?" you ask.

I push a button, but nothing happens. I push another button and your head goes down.

"No, no!" you cry. "Up, I want my head to come up!"

I push another button, and both your legs and head start to rise, causing you pain.

"Ow! Not that way, just my *head*!"

As you can well imagine, this process will generate an extraordinary amount of frustration and tension in both of us. You would be panicking and yelling at me, and I would be frantically stabbing at the buttons trying to control or reverse whatever motion was giving you such discomfort.

Now imagine further that at some point, we discover that I am actually pressing the controls of a bed in another room, and the reason that your bed is moving "randomly" is that you are in fact sitting on the controls for your own bed, and your shifting around is what is causing the uncomfortable movements.

Clearly, the first thing that you would do is apologize to me for blaming me for your discomfort, and for railing against my "incompetence."

This is the typical experience of someone who finally understands that using other people to manage his anxiety only makes his anxiety worse, causing him to further attempt to control and manipulate others, when the whole time he is "sitting on the controls" that only *he* can reach.

Why is this so important?

The reason that we are spending all this time focusing on how abusive tendencies come about is because it is essential to understand the genesis of the mythologies that separate us from each other.

When we look at the interaction between Wendy and Sally, we can understand that Wendy's bad behaviour *predated her justifications for that bad behaviour*.

Due to her rejection of her own history, Wendy ended up attacking her daughter.

This shameful action produced a great stress in Wendy, because she wants to be – and believes herself to be – a good, fair and just person.

However, continually snapping at a child, or verbally abusing her in some other manner scarcely sits well with a benevolent and virtuous self-image.

Self-Mythology

When we perform actions that we cannot justify to ourselves, we have one of two choices. We can either recognize that we have a significant moral flaw and go through the painful work of starting to correct it, or we can say that our actions resulted from a significant moral flaw in someone *else*, and go through the far *less* painful work of starting to "correct" the *other* person's flaws.

In other words, if I am angry at you, and I cannot believe that I am unjustly or abusively angry at you – which would be the case if you did nothing to provoke my anger – then I must convince myself that my anger is a *just* response to injustice or abuse from *you*.

As mentioned earlier, this shifting of moral blame is called *projection*, which is a wonderful word on many levels – not only does it connote the shining of an image onto a blank surface, but it also invokes a "movie" metaphor, which includes the artistic fiction that it so often actually represents.

The Crossroads

When Wendy stands over her child, her voice hoarse and her hands shaking, looking down into Sally's bewildered and frightened eyes, it is a moment of truth for her very soul.

If Wendy recognizes that she has just attacked a helpless and dependent child – which can never be justified in any terms – then she can begin to take the necessary and humbling steps of learning how to control her temper and hopefully, over time, win back the trust of her child.

However, the majority of parents feel the terror and vulnerability within their own hearts when looking into the horrified eyes of their children – and then take the terrible step of inventing a fiction wherein the *children* are the perpetrators – and they, the parents, are the *victims*.

Remember, in the religious approach we are always taught to create sinners to blame for our mistakes – and the more immoral our errors, the worse the sinner must be.

"Look what you made me do!" is the brutal and vengeful cry that erupts from the tortured souls of the parents.

*"Only a bad child would turn me into **this**!"*

Religion and Mythology

Why is it that we are so invariably drawn to making up self-justifying stories, rather than accepting the truth about our own capacity for doing harm?

Child abuse is just one of the many, many destructive fallouts that result from our addiction to the superstitions of religion.

Religion completely externalizes the moral – and immoral – decisions of mankind. "Virtue" is obedience to the whimsical dictates of a self-contradictory deity, while "vice" is surrender to the whimsical temptations of a self-contradictory devil.

"The devil made me do it," (often supplemented with "I was weak!") is a constant cry among the religious – while these cultists often believe that they have the choice to reject temptation, the devil is very strong, and human flesh is invariably weak.

Furthermore, children are not only born un-abused, they are also born fundamentally anti-religious. (If you doubt this, try taking away a four-year-old's Halloween candy and saying he will get 100 times more candy after he is dead!)

Children are empirical, secular, rational and fundamentally scientific. In fact, the progression of competence in a child's mind directly follows the scientific method. For instance, in the first few years a child develops the recognition of causality, by tracking an object with his eyes or turning his head at a sound, followed by "object permanence," such as recognizing that a ball placed under a blanket still exists, which then develops into basic problem solving with these objects. As the child continues to develop, these basic problem solving skills are refined by more formal use of logic in every aspect of life: identity, language, values, etc.

Just as it takes an enormous amount of statist propaganda to turn a child into a dogmatic Soviet Marxist, it takes an endless amount of *religious* propaganda to turn a child into a dazed "worshiper" of imaginary ghosts.

Children are not even naturally agnostic. To test this proposition, simply give a child an empty box as a birthday present and tell him that there *may* be an iPod in it, but there's just no way to know for sure, so he cannot really tell you that there is *no* iPod in there!

See if he thanks you for this "gift" or not.

Thus, the subjugation of children in terms of religion is based on the subjugation of children to *stories* – exploitive, abusive, ghastly, disorienting and manipulative *stories*.

In reality, of course, it is impossible for a child to obey the Bible or the Koran or the Torah, because they are simply dead books with no capacity to reward or punish.

No, the subjugation of children is fundamentally the enslavement of children to storytellers – their obedience to the whims of others, presented as absolute moral and metaphysical *facts*.

Enslavement to the idea that the stories of others are absolute facts is a crushing blow to a child's capacity to process objective reality – and, to the great benefit of those in authority, to criticize or question the errors of those who "teach" them.

Thus, since children are trained to automatically obey "stories," when an abusive parent aggressively tells a new "story," which is that the aggression of the parent was directly caused by the actions of the child, the child can only nod numbly and blame himself.

The parable of the apple, or how to control a human soul...

(*A transcript of Freedomain Radio Podcast 70*)

Good afternoon everybody. It is Wednesday, at about 4:27 on January the 25th. I hope you're doing well. We are going to chat about a most exciting topic today. Not that they're all not exciting, but this one in particular is juicy to the point almost of being overbearing to one's intellectual taste buds, to mix metaphors so much that I might as well put my brain on frappe.

So, the topic that I'd like to chat about today is the question of exercising power. How do you exercise power over another human being? How do you corrupt them? How do you take his natural integrity, intelligence, and all the wonder that is the human mind, and turn it against itself and get it to eat itself and get it to be sort of a snake consuming its own tail? How do you wrap people up in neuroses, and how do you make them obedient? How do you get them to subjugate themselves to your will without you even having to lift a finger, barely even an eyebrow? And the reason that I want to talk about this is that I'm very interested in starting a cult. No, actually, I think you've got to know the weapons of your enemies if you're going to successfully oppose them. You need to know what they are doing so that you can unravel the damage that historically we've all had done to us in this rather messy culture that we live in, so that we can not only begin to reverse the effects of this kind of power structure within our own minds and hearts and souls, but also so that we can help other people unravel the mess that they have become.

I view certain damages that are done early to the mind in life as pretty irrevocable. The mind is not so plastic that you could, say, for instance, be locked in a cupboard for your first twenty years and end up as a normal human being. You do experience some particular phases in your brain development which are pretty central and may or may not be reversible, and generally the earlier the experiences the less reversible they are.

Thus I am not saying that we can lickety-split fix ourselves up and be right as rain, but we can at least learn to strengthen where we are weakest. There is always adaptability within the human mind, as we know from seeing people who have terrible brain injuries who find other ways of adapting. So I think that it is well worth having a look at the methodology by which one twists the human mind so that we can to some degree allow ourselves or invite ourselves to become *untwisted* – which is quite a bit of work, let me tell you! But it is entirely satisfying in its conclusion.

I myself make no claims to be perfectly sane by any stretch of the imagination. I suffered, in a sense, my own intellectual "foot binding" just like everybody else, but what I have done is explored the aches and creaks of my mental joints, to the point where I think I have a pretty good idea or fairly good idea of how a straightening out could occur and what it might look like.

So, let's start at the very beginning, which is: *how do you get people, how do you get children, to detach themselves from two basic things: sensual evidence and simple facts?* It really is amazing, when you think about it, how power structures work to do this, and the fantastic success that they have in this area.

So: how do you get children to ignore the evidence of their senses, the evidence of the senses transmitted through the autonomous nerve system which is absolutely outside of our control? We can choose to open our eyes or close them, but we can't choose, if we open our eyes, *not* to see

– I mean other than pulling a King Lear or, I guess, a Gloucester, gouging out eyes.

We don't have any control over the actions of our autonomous nerve system in the perception and transmission of external, material reality, or in providing the evidence of external, material reality. So it would seem fairly hard to get children, who love to explore the world, and curl and uncurl their limbs, and figure out object constancy, and figure out how the world works, and so on to stop processing reality. It's just what children love to do – that's what a lot of logic games are all about. That's what a lot of physical games, sports and so on, are all about – exploring the world, controlling one's body, controlling one's mind, focusing, and becoming disciplined in a sort of happy way towards the exercise of one's creative and intellectual powers.

This is a perfectly natural development for children, so how on earth is it so possible and seems so easy to twist children into these obedient neurotic slaves to power, which so many of us end up becoming to one degree or another – not just slaves to power, but infected with this wild Stockholm Syndrome, wherein people end up *loving* the state? They love religion! They love God! They love all this stuff! It's more than just, "Well, you know, I was raised this way, and so I guess this is what is considered normal, and what do I know?" I mean, people will go out and have banner-waving, cheering, standing ovations, mad stampede crowd lunacy for the president or for the Pope or for leaders or members of the cultural elite or the political elite or even the economic elite to some degree.

I mean, they are not just hammered down. They are hammered down, re-forged, reshaped, recharged, re-energized, and *reformed* as people who love slavery to the point where they think slavery is freedom! I mean, we live in a 1984 universe intellectually, and the only reason we don't live in a 1984 universe physically is because there's some leftover still from the Enlightenment and from capitalism which have managed to keep us going to some degree, in a diminishing kind of way. But intellectually, we're are just… It's "Spanish Inquisition time" as far as people's ability to *reason* goes.

So how is it possible that human beings who are so constructed to love freedom, to love the exercise of ability, to love rationality, to automatically transmit or receive the evidence of the senses, how is it that human beings are so turned against all of this as children?

Well, the first thing that you need to do in order to begin the process of destroying a child's mind is you to set up *categories*, empty categories, which are *moral absolutes*. I know, it's not exactly in the kindergarten book, but trust me – well don't trust me, let me reason it out and see if you believe me. This is how it works: You, with great reverence – as the corrupting teacher, or parent, or person with authority – with great reverence, *you vividly describe and are enormously passionate about things which the child cannot see.*

Of course the first example of this that leaps to mind for most people is God, but that's just one aspect of these crazy kaleidoscopes of fantasy that children's brains are squeezed into and cut up on. So, of course, God – people all say: "Let's have grace, let's pray, let's *worship.*" Of course, Santa Claus is just one thin edge of the wedge in all of this.

So first you speak with enormous reverence and passion about things which the child cannot see. And the child, of course, is baffled. You are playing enormously on the power that you hold over the child – I mean, you hold the power of life and death over this child, there's simply no way to get around that. That is just the nature of biology: children will cleave to the wishes of their parents above all else, because without the parents there's no survival, and so, biologically, those children who fought the moral absolutes or commandments of their parents just tended to die off. Parents have absolutely no problem sacrificing children to abstract moral ideals, as we see throughout the history of the world in terms of wars and religious torture and even beatings.

That child is going to inevitably cleave to the will of the parent – and so what you do, if you are this evil, corrupting parent, is that you will – wild-eyed, or calmly, or passionately, but with *some* kind of reverence – talk about things that aren't there, as if it's perfectly natural that you would talk about these things that don't exist.

You basically say that there's *an invisible apple on the table* – and this would be your basic approach to wrecking a child's mind very early on in life.

The child knows apples, and he knows oranges, and he's getting the hang of that stuff. So he's maybe two years old, two-and-a-half years old – maybe, if he's bright, eighteen months – so he's getting the hang of material reality, and how to describe things, and categorize things, and understand them.

So what you do to start to undermine the child's sense of competency in the physical realm, in the realm of the senses, is you all sit down to dinner – and there is *nothing on the table*.

Then you, with great solemnity, reach over and pick up an "invisible apple." You pick up this invisible apple, along with the whole family, and with great solemnity you all take a bite out of this invisible apple, and you say, "That is the best apple I have ever tasted in my life. It tastes like all the sugar and chocolate and glucose and fructose and caramel you can dream of all piled together. It's a mouth orgasm that I just can't even *speak* about!"

And everybody agrees. This is "The Emperor's New Clothes syndrome."

Everybody agrees, and then everybody mimes, and so on.

The child, of course, is completely bewildered – let's say is the youngest child. The youngest child is just completely baffled – he can't *for the life of him* understand what on earth is going on. Everything has kind of made sense so far. Every sort of concept or abstraction that he are building on based on the evidence of his senses kind of makes sense.

In the beginning, when you're playing with a little baby, you roll a ball that they can see. You roll it under a blanket and they just lose interest, because they think it's ceased to exist. At some point – a couple of months, six months, seven months, eight months – they begin to develop *object constancy*, where they go, "Ahah! The ball that has rolled under the blanket has not ceased to exist, it is simply under the blanket!" And then they pull the blanket off the ball and continue to play with it, if that's what they want.

Every abstraction that the child has built up on – that letters mean things on the page that mean objects that are transmitted through the senses, and there's a correlation between concepts and instances – all of the amazing and fantastic developments of neuron complexity and brain complexity that is going on in a child's mind for the first couple of years – it all sort of comes to complete shuddering halt during this imaginary fruit eating dinner table conversation, because everything that he's eaten before has substance, and tastes, and he can see it, and everybody else can see it, and now the whole family, everybody around the table is "eating" something and *he can't see it*.

So then you think, as a child, "Well, maybe everyone else *can* see it!" So you reach out to where everybody seems to be taking the fruit from, and you can't feel anything! Well what you gonna do? I mean, it's a bizarre and deranged situation!

There was a play that was put on in the 1930s – I think it was "Gaslight" – where a man was trying to drive his wife insane, so he just rearranged things within the house. He would put a picture up and they would all comment on how lovely the picture was, and then he'd take the picture down off and she would then say, "Well, where did the picture go?" And he'd say, "What picture?" And she'd say, "Well, the picture we were talking about." And he'd say, "Well, we were never talking about a picture, what you mean?" He would be completely baffled, and he'd continue to do this over and over again and, of course, completely messing with her sense of reality.

This kind of behaviour at the dinner table is just so astoundingly corrupting and destructive of the child's mind.

The child's first reaction is horror and fear, because one of two things is occurring. Either he's lost the ability to process essential sensual information – which, to living organism, is a death sentence – and a murderously horrible death sentence, because it's going to be a slow, horrible death. You either can't figure out what to eat, or you try to eat a pinecone or you can't hear the lion coming, or you try to drink water and it turns out to be blood or urine, and it just becomes a horrible death sentence if you lose the ability to process essential sensual information – that's just a terrible thing to happen! There's almost no worse fate to an organism other than simply a quick death.

So, either the child has lost the ability to process sensual information, or the child has the ability to process essential information *and his entire family is lying to him about a very essential fact.*

Those are two absolutely, unbelievably terrible options for a child, a young child, to face. "Either I've lost the ability for my brain to work effectively with reality, and therefore I'm going to face a life of incredible struggle, danger, and death, and it's going to be very short life at that, too. Either that has happened, or my family is lying to me in such a fundamentally destructive way that I would actually prefer it if they just beat me across the head with a stick!"

At least you feel *that*, it doesn't interfere with your ability to process reality, it doesn't make you doubt your senses, it doesn't make you believe in things that aren't true, it's just like, "Ow, that hurts," and you take cover or go for shelter or whatever, but *this* is much worse! This is worse than a direct assault on the body – which at least reaffirms the evidence of the senses in a brutal kind of manner. This is a *direct assault on one's capacity to trust one's own senses and one's own mind to perceive reality!*

We can't survive without a successful or accurate perception of reality at the material level. So it's a death sentence that the family is passing upon this young mind that is opening to all the wonders of the physical world when they are miming and saying, "Mmmm, that tastes *wonderful*," and everyone's pretending that that they're eating, and if they're *not* eating and they're *lying*, it's unbelievably destructive! It's the worst kind of abuse, to tell a child that his entire brain has ceased to function correctly!

So the child is placed in an *absolutely impossible situation* – and if you want to look at the foundation of all the corruption of power that exists within the material world, within human society – everything from a cop pulling you over when you're going 1km an hour over the speed limit and giving you a big fine because he's got to meet his quota, all the way to the deaths of millions in the gulags – you can trace it right back, all the way back, to this one core central moment when the child is faced with people he has to trust, creating a situation where he either has to hate them for their direct assault upon his capacity to understand the world and to live within it – because they're lying to him – or he has to look within himself and say that he is insane and deranged, and reality no longer makes any sense, and that as an organism he is not going to survive.

Every single aspect of human corruption, and human evil, and human madness, and human hatred, and human fear that is existential in nature, goes directly back to this fork in the road that every child faces when he is in a society, when he is in a family that pretends to believe in things that are not sensual, not rational, not provable, not logical, not *true*.

Even more horribly, the child *also recognizes that his parents and his siblings have no problem doing this to him*! How is this going to affect his capacity to love them, and to love himself, and to love the world, and to love the society he's in if people are perfectly willing to do this to him. In fact, they *want* to do it to him! They're not even being forced to it, they're not even indifferent. It's a staged show, because every human being that comes into society who is not insane by nature is capable of blowing this nonsensical, irrational, crazy scheme right out of the water, and thus must be inoculated against empirical reality, truth and reason, from the very beginning. Everybody recognizes the risk that is involved in this, and everybody recognizes the danger of somebody breaking through this sick ice and actually finding out the truth about the nonsense that people call truth and reality, socially. So every child goes through this horrible fork in the road where they're told things that directly contradict the evidence of logic and their senses — which they *need*, which they must *rely on* in order to survive as an organism, which they are passionate about, and enjoy the exercise of and development of. This *direct assault* on one's identity as a species, as an animal, as a rational creature...

Every child faces this fork in the road, and the destruction and corruption that is everywhere in society flows directly out of this particular fork in a way that we will talk about a little bit further as we go along.

Let's continue with the steps to destroy a child's mind. So — there's this child at the dinner table, and everyone is very seriously telling this child that there is this invisible apple to eat and that they are eating it and it tastes *goooood!*

What is the child to do?

There is this unbelievable fork in the road, where he either has to hate those who are attacking him in such a fundamentally destructive manner, or he has to doubt his own sanity and capacity to survive as an organism, as a life, as a human being. It is this fork in the road that triggers the true destruction of what a psychologist might call the "true self," or our honest self, or our integrity, or what I might just call our actual personality, our real personality.

Our bodies have a natural growth to them. We're going to grow, going to get to a certain amount of height, a certain amount of the average weight. But if we're put in these horrible contortion machines, then we're going to end up with an unnatural body, which is all we've got to work with. It's like the foot binding metaphor I've used before, that if you're like these Chinese women in the 19th Century and you have your feet bound for a number of years, you end up with these horrible little curled-under stumps — and that's what you have to work with. There's no "original foot" for you to get back to, but there is an "original foot" that you *could have had* if they had not been bound.

That's sort of how I feel about the personality structure of a human being, that we're sort of warped by these insane experiences, but we can get back to something a lot healthier, and that's the purpose of my conversations with the segments of the world who enjoy this conversation.

The fundamental break that occurs, is a *reality break*, or a *break in belonging*, or break in attachment, that occurs at this "dinner table from hell." The problem that the child is facing is, the statement that sort of scrolls across our minds at these moments. (And I don't know if you can remember yours. I can sort of remember the after effects of mine. I don't remember the one directly, but I remember very shortly thereafter. I can mention later if it comes back to my mind.) The statement that is going to scroll across the child's mind when he or she is at this dinner table is, "*I am now doomed to live in an asylum.*" And that asylum is called "the world." That asylum is called "my family." That asylum is called "those who are close to me." That asylum is called "society" or "normalcy" or however you want to put it. The basic statement is that, "I am now condemned to live in an asylum."

That terrible statement encompasses both the options that the child is really facing. The first option is that those around him or her are trying to harm the child and undermine the child's capacity to have any kind of trust in those who claim to care about him, and that is, as you know, a horrible thing to contemplate or face.

That is one aspect that is going to occur.

The second aspect that is that people are lovingly and actually *seeing* these apples, but that the child is in no way capable of perceiving them, and is therefore fundamentally flawed, dangerous, and sort of mentally ill as a living organism, as a human being.

So the asylum that the child is now facing is that he lives in a world of insanity, and either *he* is sane but those *around* him are telling him or pretending to him that he is insane – which means that the asylum is composed of those around him – or, the asylum is actually that everyone else around him *is* sane, and that *he's* the only member of this asylum.

However, the asylum is absolutely there – the asylum is either his own mind or everyone around him. *This* is the break in belonging that occurs for a child when people around him tell him that things are there and exist and are real that he can clearly and plainly see are not there, don't exist, and are not real.

Now, of course, the question becomes: "Why does he of often believe that it is *him*? Why doesn't he just believe that it's everyone else around him who is just messing with his head, and just take *that* approach to the problem of being lied to?"

Well, that is a perfectly valid and logical response, and we'll get back to that in a second, but first I would like to deal with the problem of virtue.

The problem that power has is not with other people who want power, but rather with people who are *moral*.

Morality is the opposite of power. Morality is the opposite of dominance. Morality is the opposite of subjugation, or exploitation, because morality is all about finding what is common and true in the world – common to all human beings and true empirically and also biologically – and therefore it's not about subjugation, because it is creating one rule for everyone, and the only way that you can have subjugation or exploitation is if you create different rules for different people.

Thus the real threat that power structures face is not from those who would wrest that power structure away from them, because they can be beaten or even if they can't be beaten, the vast majority of those who benefit from a power structure are not those at the top, but those in the hazy middle – you know, the money changers, the legislators in the background, the middle managers and so on.

This sort of bureaucratic parasitical power structure feasts on subjugation and is deathly afraid of morality, because if morality is applied to the situation, the whole gig is up. That's why they focus so much on *owning morality* in these power structures.

So who they really have to worry about are those concerned with goodness, who are concerned with morality and righteousness, with brightness and logical consistency.

So – how does this invisible apple eating madness contest, how does it deal with the problem of somebody saying, "You know, you guys are just immoral! You're trying to harm me, you're trying to exercise power or control over me!"?

(I mean, obviously that would be highly unusual for a child to say – in fact, I think it would be fairly unprecedented for child to say that, but you never know, they might, as they get into their teenage years or so on…)

So those who are keen on destructive and exploitive power structures, those people are deathly afraid of the moral man, the moral woman, the person who logically points out the inconsistencies in what they're doing, and the hypocrisy, and the immorality. So what they have to do, the gradient that they have to mix in, is that *only bad people can't see the apple.*

Seeing the apple is thus always portrayed as *synonymous with virtue.*

Thus – if you say to this child, "Mmmm, mmm, mmm! That invisible apple tastes *fantastic!*" well you're not going to get a lot of allegiance from the child because the invisible apple doesn't exist, so it's not going taste good to them. So why on earth would they involve themselves in this charade?

Well, of course, what you do is say: "*Only a only a good little boy or a good little girl can see this apple!*"

Again, we're back to "The Emperor's New Clothes," which is fantastic – one of the most amazing stories in all of literature, in my view, and entirely unappreciated by those who study politics, because it *is* politics. I mean, it's *exactly what politics is* – and religion, for that matter, and nationalism, and racism, and sexism, and all of the "isms" that so corrupt our natural and common humanity and interconnectedness.

So you say that only a *good little boy* can see the apple – and the more good you are, the better the apple tastes!

This, of course, is the false dichotomy that is used to trap those children who have a natural inclination towards logical consistency or morality, who are the people that they are most concerned about or afraid of. So the elders say, "Only good little boys can see the apple!"

So, of course, you're faced with another choice, but now you have a *moral* element.

You're not faced with either "I'm insane or they're insane – either I'm unable to survive or they are trying to kill my mental development." Now you have an additional element layered into the sickness – or in this case the inculcation of an illness in another – it sort of follows the same pattern as a viral invasion in your body would.

Now you have an additional layer, which is: *this lie only enslaves you if you want to be good.*

What if you don't care about being good? We'll get to that in a second – but if you *do* care about being good, if you have that sort of empathetic sensitivity and moral nature, it's sort of innate within you (and I'm not saying this is by any means the majority of people, but it certainly does exist), then you're going to be *very interested in being a good person.*

This moral lie also raises the stakes of questioning those who are "totally sure" that there is an apple there and maybe you just can't see it. You could at least stay at the level of sensual error, an error in the senses or in interpretation of the senses, so maybe they really *can* see the apple, but if I tell them that they're wrong, I'm telling them that *their* sense apparatus is faulty, or *their* conclusions are faulty, or maybe they've been struck with some sort of ailment that they are not aware of that is affecting their vision or their ability to process physical or visual stimuli.

The child obviously isn't going to say it in that sort of manner, but that's still a thought that can occur in the mind of a child, how can something "exist" that patently does not exist? They can still trust their senses, and then they can say, "You people who are telling me that this thing exists, you're obviously not doing very well in terms of your ability to process things, because it quite obviously doesn't."

The wonderfully invasive and horrible thing that happens when you begin to say, "Only good boys can see the invisible apple," is you now raise the stakes for that boy to contradict you. If you're the evil, corrupting parent, you've now raised the stakes for the boy to contradict you, because now you've said that only immoral people cannot see the apple.

Thus if you're the child, you're then faced with this choice: you then either say, "I'm an immoral boy and I can't see the apple," which is sort of surrendering the premise and giving up something even more important, in a sense, than sensual competence (or the ability to process information correctly), which is your moral nature, your goodness.

I would rather be blind than evil, so let's just say that it would be pretty catastrophic for anybody interested in or with a natural bend towards morality, empathy, and an ethical approach to things to label themselves as evil because they can't see the apple.

So then, if you *don't* want to label yourself as evil – and you can't approach the parent who is telling you that the apple exists from the standpoint of error, because the parent has said, "Only evil boys can't see the apple, evil people cannot see the apple. Good people can see the apple" – you are truly stuck.

If you say, "Dad," or "Mom – I don't think that you can see the apple because *there is no apple there!*" – you're automatically calling them evil, and you're not going to have a whole lot of luck when you are a child calling your parents evil.

That's why they layer in this moral dimension. They raise the stakes to the point where if you say you can't see the apple, then you are evil, but if you say that the apple doesn't exist and "you guys are trying to screw with my head," then because the parents have layered in the moral dimension, they cannot withdraw from the position. They have now used the *argument from morality* – and once you take the argument from *morality* out of its scabbard, it's a sword that you just can't sheath again. It's out there, and it's just a fact. You simply cannot withdraw from that; you lose all parental authority.

So that is a pretty important aspect to what happens in this particular realm. You can't call those who are telling you all this corrupting, immoral nonsense evil, because they simply won't accept it. And of course, even as a child, the horror of what is occurring at this moment is so hard to understand. It is just so hard to understand and to process this kind of unbelievable destruction of your identity and complete rejection and repudiation of your mental development and crippling blow to your self esteem. I mean, *this* is the root of neuroses and religious fanaticism and people who grow up to become dictatorial or bullying or overly subservient, this is where the root of all of this starts from.

So if they can get the person who is moral, who's interested in morality, or the child who is sort of good by nature, wants to please, wants to be a good person, then, by getting the person to believe that if they *can't* see the invisible apple they're *bad*, well then you torture them and you set them up with this lifelong quest to see an invisible apple which they *just frickin' well can't do!* You've put them into this mode of a dog chasing its own tail for the rest of its life and that person is then going to pose absolutely zero threat to the power structures that exist in the world, because he's going to be so consumed with his own inability to see this invisible apple that he's not going to raise any sort of basic or sensible questions to those in power.

So that's how you defuse the moral kid.

There's another kind of kid who doesn't necessarily – let's just theoretically call that person "the older brother" – that person does not have the same amount of natural empathy, probably because that person is now complicit in the destruction of their younger siblings' minds, and so they have a lot more aggression and a lot more natural dominance built into their personalities. (Whether that's innate, or based on the fact that they're an older sibling, I don't know, but it does seem to follow that pattern; I mean, the birth order is pretty important. Of course there are exceptions, but that's fine, I can live with exceptions. As long as there's a general trend that can be identified, that's good enough for me.)

So this naturally aggressive person becomes, in this moment, when this occurs to him or when he's inflicting it on someone else, this person becomes *cynical*.

And that's perfectly fine for those in power.

If you're chasing your own tail and wondering why you can't be a better person and see this magical, invisible apple that everyone else can see, you're no threat. You're going to work, you're going to pay your taxes, you're obedient, and you're always like, "Oh, what else can I do to become a better person? I really wanna be a better person!" Blah blah blah." You're just running around chasing your own tail, you're no threat to anybody in power because you're just sort of a complying weenie.

If, however, you are a more *aggressive* person, then you're going to look right through that invisible apple and say, "Everyone's a jerk, there's no such thing as goodness, everything's just about power and control."

But you can't use the argument from morality, because you've given up your values, you've given up the idea that there's such a thing as right and wrong, good and evil, and you're just saying, "Yeah, well, this is what they tell you just to control you."

(I wanted to mention this point earlier but it escaped my mind, one of the ways that you would test the theory of the fact that a lie that is told to children that is not moral in nature can be withdrawn, but a lie that is told to children that is moral in nature or is presented as moral in nature, that it *cannot* be withdrawn, you would obviously contrast something like Christianity — which is a lie told to children that is moral in nature, or thought to be moral in nature, or fantasized to be moral in nature — versus the Easter Bunny and Santa Claus and so on — which are lies told to children that are not moral in nature — whether parents end up withdrawing this and sort of "Hah hah," but you don't get this with religion, because religion is presented as moral in nature, therefore it can no longer be withdrawn from the discussion, because then you've portrayed yourself as an unbelievable, destructive hypocrite, which parents generally aren't that keen on doing, because they want to continue to pillage their children's time and attention for the remainder of their natural born lives.)

So if you do have this more aggressive style of personality, then when you're faced with this terrible choice at the dining table, which is to believe that you are insane or other people are bad or trying to control you, then what you do is: you say, "Well I don't care about the moral argument, that just is nonsense, because I don't believe in morality, I don't believe in right or wrong, everyone's just trying to mess with me!"

So then you become sort of pugilistic and aggressive, and you're mad, and you're angry, and you're cynical, and you're nihilistic.

Again, you're absolutely *zero threat* to those in power. I mean, you can rail if you want, you can fight the cops, you can get mad at them, you can yell epithets at them and so on, you can throw rocks at the police cars — *zero threat* to those in power. I mean, just absolutely no threat. You might as well just be spitting in the wind and hoping to bring down a cloud with your thoughts.

This is sort of the duality that occurs, and this is somewhat dependant, perhaps, on what occurs, perhaps on birth order, on personality type, the way that in which it's applied.

You could just have jerky parents who are overbearing… "orifices," let's say, to keep my iTunes rating… *Those* parents are sort of going to yell at

REAL-TIME RELATIONSHIPS

you and bully at you and drag you around, and that may produce somebody who's more aggressive.

And then you have the other type of parent, generally it's more associated with the feminine, who's sort of soft and gentle and just sort of *disappointed* if you don't see the apple and wants you so *desperately* to be a good person and guilts and manipulates you and so on – and that is the type of person who's going to be more of the compliant woman or man through that kind of emotional problem...

Once you have created this invisible category of virtue that is not associated with *any* logic, is not associated with *anything* material or *anything* verifiable, or *anything* rational, or available through the senses, once you've created this incredible imaginary category of virtue, and you have forced your child to have to kowtow to that concept – well, you're set! I mean, you're absolutely set!

This child, who grows into an adult, is going to be completely compliant for the rest of his or her natural life. You have won the battle. You have completely realigned their reality processing to not have *any* concern with things like facts, except as sort of a lesser kind of way, like "I've got to drive and put my signal on, and I've got to get groceries and I've got to eat when I get hungry and wash when I'm dirty." I mean they'll deal with it at that sort of basic level, but when it comes to anything to do with the virtue, they have no interest in fact. In fact (haha), facts are a direct *threat* to them, because they have now had to swallow this whole lie and base their whole attachments on their family and their basis of their identity and, if they're moral in nature, the root of their morals on a *falsehood*!

So any time you start bringing up facts, these people are going to get angry, or petty, or pouty, or withdrawn – they're going to use some negative emotion to try and coat and repel anyone who gets close to talking about the truth with these people.

This is what Noam Chomsky calls the "narrative." (I mean, he's a crazy lefty, but he's got some good points!)

The "narrative" is the *story* that people are told about the moral history or the nature of their country, good versus bad, us versus them. The British are great, the Germans are evil, we have nothing in common except right after the war, then we're going to give money to the Germans.... I mean people just make this stuff up all the time – 90% of the e-mails I get is people just making up stuff and thinking that it's got something to do with reality.

But when you start bringing *facts* to bear on these people, they start getting hostile in one form or another, either passive-aggressive or otherwise aggressive – and that's because once they had to swallow this madness of the invisible apple, what relationship to facts could their ethical reasoning ever have in the future?

It simply can't exist.

Once you believe that something that is invisible is the center of morality, and the center of truth and right and all that is good in the world, what possible reference could you have to facts about ethics in the future? Or about *anything*, for that matter? About the existence of things? You're going to be drawn toward emotionally compelling stories, you're going to be drawn toward emotional bullying, and you're going to be drawn towards just making other people feel guilty for not believing you, or being aggressive and basically saying, "Well if you believe this or that you're a bad person." But you're not going have any reference to a single fact, or a single statistic other than those that are made up by people with a like-minded view.

But you're not going to have any reference to any *facts*. You're going to have instantaneous answers that you make up on the spot based on prior prejudices. How could it be otherwise? You've already accepted as the core of your reality processing that invisible things exist and have supreme value and ultimate moral authority. How on earth are you going to process anything from even a remotely reality-based or empirically-based or fact-based standpoint ever again? Well, you can't!

And that's *fantastic* for the people in power, because if you can't track anything to do with material reality, if you can't track anything to do with facts, if you can't apply logic and empiricism to something like morality, you're completely helpless. You are a lamb in a slaughterhouse when it comes to being abused by power, by those in power, by those willing to use violence to achieve their ends.

You're absolutely without defenses in this realm. You can groan and you can grumble and you can roll your eyes and you can write in your blog that you're mad at things and so on. But it really doesn't matter: you're fundamentally, absolutely, and completely helpless, because how are you going to question the morality of those in power with reference to logic and facts and our common humanity, when at the very beginning of things, you swallowed this invisible apple and called it tasty? Your reality processing and your logical processing and your central processing is completely wrecked. You might as well drive a car off a cliff and then try and win a race with it. It's just wrecked, it's smoking, it's wheels have fallen off! I mean, it can be repaired, of course, but it takes a lot of work, and the first thing you have to do is recognize that it's broken.

You've got to recognize that your mind is kind of broken, your mind is kind of damaged. What they call "the norm" is an asylum, what they call the norm is mentally ill. What they call the norm is people who believe in things like a government. Government doesn't exist! There is no such thing as the state! There's people with guns, and there's people who obey them. That's it. There's no such thing as the state, no such thing as countries, no such thing as gods, or demons. It's all just such a complete nonsense. Even *gender* exists in reality. You have biological differences that you can categorize. But nations don't exist in reality. Culture doesn't exist in reality.

Culture is just – and I'll do another podcast on this – culture is just the scar tissue of the child abuse of the invisible apple. I mean, why do Americans believe different things than French children? Why does everyone love their own country and love their own culture? Because of child abuse! Because that's what they're *told*, they're told all these false things!

My wife is told, "Oh, the Greeks are the best, we gave the world this and that and the other," and the Italian kids, "Oh, Italians are best," the

British: "Oh, the British are the best." It's all just nonsense. You're filling your children up with complete idiocy and falsehoods and telling them that it's all "morality" and self esteem based. It's complete child abuse. All culture that is not based on this simple observable facts of reality is just scar tissue that grows over being lied to as children. But we can deal with that another time.

I think it's very important to understand the number of things that you're told as a child that don't have *any* kind of reality, that you are told to be loyal to, that you are told to believe in, that you are told to infuse with some sort of moral energy – they're all complete falsehoods. And the wonderful thing about it is that *concepts have no voice*. This is the sort of nail in the coffin as far as obeying things like this state and politicians and priests and the military. If "the country" is virtue – my country right or wrong – if the country is virtue, if the country doesn't exist, then the country obviously can't tell you what to do. If God is goodness, but God doesn't exist, then God cannot tell you what to do. So who gets to tell you what to do? Well, the person who claims to *represent* this fantasy abstract. So it's how one human being bypasses another human being's legitimate anger of being bullied and told what to do.

The priest doesn't say, "Give me your money because my name is Bob and I want your money." The priest says, "Give God your money, because God wants you to give him your money, because God says 'help the poor.'" It's not, "Obey *me*," its, "Obey this abstract entity that I made up – because only *I* know what it wants!"

I mean it is ridiculous! It is absolutely insane! These things *don't exist* – and because they don't exist, they can't voice anything, and so the people who make them up and get you to believe in them say that you have to obey: "Oh not me. It's not me. It's for the good of the *country*. The country. Your *country* needs you!" No! Roosevelt needs you! People who profit from the war need you to go and get killed. Your country does not need you because countries don't exist! *God* is not telling you to do anything, the *priest* is telling you to do things! Crazy lunatic monks 5,000 years dead are telling you to do things! There's no such thing as God, or country, or state. They can't tell you to do anything because they don't exist! It's like trying to get paid with the *idea* of money – it doesn't exist! It's a mere conceptual tag that is imperfectly derived from physical instances – and in the case of country, it's not even derived from anything. It's a line in a map in somebody's head. Your country doesn't need you – countries don't have needs because countries don't exist!

And that's how they bypass your natural resentment at being told what to do, and it's time that we got that natural resentment back. Your country doesn't "need" you – George Bush needs you to go shoot people, or he wants you to. If you reframe that a little bit more accurately in your head, you'll just see why I say it's so insane.

George Bush says "I want you to go shoot that guy," you're gonna be like, "Well who the hell are *you*?" But you drape him in all this pomp and circumstance and he is the President of the United States. Well "President" doesn't exist, it's just a weird little conceptual label for a political fantasy. The "United States" doesn't exist, "Iraq" doesn't exist. There's desert and there's people, there's no such thing as Iraq, no such thing as the United States, they simply don't exist. A tree exists; the concept of tree, or the abstract notion of a forest, does not exist. A tree exists, a forest does not exist. A forest is an aggregate, it's a collection, it does not exist.

But if they can get you to believe that these things *do* exist, then they can say, "Your country needs you to do this, God needs you to do that, your father needs you to do the other!" Tell you what: "father" does not exist. There's a guy who had sex with your mother whose name is Bob who's telling you what to do. "Your father, your mother." I mean, in order to speak sensibly about Christina's family, we had to start referring to them by their Christian names. You can't refer to these things in any kind of abstract way that makes sense. "Father" is a category, it doesn't exist. It's like "forest." It applies to more than one person, therefore it doesn't exist.

"You *listen* to your father." "You listen to Bob." Which one sounds more compelling? If you obey a category, you feel like you're obeying something larger than the person who inhabits it. "I'm obeying a priest, I'm not obeying Ralph." Because if you say that you're obeying Ralph, you kind of feel like a slave, right? But if you say, "I'm obeying the will of God," you feel a smug kind of virtue creeping over you and fogging up your head. And that's exactly what the *point* of all of these abstract moral abstractions are. They're *designed* to bypass your natural animal resentment at being ordered around by idiots. And as soon as you stop believing in this nonsense, then you get some healthy anger which allows you to push back at these people who just make up all this stuff to cripple your minds and to cripple your animal instincts, to cripple your natural self esteem and feel a healthy push back at people who tell you what to do.

And that's why I dislike these categories so much, because they are the root of abuse. They are the root of exploitation. They are the root of the destruction of the human mind and the human personality and human morality. Humanity's capacity for morality is completely destroyed if you come up with these all-powerful, overarching moral constructs that have no existence and therefore have to be "interpreted" by individuals who are only doing it to exploit you. I hate these things! They are the cancer of the human soul. As Solzhenitsyn wrote in "The Gulag Archipelago," *secrecy is our cancer*. And in this case, *dishonesty* is our cancer.

There is no invisible apple. Your family was brutalizing you. There is no state, there is no God, and there is no country. There is no such thing as a municipality or a city. There are things, there are buildings, there are people, there are guns, and there are trees. There are no concepts that exist anywhere in the world. They exist in our minds as useful ways to organize physical objects and that's it. They mean nothing. They have no existence whatsoever. And to obey a concept is as ridiculous as trying to eat the idea of food. It is as ridiculous as trying to chop down a forest without touching any single tree. It is completely insane! And this insanity is a sickness that human beings have to outgrow, we have to fight our way out of this fog that is placed here to exploit us.

We do this in compassion for ourselves and compassion for those who are our fellow exploited, but perhaps it's possible also to find just a shred of compassion for those who claim to be our masters and are as absolutely enslaved in this sick fantasy, as enslaved as everybody else. George Bush is not a free man. Vladimir Putin is not a free man. They're slaves! They're slaves to this illusion that we all feed into and try and live on. I mean, it's not about fighting the rulers; it's about fighting the falsehoods. It's not about bringing down the government; it's about exposing the facts. It's not about overturning authority; it's about affirming the truth.

And if we can do that, if we can affirm the truth, if we can simply state the facts that have been so long obscured to us in our own hearts because of the corruption that we all faced as children, the lies that we were all force fed as children, the terrible and horrible choices that we all faced as children, if we had the strength to face up to that, and to speak the truth, and to stay in the conversation about what is real, and what is true, and what exists in reality, rather than what exists as sick exploitive fantasies in other people's minds, then by god we *can* free the world! By god we *can* wake humanity up from this nightmarish ten-thousand-year slumber of the damned! We can end war, we can end poverty, we can end hunger, we can end violence, we can end murder and theft and rape! Because all of these sicknesses can be traced back to that awful crossroads early in life when we are forced to choose loyalty to lies and corruption over the truth. And if we can reach back to that part of us that could never believe in such sickness, that could never believe that the world is an asylum peopled by those who have power over us – who are insane.

If we can reach back to that part of us that never believed, reach into that part of us which never believed those lies, then we really *can* remake the world. We really can bring a new light to humanity – ha, new light? – it's the first light! The Enlightenment came close, but they all backed away, because they couldn't get rid of the state and they couldn't get rid of God. They all became Deist and allowed it to trundle along, and so the cancer grew back.

We *can* make a new world that will be as unrecognizable to us now as we are to people in the fifteenth century. We made that leap in the past because we started to recognize things like property rights and the common humanity of all, and we began to question authority, and remove the state, and remove the intertwining of state and religion, and there's absolutely no reason why we can't continue to do it, but we have to continue to tell the truth at all times. So thank you so much for listening, I hope this has been helpful. It's been quite exciting for me, and I will talk to you soon! ☺

Virtue and Love

Honesty is the First Virtue

Honesty is the first virtue in every relationship – and most importantly our relationship with our self.

Mythology is the *opposite* of honesty, because mythology provides the *appearance* of truth, which prevents us from actively continuing to *pursue* the truth.

In this section I will put forward the thesis that our existing relationships are not primarily with each other, but with our own mythologies, with our own *stories* about our interactions with each other.

Mother Theresa used to say that she was not administering to the poor, but rather to *Christ in the poor*, which is a very different thing. Since Christ "the man-god who strolled the waves and came back from the dead" is a mere fantasy, Mother Theresa did not have a relationship with the poor as individuals, but rather with her own projected fantasy of "service" to a nonexistent deity. This is a form of spiritual "stalking."

I may as well say that I do not have a relationship with my girlfriend, but rather with the "leprechaun in my girlfriend."

Clearly, if I say that, I am openly admitting that I do not have a relationship with anyone or anything – outside my own fantasies of course.

"Not Even Wrong"

In the world of science, the worst judgment that can be passed upon a theory is that it is "not even wrong" – in other words, it is so incomprehensible or self-contradictory that nothing can be even learned from its mistakes.

"2 + 2 = 5" is wrong; "2 + blue = unicorn" is "not even wrong."

If I am patriotic, then clearly I am not in love with "the land" itself, since that is just earth and rock. I am not in love with the grass, or the trees, or the mountains or the clouds. I can say that I am in love with the *ideals* of the country that I live in, or its best and most virtuous principles – but clearly, those "ideals" exist *only as ideas within the minds of those around me.* If I say that I love "America," I am really saying that I love *my fellow Americans*, since "America" is a concept, and has no real existence in the objective world.

Since "America" does not exist, I cannot love it, any more than I can marry a leprechaun or send the concept of "children"" to school. Thus if I claim to love my fellow "Americans," I am not claiming to love any particular individual for his specific virtues, but rather a general group in relation to a concept that does not exist.

Of course, a "general group" is also a concept that does not exist in reality, and so when I claim to be patriotic, I am in fact expressing affection with regards to a generalized and abstract "group" (which does not in fact exist) in relation to a "country" (which does not in fact exist).

"Patriotism" is thus a mythology which separates us as individuals, because the primary relationship of the patriot is to a projected abstraction, rather than to any individuals in particular. The patriot "loves" his fellow countrymen in the same way that Mother Teresa "loves" the poor – it is a narcissistic projection, not a mature acceptance of another individual soul.

The sad thing about this is that we cannot in fact have any relationships to our mythologies, any more than we can soul-kiss our reflection in the mirror, or sit down with "the country" for nice cup of coffee and a chat.

Mythology always isolates – we can only meet in *reality*.

Relatedness

To be "related" to someone – to have intimacy – clearly requires that both parties feel free to speak their minds, commit to listening, and strive to understand each other.

In other words, relationships are fundamentally defined by *reciprocity*.

Clearly, you and I do not have a "relationship" if you forbid me to provide any feedback about anything you say or do. If I am not allowed to change my facial expression, open my mouth and say anything, or provide any response or feedback to your words or actions, then clearly I cannot be said to be having a *relationship* with you in any way at all.

Clearly, any intimate relationship also requires that both parties respect each other's thoughts, emotions and opinions. I cannot say that you and I are "close," while at the same time disagreeing with everything that you say, and criticizing everything that you do.

Similarly, intimacy requires feedback that is objective. If you show me a portrait you have painted and I tell you that it is terrible because I am jealous of how good it is, clearly the feedback that I'm giving you is not objective. This is equally true if I tell you that your portrait is wonderful when it is not because I am afraid of hurting your feelings.

This requirement for objective feedback does not exist only in relation to external objects.

If I am angry with you, and you ask me how I am feeling, and I tell you that I am "fine," then I am not giving you objective feedback. Expecting any relationship to flourish when you mislead your partner is like expecting a doctor to cure the pain in your arm after you tell him that your leg is hurting.

Thus if you and I have an intimate relationship, it must be true that we are giving each other objective and authentic feedback. We cannot be "close" if everything I say to you is a lie, or if every emotion that I claim to feel is manufactured – or, of course, if I only tell you what I think you "want to hear," or keep silent out of fear, or actively mislead you.

Intimacy and Value
Similarly, intimacy cannot coexist with any sort of "third-party validation" of each other's value.

If I date you only because you "look good on my arm," then it is not because I find particular value in you, but rather because I imagine that other people will find "value" in your appearance. If a woman marries a doctor because she primarily desires the prestige of being a doctor's wife, then the value of the man she is marrying is defined by the possible judgments of other people – not the man in and of himself.

An actor who befriends an agent in the hopes of gaining representation cannot claim to be "close" to that agent, but rather is using him as a means to an end. This is not always bad, of course – economically, I "use" my grocer as a means to the end of getting food, just as he "uses" me as a means to the end of getting money – but I would certainly not claim that I am "close" to my grocer!

Reciprocity
Without reciprocity, relationships are empty, manipulative, meaningless – and somewhat delusional.

We would not look at a ventriloquist who said "I have a close relationship with my dummy," as particularly sane or healthy, because his dummy, being functionally inert, clearly cannot provide any objective reciprocity in such a "relationship."

Also, if the primary "reciprocity" in a relationship is based on *third-party validation*, then clearly individual, or one-on-one reciprocity, is not particularly present.

If a woman dates a man because he is "so cute that her friends will be envious," then obviously her primary relationship is with her friends, not with the cute man. He is merely a means to an end, which is the envy of her friends. Thus the primary reciprocity she experiences is not with him, but with others.

In the same way, a man who dates a woman because he fears solitude does not have a positive relationship with her, but rather a "negative" relationship with his own fears. She is an anxiety-avoidance mechanism, and only has "value" as a human shield against his own low self-esteem. He has the same motives as a bank robber who grabs a hostage in order to avoid capture.

Intimacy

As we take a step back from our detailed brickwork, and look at the shape of the house we are constructing, we can begin to see what it looks like as a whole.

Love requires honesty, courage, integrity and virtue, both because these traits are admirable, and also because they foster predictability and security in intimate relations.

Love does not require perfection, but honesty – particularly in relation to mistakes, since perfection creates impossible standards and inevitable frustration, and love is fundamentally about sustainable pleasure, just as nutrition and exercise are fundamentally about sustainable health and well-being.

Love requires two parties that are drawn together by an objective standard – virtue – just as science requires two parties that are drawn together by an objective standard – the scientific method – and economic interactions require two parties that are drawn together by an objective standard – the voluntary exchange of economic value.

True intimacy is driven by a delight in gaining knowledge about the other person, just as scientific knowledge is driven by a delight in gaining knowledge about the material world.

Intimacy is the natural process and result of *pleasurable curiosity*.

A man who loves history will enjoy learning all about history.

A woman who loves a man will enjoy learning all about him.

If a man claims to "love" history, but scorns and rejects the study of history, we would not take his claim very seriously. If a man claims to "love" exercise, but never gets off the couch, and constantly mocks athletes on television, then we know that his professions of "love" are mere narcissistic foolishness.

However, active hostility is not required to repudiate claims of "love." Mere indifference is an effective argument against protestations of affection.

If a man says: "I love yoga," but never takes a class, watches a video, or practices, then clearly he does not love yoga, but rather is indifferent to yoga. What he "loves" is *saying* "I love yoga," rather than yoga itself.

In the same way, many people say that they like classical music, although when you hunt around their music collection, there's not a whole lot of classical there. The reason that they say they like classical music is that they like being *perceived* as someone who likes classical music, because it makes them appear cultured and refined.

In other words, they do not "like" classical music, but rather "like" lying, thus confirming that they are not cultured and refined – at least in this area – but rather shallow, insecure and manipulative.

I Want!

Love is a statement: "I want."

I *want* to get to know you better, I *want* to spend time with you, I *want* to share myself with you, I *want* to see how you will react to this or that. I *want* to know your thoughts and feelings.

I *want* to run downstairs and greet you with open arms when you come home.

I *want* to take care of you when you're feeling unwell.

I *want* your happiness.

I *want* you to feel safe, protected, loved and cherished.

The list goes on and on, of course – the essential aspect of "I want" is: *compared to what?*

All desires are limitless; all resources are limited. This fundamental principle of economics applies equally to questions of preference and prioritization.

I can say: "I love squash," but that does not mean that I want to play it 18 hours a day, since that would leave me injured and unable to play squash.

I can say: "I want to lose weight," but that does not mean that I *really* want to lose weight, if my following statement: "I want another piece of cheesecake," takes precedence.

I can say: "I want to be a millionaire," but that does not mean that I'm willing to sacrifice my leisure in order to achieve that goal.

Thus preferences must always be measured relative to each other.

In the example of Bruce and Sheila at the beginning of this book, we can see their initial meeting was characterized by a form of "fusion," wherein they developed a kind of one-dimensional "intimacy" by isolating themselves from the world, thus largely rejecting the ecosystem of competing demands. In this way, they really did not get the chance to see how they really "competed" with other priorities, which did not give them an objective way to really determine each other's value.

I used to work as a software executive, and traveled fairly regularly. I would say to my wife: "I love spending time with you," but that did not mean that the only thing I ever wanted to do was to spend time with her. I certainly preferred spending time with her to going to work, or on a business trip, but it was in order to retain my pleasure in her company that I felt it incumbent upon me to contribute to the household income.

Life is a balance of competing pleasures, as we all know. I have to get up early, but I want to finish watching a midnight movie. My wife is calling me for dinner, but I am right in the middle of a video game. I want to continue working on this book, but a Freedomain Radio listener has an important question.

In the absence of outright evil and corruption, there are no particularly objective "right" answers. Should I continue working on this book, or take a call from a listener with a problem? There is no totally objective way to answer this. We do not receive medals in the afterlife for the actions we take in the here and now. No one is "taking score," or giving us marks for right or wrong behaviours (except our conscience of course). We do not answer to an objective and conscious "higher power."

We do have an inbuilt desire and drive for the truth, since we live in objective material reality, which consistently reinforces the objective and rational principles that define the truth.

We do have an inbuilt desire and drive for moral justifications, because all human beings feel a fundamental need to be virtuous.

We always have the choice, of course, to either be virtuous or to just define whatever we're doing as "virtue," and thus corrupt both ourselves and the world.

In the same way, we always have the choice to either love honourably, or to just define whatever we're doing as "love," and thus corrupt both ourselves and the world.

Love is a Verb...

"Love," like "virtue," is *derived from actions, not defined by words.*

A man who claims to "love" a woman, but scorns and denigrates her – even on occasion – not only does not "love" her, but rather hates her.

In the same way, a man who claims to "love" his country, and then puts on a costume and points a gun at whoever his leaders tell him to – foreign and domestic – clearly does not "love" his country, but rather "loves" violence – which is the opposite of love.

A superstitious man does not "love" God, but rather "loves" controlling others through morally poisonous fantasies.

A statist man does not "love" government, or his fellow citizens, but rather "loves" controlling others through morally poisonous fantasies.

In the example above, Wendy does not "love" her daughter, but rather "loves" managing her own anxiety by controlling her daughter's behaviour.

Similarly, Bruce does not "love" Sheila – or vice versa – they just "love" managing their own anxieties by manipulating each others' behaviour.

In my first book, "On Truth: The Tyranny of Illusion," I argued that authority figures use morality to control us, thus affirming the power of morality – and our desire as children to be good – and then use that power to corrupt us and "justify" their own actions.

In the same way, any person who uses the word "love" to manipulate other people is acting in a highly corrupt manner.

The word "love" is used in many contexts, both within our personal relationships, and in our "larger" relationships to state, church and "morality."

Before discussing how we can begin to undo these destructive fantasies in our own lives using the Real-Time Relationship, let us look at how these pious lies have corrupted our social, religious and political environments, so that we can understand the difficulties that we will face when we finally begin to really speak the truth.

Social Lies: Love, Power and Manipulation

In the absence of nutritional knowledge, human beings tend to eat what tastes good in the moment.

In the absence of philosophical wisdom, human beings tend to become mere "anxiety avoidance machines."

Let us look at a few examples of this in various fields, before we see the enormously destructive impact this has on people's personal relationships.

Religion and Anxiety
Religious mysticism, or superstition, is almost always driven by a fear of the unknown.

If we look at the example of epilepsy, we can see that the incomprehensible foaming and thrashing behaviour exhibited by epileptics during an attack can create great anxiety in others. *What on earth is happening? Why is it happening? Could this happen to* **me**?

Whenever we are confronted by something that we do not understand, we can either roll up our sleeves and begin the hard work of striving to understand it – a work that will doubtless remain uncompleted in our lifetime – or we can simply make up an explanation that gets rid not of our ignorance, but of our *anxiety*.

Clearly, sacrificing a goat in no way affects whether or not the rains will come. However, if you can *convince* yourself that sacrificing a goat can indeed control the rain, the brutal ritual allows you to live with less anxiety, because you have "done something" to control your environment.

The Pitfalls of Mythology
Unfortunately, every moral illusion we create for the sake of immediate anxiety avoidance tends to harden into cultish dogmatism.

If we end up convincing ourselves that slaughtering the goat controls the rains, we are usually the one who slaughters the goat. All too often, our ability to spin comforting fantasies and kill animals becomes our profession. Our livelihood then becomes based on lies.

When this occurs – when the priestly class emerges – our greatest enemy then becomes scepticism and rational curiosity. Since we make our living by lying, anyone who starts objectively looking for the truth threatens our livelihood, our sense of virtue, and our position in the community.

If it becomes revealed that we have just made up our answers to prey upon others – and that we have provided only the *illusion* of security and control, to the great detriment of the community – then we are also likely to be attacked in retaliation, or banished from our community as liars and con men. We will be revealed to our children as shallow and manipulative thieves, and will be cast out into the wilderness, subject to all the whims of nature, beasts and men.

This is why mythologizing is so elementally destructive. Whenever you create a group of people who profit from lies and violence – the church and the state, respectively – you create a hardened caste whose self-interest can only be maintained through brutality and a willingness to attack virtue.

Mythology always becomes cancer.

Mythology and the Appearance of Control

Mythologizing, then, masks anxiety by creating the *appearance* of control.

Like any drug, this temporarily reduces anxiety in the moment, while continually escalating it in the long run.

Mythologizing is in essence the creation of an *unsubstantiated link between cause and effect*. Why does Bob have epilepsy? Why, because he is *possessed by a demon!*

Naturally, since this supposed "cause and effect" is entirely illusory, it cannot rest on its own empirical merits, but must be aggressively inflicted and defended through propaganda and force.

There is no "Church of Gravity," which drags young children into Sunday school to repeat to them over and over that gravity exists, that gravity is real, that gravity has an effect on matter – and that the children will be sent to hell for disbelieving in gravity. Similarly, there are no "Temples of the Hot Stoves" which strive over and over to inculcate the belief in children that a hot stove will burn them if they touch it.

The reason for this, of course, is that children have direct empirical perceptions of gravity and heat – the cause-and-effect is very immediate, very testable, very powerful, perfectly consistent, and so perfectly real.

It is only when the cause-and-effect is *imaginary* that moral and physical aggression need to be deployed against anyone who questions it.

Statism and Anxiety

The mythology around "the state" in many ways exceeds – particularly in the modern world – the mythology that surrounds superstitious religiosity.

The question: *how can human society be organized?* is not answered by the state, any more than the question *where did the world come from?* is answered by religion.

If a man says, "My wife loves me," and then locks her in the basement and threatens to shoot her if she tries to escape, do we believe him?

A "theory" cannot be considered "proven" if all it does is shoot anyone who disagrees with it.

In fact, any theory which requires violent defense is by any rational standard of proof utterly wrong or false to begin with.

Thus the thesis that "a state is required to organize society," is demonstrably false, because it is not in fact a thesis at all, but rather a *violently aggressive dogma*.

Shooting those who disagree with you does not make you right, but rather proves that your position is wrong, corrupt and evil.

The State and Society
Since the state uses compulsion to "organize" society, it repudiates the very concept of "society," just as rape repudiates the very concept of "love making," and robbery repudiates the concept of "property."

Using "the state" to answer the question of how society should be organized is morally identical to using kidnapping and imprisonment to answer the question of how to get someone to "love" you.

It is the mere *illusion* of an answer, rather than a real answer – and like all illusory answers, not only is it brutal in the extreme, but it also actively prevents the pursuit of true answers.

The False Answers of Statism
When people ask, "How should children be educated?" – the answer, inevitably, is: *we should educate them through the state*.

This is not an answer at all.

We may as well answer the question *how should people get married?* with the answer: *we should force them to cohabitate at gunpoint.*

However, the moment that force is used, voluntary descriptions must be abandoned.

If I steal your wallet at gunpoint, I cannot logically call the transfer of money "charity."

If we force people to get "married," it is not *marriage*, but rather *institutionalized rape.*

If we force children to get "educated," it is not *education* but rather *institutionalized indoctrination.*

In the same way, if we bully, force, manipulate or threaten children to get them to believe in God, what results is not *belief*, but frightened conformity, which can also be termed brain-rape or brainwashing.

And the same is true of love.

Love and Anxiety

True knowledge reduces our anxiety, because true knowledge allows us to predict consequences, accurately manage cause-and-effect, and thus gain some objective measure of control in our lives.

Thus, when we correctly view epilepsy as a neurological disorder, we can predict that attacks will occur in the future, we can examine the causes of these attacks and develop medications to prevent recurrence – or at least manage the symptoms.

Even if we cannot control epilepsy, understanding that it is a neurological disorder at least reduces our anxiety with regards to the unknown. Even if we cannot turn on the light, once we understand that the "giant skeletal hand" scratching at our window is in fact a tree branch, our terror is sharply reduced.

On the other hand, if we believe that epileptic attacks are the result of demonic possession or invasion, then we will take the epileptic to a priest, who will sprinkle water and chant words, which have absolutely no effect on the cause of the attack, and prevent rather than provide understanding.

Trial by Fire
In the Middle Ages, there was a ritual known as "trial by fire," wherein a person accused of a serious crime would be forced to reach into a fire and

pull out a metal bar – being terribly burned in the process. If the burns became infected, then the person's guilt was considered established, since infection was a sign of moral corruption, inflicted by God only upon the guilty.

Of course, the presence or absence of infection has nothing whatsoever to do with a person's guilt or innocence, but is mere random chance. Inherent in the "trial by fire" was a complete understanding of this, insofar as the person had to be burned in order for the infection to possibly occur – in other words, they did not wait for a spontaneous infection to afflict a healthy person.

We may feel that we are far above this primitive brutality, but of course we are not. Governments the world over – including the United States, and other "civilized" Western nations – regularly torture "confessions" out of people. This can occur through "extraordinary rendition" programs, wherein people are kidnapped, flown to Egypt or Syria, and tortured or murdered – but it also happens countless times daily, when people are offered reduced sentences or plea bargains, in return for "confessions."

During the Salem witch trials, women were tortured into "confessing" that they were witches – and then they were offered a quick death if they would name other witches in their "coven." Dazed, bleeding, broken, mutilated, they coughed up the names of anyone they could think of, in order to gain the sweet release of death.

In our times, such "confessions" are also extracted through the threat of torture – since modern prisons in every country are certainly torture pits of brutality and rape – in return for "testimony" against others.

This "testimony" usually results from a person facing years or decades in prison naming whoever he can in order to reduce his sentence, and has nothing to do with establishing any sort of reasonable innocence or guilt. These "named" people are then picked up, and the process continues.

The only difference is that in the medieval "trial by fire," at least you had a chance of *not* developing an infection.

Through this process, the number of crimes that are genuinely prevented is far outstripped by the number of crimes certainly committed, through the sending of innocent and terrified people to the brutal rape rooms of modern prisons.

Furthermore, since the government can invent any number of "crimes" and "criminals," this sick and evil process both allows the government to claim that it is really *good* at catching criminals, and also terrifies the population through the invention of a "criminal underclass" that citizens believe they need the government to protect them from.

False Knowledge and Crime
This whole process is a vicious example of how "false knowledge" (i.e. *you have committed this "crime"*) both enables and exacerbates real crimes. By creating "facts" through the threat of multiyear torture, only the *appearance* of guilt is established.

We may as well imagine that the Salem trials were really about finding witches. While many women certainly did "confess" to being witches, that was only because they preferred a relatively quick death to the endless tortures inflicted on them by superstitious fanatics.

We can see countless other examples as we look across our intellectual landscape, from the bitchy and greedy fear-mongering of "global warming" to the filthy and viciously corrupt fear-mongering of the "War on Terror" to the exhausted and numbly-repeated fear-mongering of the "War on Drugs," "War on Poverty," "War on Illiteracy," etc.

Whenever a disaster strikes a statist or religious society, the brutalized mob's first instinct is not to find the root cause, but rather to identify a scapegoat.

New York, 2001

For example, in the case of the attacks on New York in 2001, everybody's first desire was for vengeance, not knowledge.

This is exactly the same reaction as the superstitious desire to "attack" the demon that is causing epilepsy, rather than struggling to understand the root causes of epilepsy, and working to alleviate them.

If we refuse to understand the root causes of epilepsy, but rather just attack the epileptics, anyone suffering from epilepsy will do anything he can to shield knowledge of his symptoms from everyone else. In the same way, the president of Iran can, with a straight face, say, "We have no homosexuals in our country." Given that homosexuals are regularly tortured and killed in Iran, it hardly seems surprising that they would be a challenge to find.

When epileptics are attacked, and then the symptoms of epilepsy mysteriously "vanish," the attackers generally raise a cheer and toast their own effectiveness.

However, all these monsters have done is to make the study of epilepsy highly dangerous. They have eliminated the "symptoms," but their definition of epilepsy as an "evil possession" simply makes anyone who strives to understand it scientifically "evil" as well, and thus subject to attack.

In this way, not only do they merely eliminate the symptoms of epilepsy, but they ensure that epilepsy will continue – and likely increase – by attacking anyone who displays the symptoms, as well as anyone who investigates those symptoms scientifically.

Just as refusing to investigate the aetiology of epilepsy causes one to act in a way that does nothing to alleviate the problem of epilepsy, refusing to understand the root causes of "terrorist" attacks does nothing to alleviate the problems of violence.

If fact, it only makes those problems worse.

Empathizing with Vengeance
If we are attacked, it is generally very easy to understand why.

We are attacked for exactly the same reasons that we want to attack others.

When we want to go and bomb Afghanistan after 9/11, we fully understand the mindset of the "terrorists" already.

To understand why people would want to fly planes into buildings, all we need to do is understand why we want to bomb Afghanistan.

Since we want to bomb Afghanistan because we have been attacked, we can then easily surmise that planes must have been flown into our buildings because we have attacked others.

It's really not that complicated, and it takes an enormous amount of effort to avoid this simple and basic understanding.

The Golden Rule – do unto others as you would have them do unto you – serves us well here. "Others are doing to us as we have done to them." (I use the word "we" here very loosely of course, referring rather to the foreign policy of the US government. Also, please note that I use the word "policy" here equally loosely, referring rather to its terrorist attacks on foreigners.)

To understand the "terrorism" of foreigners, all we have to do is understand our own response to "terrorism."

When "terrorism" is inflicted upon us – paramilitary attacks without a declaration of war – we have a desire to lash out and murder others.

Thus since we wish to attack when we are murdered, *we must have been attacked because we have murdered*, since Muslims do not belong to another species, and human beings have similar reactions to similar stimuli.

How long does this take to figure out? Not very long at all.

A few minutes on the Internet will reveal a massive bombing campaign throughout Iraq in the 1990s, conducted by the British and American military, which resulted in the economic decimation of the middle class and the physical destruction through malnutrition and illness of upwards of half a million Iraqis.

Going further, it does not take very long to find out that the United States has tens of thousands of troops stationed in Saudi Arabia – and it also does not take an enormous leap of imagination to understand how this must make certain Saudis feel, given that many Americans would doubtless find it highly objectionable to have Muslim nuclear weapons stationed outside Washington, pointed at the White House.

Also, the US still occupies Japan, more than a half-century after conquering it, and has 700+ military bases throughout the world, and extracts billions of dollars from foreign governments to pay for these occupations – like any other criminal shakedown.

Going just a little bit further, it does not take very long to find out that America subsidizes the Israeli military to the tune of several billion dollars a year. Regardless of how one views the division down the Gaza Strip and the creation of the occupied territories, it certainly is the case that America finances the oppression of Muslims through the Israeli occupation.

Given that America was founded through the violent overthrow of a foreign "dictatorship," it should not be hard for Americans to figure out that when you cause the deaths of those in another group by the hundreds of thousands – particularly children – and when you station "infidel" troops on the "holy land" of a highly volatile and superstitious gang of oil-rich thugs – and finally, when you subsidize a group that is viciously oppressing members of the same volatile gang – that reprisals, or "blowback," will be inevitable.

Americans make up stories about how the Muslims "hate us for our freedoms" – and then condemn Islamic societies for their lack of freedoms. When I ask Americans if they hate Islamic dictatorships – and they say, "yes" – when I then ask them why they are not out committing acts of terrorism against those Islamic dictatorships, they just stare at me blankly, as if I were insane.

In other words, the blatant conflict between, "They attack us because they hate us in the abstract," and, "I hate them in the abstract, but I would never attack them," must be repressed, like all mythologies.

Hellish Reciprocity
If they come to kill us, and then we want to kill them, then logically *they must have come to kill us because we have already been killing them.*

If Americans stare around in bewilderment, asking "Why do they hate us?" the first person to ask, of course, is the person who attacked them.

If I sit minding my own business in a restaurant and a man comes up and slaps me across the face, my first question would be: "Why did you slap me?"

If the man says, "Because *here* are the pictures of you sleeping with my wife!" then I cannot claim to be ignorant of why he has hit me. I may oppose his use of force or consider it an unjust response to my actions, but I cannot claim to be ignorant of his motives.

On the other hand, if the man says: "I slapped you because you killed my entire family," then any vengeance that I would take would seem wildly unjust to everyone else, since the wrong I had done this man far outstripped the wrong he had done me in return.

People always ignore, repress or bypass questions for which they already have answers that they do not like, or which do not serve their needs.

If the man in the restaurant slaps me, I can only take vengeance upon him if I claim that I have never done anything to harm him.

If he claims that his slap was a retaliation for my far more grievous attack upon his family, then I must not respond to that accusation in any way – neither to deny nor affirm – but must continue to protest my complete ignorance as to his motives for attacking me.

Only by ignoring *his* motives can I justify *my* vengeance.

In the case of the September attacks, this "bewilderment" reached truly ridiculous proportions. The man who claimed to be behind the attacks openly stated that his three reasons for attacking America were exactly those described above – the US occupation of Saudi Arabia, the funding of Israel, and the blockade of Iraq,

He repeated over and over that his attack was a retaliation for the far more egregious American attacks upon his fellow Muslims.

Yet still Americans claimed that they had "no idea" why they were so hated – or, that they were hated for their "virtues" – which is even more offensive and provocative.

If a man rapes a woman and then claims that she is fabricating charges against him, because he is just so "wonderful and loving," then he is egregiously and provocatively adding insult to injury. By claiming that she is reacting in rage and hatred to his benevolence, love and virtue, he is not only rejecting the fact that he brutalized her sexually, but he is also claiming that she is emotionally corrupt and viciously anti-virtue.

Backup Lies

Of course, after the mythology of "we have no idea why we were attacked" is invented, a secondary mythology must also be created, in order to protect the first.

As described earlier, false cause-and-effect "relationships" such as "*sacrificing a goat = good rains*" must always be defended through the use of emotional and/or physical brutality.

After the September attacks, the backup mythology – the "thug" story – was that any attempt to understand the root causes of the attacks could only be motivated by sympathy for the attackers, and a desire to justify their murders.

This is all pure, vicious nonsense – the direct equivalent of accusing an oncologist who studies how to prevent a recurrence of cancer of being a big fan of the cancer you already have.

Clearly, someone who wishes to get to the root causes of an affliction cannot "cure" those who already *have* that affliction, any more than an anti-smoking campaign can reverse lung cancer.

It is precisely *because* lung cancer is largely irreversible that prevention is far more valuable than attempting a "cure."

Love and Ego Identification

Why is it that the average American would be so resistant to discovering the truth about the September attacks?

What would it cost him emotionally if he discovered that those who claim to represent "his government" had done unspeakably evil things, which had brought about unspeakably evil retaliations?

If the average American reads about a Mafia hit-man who gets "whacked" in return, or some gang banger found shot dead in a gutter, does he immediately rush to the defense of the Mafia, or the gang?

Of course not.

If a mugger gets shot, the average American most likely shrugs and says, "Well, don't mug people!" If a hit-man gets whacked, we often feel a grim, unpleasant but generally-inevitable sense of justice.

Ah, the average American might say, but in the case of the September attacks, the people who were killed were *not* the people responsible for the decisions of the leaders.

This is very true, of course – but it is equally true for the Iraqis, who starved and died under an embargo that supposedly resulted directly from the decisions of *their* leader – Saddam Hussein.

Furthermore, the Iraqis who died had no chance whatsoever to change their leader or to affect their political system in any way, shape or form. The people who died in the World Trade Center were educated, affluent, well-spoken and old enough to vote. This does not mean that they brought about their own deaths, of course, but it *does* mean that if the standard is brought forward that people should not be killed for the actions of their leaders, then we must have more sympathy for the helpless Iraqis, who lived in a dictatorship, than the adults of New York, who lived in a democracy.

Furthermore, it was the Iraqi *children* who suffered and died the most under the UK/US blockade. Should we primarily blame *children* for the actions of a dictator? Would it have been *worse* for the Muslim hijackers to target Disneyland?

Finally, what is the average Muslim to make of the simple and brutal reality that, even after the "reasons" given for the invasion of Iraq in 2003 turned out to be totally fraudulent, the sitting President was returned to office with a clear majority of the popular vote? What could it mean that, *after committing a genocide against Muslims, Bush won the Presidency more decisively* in 2004 than he did in 2000?

Are those who vote responsible for the decisions of their leaders?

The "Stockholm Syndrome"
The only way to truly unravel this unholy knot is to understand that the average American feels a very strong ego identification with "his" leader, "his" government, and the political ruling class as a whole.

Why is that?

Well, of course it is partly due to the endless propaganda that every citizen of every country is endlessly subjected to, particularly in government schools.

However, there is a far more central reason that we rush to the defense of our leaders, which has great ramifications for our own personal relationships as well.

Sympathy and Integrity

What would it mean to have sympathy for the victims of our own governments?

What would it mean to dispassionately survey the political and military landscape of the past generation or so, and realize the degree to which our own governments have committed unspeakable crimes and genocides throughout the world?

What would it mean?

The reason that we avoid knowing evil is not because we wish to avoid that knowledge, but rather because we wish to avoid another knowledge which is far more dangerous to us.

Imagine a prisoner who wakes up to a silent and empty prison, with the door of his cell very slightly ajar.

He calls out, but no guards come.

He rattles the bars of his cage, but no other prisoners respond, and no other sound can be heard.

Everyone has left. He is alone in an empty prison.

If we imagine that we are this prisoner, can we picture how terrifying it would be for us to *actually try to open the door of our cell*?

If the door *opens*, we at least have the chance to escape.

If the door is locked, however – ah, then we will suffer the agonies of thirst and starvation for days, and die a terrible death, alone in our locked cell.

With the stakes so high, how would we *feel* about actually trying to *open* the door of our cell?

The reason that we would avoid trying to open the door of our cage is not because we were afraid of the door being locked, but rather that we were afraid of dying of thirst and starvation, over days, agonizingly slowly.

By avoiding the door, we are avoiding the knowledge of our death.

And – the more certain that we are that the door is locked – and thus that we will die - the more terrified we are of trying to open it.

In the same way, we flock to defend our leaders, because if we objectively survey their actions and realize the violence and evil that they have committed, we are led to some terrifying and terrible conclusions about the world that we *actually* live in.

Democracy?

The vast majority of people in the world did not want America to invade Iraq – and even the majority of people in America did not want the invasion, or if they did it was only because of propaganda.

Yet still, the invasion occurred – even though Saddam Hussein had nothing to do with the September attacks, had no contacts with Al Qaeda, and did not possess weapons of mass destruction.

What does this say about the true nature of the society that we live in?

If our leaders are capable of ordering a blockade that results in the deaths of half a million Iraqis, what does that say about their capacity for ethical action?

What does that say about their capacity for empathy?

What does that say about their moral values?

What are we avoiding when we do not ask these questions?

Furthermore, if our leaders perform these unspeakably evil actions and then profess "bewilderment" when their victims strike back, then clearly our leaders fully understand the ethics of "virtuous self-defense."

Thus they cannot be mad – or at least, not *morally* mad.

If they are not morally mad, but perform evil actions, then they are truly evil.

And these are the people that we give our children to, to become "educated."

In a democracy, if the leaders are evil, it is either because the people are evil, or because it is not really a democracy.

If we live in a true democracy, and the majority of people elect evil sociopaths as their leaders, then clearly *the majority of people are evil*.

If the majority of people are evil, and their leaders are also evil, then the attacks of September become understandable – it is just one Mafia gang attacking another in retaliation for a previous attack. There is no honor, no reasonable self-righteousness – it is just one more dirty murder following another dirty murder.

In this case, retaliation becomes impossible to justify in moral terms – and so the cycle is broken.

If, however, the people are *not* evil, but their leaders *are* evil – as surely they are – then clearly the leaders do not represent the will of the people, and thus society cannot be called a "democracy."

If the majority of the people are good, but the leaders are evil, then clearly it is immoral to have any sort of allegiance to this corrupt and exploitive gang of political thugs.

If we saw innocent bystanders being gunned down in a drive-by gangland shooting, would we rush to the defense of the shooters?

If this type of murder occurs in a neighbourhood – dozens of people being cut down in gangland shootouts – we would tend to get angry at the gang that *provoked* the retaliation, not flock to their support, grab weapons and continue to escalate the war.

In other words, we would identify with the *victims*, not with the *perpetrators*.

However, in the case of the September attacks, the average American did not identify with the *victims* but rather with the *leaders*.

Again, *why?*

Morality and Victimhood
To start, let's trace what happens when the average American begins to apply objective moral judgments to the actions of those involved in Christian/Muslim/Jewish violence.

Clearly, ordering the death of another is immoral. Equally clearly, in terms of ordering the deaths of other religious groups, the *Christians* started the cycle of violence, at least in the 20th century. There were no Muslim attacks on America in the 19th century even though America was far freer in many ways in those days.

The Christian attacks on the Muslim world continued throughout the 20th century through the creation of Iraq by the British out of the ashes of the Ottoman Empire after WWI, and escalating in the American arming of Iraq against Iran in the 1980s, followed by the sanctions against Iraq in the 1990s.

Thus in terms of "who started it," clearly it was the Christians – initially the British, and to a smaller degree the French, and most recently the Americans.

Since ordering the deaths of other people is evil, then clearly this evil was first committed by the Western Christian leaders.

Since Westerners pride themselves on their "democratic institutions" – particularly as opposed to the dictatorial Islamic theocracies – clearly the Western citizens of those democracies have a far greater capacity to control the actions of their leaders, relative to the average Muslim.

Since in a democracy the actions of the leaders must represent the will of the people, if those leaders perform evil actions, then the people are to some degree at least responsible for that evil.

If I give a gun to a murderer knowing that he is about to kill someone, cheer him on when he does kill that person, and then give him more bullets right afterwards, then clearly I am complicit in his crimes.

Now, if the attacks of September 2001 were evil – as doubtless they were – but we apply an objective moral standard, then clearly our own leaders are far more evil than the leaders of the attackers, since they have been responsible for hundreds of times more murders than the attackers.

If our own leaders are evil, then we must attempt to prevent them from performing their evil actions.

If we live in a true democracy, then we should easily be able to prevent our leaders from performing evil actions.

In other words, the door to our cage should be *unlocked*.

Yet – we do not try to prevent our leaders from performing evil actions.

Even after the manipulations and falsehoods of George W. Bush were fully exposed – even in the mainstream media – he still won the popular vote with a margin of several million.

Since he had started a war based on false information, why was he not voted out?

The Knowledge We Avoid

He was not voted out because the people did not want to see that the war would continue.

The average American does not want to find out that no matter who he puts in government, the evils of the state will continue.

The average American does not want to find out that his cell door is truly and irrevocably locked.

The average American – like all of us – knows deep in his heart that he has absolutely no control over his government.

Deep down, we all know that the rapes, murders, tortures, predations, corruptions, thefts and brutality committed in the name of "the state" will continue as long as "the state" does.

We can sooner alter the orbit of the moon with our minds than control the actions of our leaders.

It is not knowledge of *evil* that we are avoiding, but knowledge of our own *subjugation* – of our own helplessness, of our own enslavement.

The moment that we actually emotionally understand, accept and truly *feel* the nature of our enslavement, we will find ourselves compelled to action.

And it is *that action* that we fear – not because it involves violence or physical danger, but rather because we know it will trigger the undoing of our entire world as we know it.

That is what is truly called "taking the red pill."

Implosion

The moment that we begin applying objective moral values to our own life – and to the actions of those around us – we immediately step into another kind of world – or rather, step out of a prison *that is only visible from the outside.*

So when we question the murderous desire for retribution after the September attacks, we begin to understand that we are surrounded by people who *attack anyone who speaks the truth.*

If we are surrounded by people who attack the truth, then we are in fact surrounded by corrupt and brutal individuals.

If we are surrounded by corrupt individuals, then the corruption of our leaders becomes more understandable.

The corruption of our leaders becomes more understandable when we realize that we are living in a world of pious, frightened and brutal liars.

In this way, the "country" that we formerly claimed to "love" is revealed as a frightened, tyrannical and abusive "family" that showers empty goodies on blank conformists and *attacks anyone who asks rational and moral questions.*

In other words, the moment that we speak the truth, we find out that we were only "loved" because we were silent, stupid, obedient – and productive.

We find out that we were only "tolerated" as a means to an end, in the same way that a farmer "tolerates" his cows, because he wants milk – and meat.

The Humiliation of Knowledge

This knowledge is exquisitely and almost unbearably humiliating.

When we emerge from the "matrix" of mythology, we look back and see…

…that we licked the boots of those who kicked us. That we sang the praises of those who harvested us. That we were slaves who cheered the virtue of being owned.

And – the most terrifying realization of all…

That we are far more afraid of our fellow slaves than we are of our masters.

Once this realization sinks in, we are temporarily lost in a fog of limbo… We cannot be masters, but are no longer slaves. We cannot sup at the bloody tables of the elites, but neither are we welcome any more in the cages of the slaves, to fight over scraps and call it "plenty."

This is the land between the stars, between the past and the present, where the fertility of the future takes root.

And it can be a very, very lonely place to be.

And it is this exile, this knowledge, that we are avoiding at all times.

The truth does set us free – *at the cost of revealing to us that we are all slaves.*

And – that our fellow slaves hate us most of all.

Anxiety Avoidance and Relationships

What does the above analysis have to do with our personal relationships?

It has been my experience that it is far easier to get people to understand personal topics in an abstract context first.

As the long-time listeners at Freedomain Radio well know, I began my series on personal and political liberty with long discussions of anarchistic models of social organization, as well as abstract economic, theological and political analyses. It was only after 70 or so podcasts that I began to dip into personal topics, and only in the late 100s did I really begin to zero in on personal liberty, particularly with the series 180 to 183 – "Freedom" Parts 1-4.

Most people who are interested in political liberty know that some rather terrible things have occurred since the attacks on New York. Some have gone as far as saying that these attacks were an "inside job," which I do not believe, but you do not need to go that far in order to understand that those who wield political, military or mercantilist economic power only stand to gain when a nation is "attacked," particularly when a nightmarish Orwellian "endless war" can be invented.

In other words, if you really want to hurt yourself, you do not need to stab yourself: you simply need to keep poking a bear with a stick.

Most of my writing and thinking as a philosopher has been focused on answering two fundamental questions:

1. Why has libertarianism failed so consistently throughout history?
2. Given that we can have no practical effect on a nuclear-armed state, how can we best work to bring about political liberty without compromising our personal liberty?

The answer to the first question has been the subject of many podcasts on the family; the entire answer to the second question is obviously beyond the scope of this book, but I will say that once you understand the principles of the Real-Time Relationship, you will have taken an enormous leap forward in understanding how to free yourself personally, and how it can be applied politically as well.

If we distil our analysis of the September attacks as described earlier, we can come to some very valuable conclusions, which can really help us understand the nature and challenges of our personal relationships – as well as why we spend so much time and energy avoiding the truth.

The Principles of Intimacy

First of all, I can guarantee you that examining your personal relationships in the light of what is being discussed in this book will be enormously costly.

If you continue, and move beyond the theoretical stage and actually understand these principles *personally* – whether you end up putting them into practice or not – it is likely that very few of your existing relationships will survive this transition.

I just think that you should know that up front.

Philosophy is not a toy – and in particular, *moral* philosophy is the most powerful force on the planet.

If you are going to bring this amazing power to bear on your relationships, then very few of them will actually survive. I can tell you that those that do survive will be greater than anything you can imagine at the moment. In other words, there is a light at the end of the tunnel, or "hope" at the bottom of this Pandora's Box.

Realities
First of all, I fully accept and believe you when you say that every relationship that you are involved in at the moment is based on virtue.

None of us get up in the morning, brush our teeth, look in the mirror and say: "my wife/parents/friends etc. are *evil!*"

We may get angry at them from time to time, but we do not truly or consistently believe that they are full of malevolent intent, hell bent on our destruction, and selfish to the core.

If people in our lives behave in a manner that cannot possibly be construed as virtuous or benevolent, we have an endless stream of clichés at our disposal with which to wish away our wounds and knowledge of corruption:

- "He did the best he could!"
- "His heart is in the right place!"
- "She comes from a different generation, that's just all she knows…"
- "I guess I'm just a bit oversensitive."
- "That's just his way!"
- "Oh, that's more prevalent in *his* culture."
- "He never acts with any ill intent, he's just… brusque."
- "She's under a lot of stress right now."

In other words, we explain away non-virtuous actions with self-medicating *stories*. We accept immoral behaviour by redefining it as "well-intentioned imperfection," and then proudly wear the medal of "virtuous tolerance."

In other words, as described in Part 1, we redefine our cowardice as "courage."

This is very similar to the way that people view their government. While getting upset and frustrated at some evidence of incompetent, scandalous or immoral behaviour, the "value" of government *in the abstract*, or *as an institution* remains not just unquestioned – but *unquestionable*. "A few bad apples don't spoil the barrel," we say, or, "Don't throw the baby out with the bathwater."

Thus we have a seemingly ineradicable habit of believing that those people we have relationships with are virtuous or have our best interests at heart, *but we will do almost anything to avoid applying rational moral principles to their actions.*

In the same way, theologians claim to have "knowledge" of the existence and will of some sort of deity. This "knowledge" is always presented as objective – as differentiated from their *opinions* – however, when any sort of objective principles are applied to this knowledge, it completely evaporates, and is revealed as, after all, a mere *opinion*.

This is an example of a meal that this book will take off your personal "myth menu" forever: *having your cake and eating it too.*

Virtue as "Objective Opinion"

People always claim that their relationships – with their parents, friends, governments and gods – are based on *virtue*. However, when you attempt to ask them *how* they know this and what principles they have applied to derive such objective knowledge – since virtue is surely not just an opinion – they immediately and instantaneously shy away, or become aggressive.

If I claim to have created a medicine that will prevent the spread of HIV – a pronouncement greeted with cheers of gratitude – and then, when a population takes this medicine, what results is *the greatest HIV plague that the world has ever seen*, will people's gratitude for my medicine continue unabated?

In the same way, patriots say: "I love my country because my country is the *best!*"

"Best" in this case always means *most moral*. Americans talk about the Constitution, the Bill of Rights, the separation of powers and so on. In other words, they talk about how the American system *limits* the power of government, and how right it was for the United States to break away from England in the 18th century.

When you then ask these patriots how it is reasonably possible to love a system that was designed to limit the power of government that has produced the most powerful government, with the greatest and most destructive military, that the world has *ever known*, they just shy away or become aggressive.

Furthermore, if it was right to fight against the British state in the 18th century, when it was imposing minor taxes and duties, and threatening to impose a fiat currency, how can it be possible to love the American state in the 21st century, with its crushing tax burdens, ridiculously overinflated fiat currency, massive national debt, monstrously imperialistic foreign policy and so on? That's like saying that you hugely respect the virtue and courage of a woman who leaves her husband because he doesn't take out the garbage, but that a woman should stay with a husband who half-strangles her to death every other week.

Also, if Americans love their country because the Bill of Rights and the Constitution limit the power of government, then surely they must love their country less and less, as government power grows greater and greater.

If I love sobriety and hate alcoholism, and when I married my wife she rarely drank, surely I will love her less when she becomes a raging alcoholic, hiding gin in the Listerine bottle for her morning "gargle."

If I say that I love sobriety and hate alcoholism, but claim that I love my wife equally after she transitions from teetotaler to raging alcoholic, then clearly I am just making up criteria by which I claim to "love" her.

God is Good?
In the same way, when you talk to Christians – or any religious people – and hear from them that God is good, it is reasonable to ask them: "How do you know?" – particularly because most theologies include a deceptive devil as well, and apparently it's always good to know the difference, to avoid being fooled into worshipping the wrong deity.

If they say: "God is good because that is written in the Bible," then it's worth asking them whether they believe that the Bible is the Word of God. Naturally, they will say yes.

In this case, we basically have an autobiography in which the writer claims to be virtuous. In other words, a "claim to virtue" is the equivalent of virtue itself.

If "crazy eyes" Charles Manson scratches "I am virtuous" on his prison wall using the tooth of another prisoner, does that make Charles Manson virtuous?

There were many "authorized" Soviet biographies of Joseph Stalin that claimed he was the greatest and most virtuous man who ever lived. In "Mein Kampf," Hitler also makes great claims about his own virtue, and divine mission, and piety, and obedience to God and so on.

In other words, a self-proclamation of virtue does not prove virtue any more than repeating the words "I am rich" magically creates gold in your hand.

Thus the "virtue" of a supernatural being cannot result from its own self-proclamation, but must exist relative to some other objective standard.

A scientific theory is not "proven" because its author says so, but rather relative to the objective standard of the scientific method, which is to say relative to empirical reality. A compass measures "North," not just me yelling the word "North!"

In this way, the "virtue" of a supernatural being must be determined relative to an objective standard of virtue.

"What, then," I always ask the superstitious at this point, "is the objective standard by which you measure the virtue of your deity?"

If the response comes back: "The 10 Commandments," then clearly, since one of them is: "Thou shalt not kill," I always ask if this supernatural being has ever willfully caused the death of a human being.

Naturally, any honest Bible reader has to answer in the affirmative.

We can go through the same process with other commonly-accepted moral propositions, such as "rape is evil," "slavery is immoral," "child abuse is unacceptable," and so on. If we find that the "holy" words of this supernatural being approve of – or even excuse – evils such as rape, slavery and child abuse, then clearly either these things are moral, or the deity is not.

Inevitably, the superstitious cultist you are talking to will find other, more pressing matters to attend to, rather than examining the "virtue" of his own fantasy sky ghost.

I myself would not be able to find any topic more important, more essential for my own virtue, well-being and happiness, than establishing the moral rightness of a being that I loved and worshiped – particularly if my theological model included the existence of an evil and deceptive counter-deity, such as Satan.

If you heard on the news that the medicine you were taking for a minor ailment had a 50% chance of containing a fatal poison, would you shrug and continue to take that medicine, and claim that you had more pressing matters to attend to than figuring out whether it would *kill you or not*?

Of course not.

When the superstitious claim that they have "more important matters to attend to" than determining the virtue of the being they worship, clearly they have no interest in virtue, either in themselves or others – or in their deity.

Not having any real interest in virtue is not in itself particularly problematic – oysters doubtless do not ponder ethical abstractions, yet we would not call them evil – however, understanding the value and beauty of virtue to the degree that you attempt to pass off your own beliefs as *virtuous* – and then scamper away in fear or anger whenever the topic of moral principles arises – this behaviour is morally vile, and utterly corrupt.

Ethics in the Service of Evil

In the earlier example of the New York attacks, we understood that the *moral stance of victimization* was essential to enable *the victimization of others*.

Americans – and in particular the American government – had to propagate the mythology that the attacks were utterly unprovoked, stimulated only by the malevolent evil of the attackers, and were directed at America solely as a result of America's "virtue."

America's capacity to sustain this mad fiction was a truly staggering "achievement." The leader of the attackers *clearly stated, in factual terms, the crimes that America had committed in terms of foreign policy*. No sane human being could deny that American troops were stationed in Saudi Arabia, or that the Anglo-American sanctions against Iraq had resulted in the deaths of hundreds of thousands of children, or that billions of dollars of aid were not flowing from Washington to Tel Aviv.

These were all *facts*, which were not even mentioned, let alone discussed or repudiated.

This does not mean that we must necessarily *agree* that the actions of the American government justified the attacks on New York. It does mean, however, that the mantra "we have no idea why they attacked us" is a complete falsehood. We may violently disagree with the moral justifications for the attacks, but the attackers were very clear as to *why* they attacked.

The reason that these simple explanations went instantly and irrevocably down the "memory hole" is that they threatened to bring the question of *moral principles* to bear on the interaction, in a simple one-two punch:

1. If their attacks on us are unjustified, then our far more egregious attacks on them were also unjustified. (If *they* are evil, we are *far more* evil.)
2. If our egregious attacks on them were justified, then their muted response against us is even *more* justified (If *we* are good, they are *more* good.)

The only way that the second premise could be justified is if excessive murder is considered "better" than a muted response – in other words, they are less moral than us *only because they murdered fewer of us than we did of them*. (This would be a difficult moral premise to argue for without openly bursting into sulphurous flames.)

Ethical Attacks

Thus, we can see that as a species we have a very strong tendency – I would say due to how we are raised, rather than what we are – to justify our immoral actions through appeals to morality, which is the mind-bending corruption that always threatens to drown the world in blood.

Also, as we can see in the above example, in essence *we justify our actions according to moral principles because we want to commit* **immoral** *actions.*

Because we want to attack Afghanistan and Iraq, we must pretend that we are the innocent victims of an unprovoked attack.

In other words, the *end* is evil; the *means* is false ethical "justifications."

In this way, the power of morality is enslaved to the service of evil.

Morality thus has such astounding power not only because it creates our capacity for virtue, *but also because it creates our capacity for evil.*

It truly is a double-edged sword. Evil is impossible without moral justification. This is why endless propaganda is heaped upon the breaking minds of children by the state in terms of education, by religion in terms of indoctrination, and by families in terms of hypocritical moral "instruction."

The reason that philosophy is so essential is that if we don't use it, it is used against us in the service of evil to enable the murder and enslavement – literally – of billions.

There is a gun in the room called "ethics," and either we take it up and fight for our freedom, or we surrender it to evildoers and remain their prisoners forever.

Warning Signs

One of the greatest warning signs of an impending attack is hearing a compelling "moral mythology" spilling out from someone's lips.

For instance, it is impossible to listen to Hitler's ranting oratory about the evils of the Slavic and Jewish races, and the need for defense of the Fatherland without understanding that these "moral" theories were the real weapons that he wielded – the true motive power of the war machine he launched across Europe, North Africa and Russia.

In the same way, when you hear Americans saying: "Here we were, as a country, minding our own business, when out of the blue, these goddamn Muslims attacked us for *no reason!*" you know that these words are mere preludes to evil.

These kinds of fantasy tales are what truly slips the "safety" off on the revolver. The immortal line from Hanns Johst's play *Schlageter* (first performed for Hitler's birthday in 1933): "*Wenn ich Kultur höre ... entsichere ich meinen Browning!*" ('When I hear "culture," I release the safety catch on my Browning [revolver pistol]!') – resonates because it contains a fundamental truth.

"*Culture*" *is a* **necessary prerequisite for violence**.

In other words, violence – particularly institutional violence – *requires* false moral justifications – that culture is, in its essence, a set of *ethical mythologies*.

Ethical Mythologies

Ethical mythologies are moral fairy tales created and inflicted through repetition, social praise and attacks, which are useful to those in power because they justify the extension of their power over the individual.

The table below lists some common social mythologies of the Western world, and the translation of those theories into practice.

Myth	Moral	Result
The Great Depression was the result of free-market capitalism.	Without government control of the economy, massive disasters result.	Increased government control over the economy.
The free market system was only saved by the start of World War II.	The free market profits from the murder of millions.	Increased government control over the economy – particularly the "evil corporations."
Without government schools, children – particularly poor children – would remain uneducated.	Societies as a whole – particularly parents – care nothing about poor children – only the government does.	Near-total control over the indoctrination of children for almost 15 formative years.
Democracy is the ideal political system.	You control the government.	The government controls you.
The Civil War in the United States was fought to free the slaves.	Private citizens and the free market profited from slavery; only the government could free the slaves.	Massive increases in the power of the federal government.
If Western governments had not fought Nazism, we'd all be speaking German right now.	Governments are essential for protecting freedom.	Governments destroy freedom.
Governments must control the money supply; otherwise there would be wild economic instability.	The government has your best interests at heart; voluntary private interactions are exploitive.	Wild economic instability, massive national debts and endless inflation.
Governments must intervene to provide medical care for their citizens.	Doctors will rob you blind. You will die of disease in the gutter.	Massive increases in the price of health care, utter dependence upon the State in medical matters.

As we can see, all of these cultural mythologies are put forward prior to massive expansions of state power – in fact, the net increase in violence that results from expanded state power is only possible *because* these moral "justifications" are put forward.

When you examine culture in its essence, it is an endless series of false and destructive moral positions inflicted upon children through repetition, social ostracism, and teacher, peer and parental hostility.

Culture is a form of slave programming wherein knee-jerk emotional defenses are inflicted upon the natural personality, which cause people to automatically cough up moral justifications for their enslavement – without thought, without evidence, without rationality, without basis – and to their endless detriment.

Cultural Programming and Predictability
When you bring up the coercive nature of government to your fellow citizens, the responses that you will receive are *utterly predictable*.

"Taxation is force," you say – and hear the exact same arguments back, every single time:

- *It's not force because we get to vote!*
- *It's not force because we have the choice to leave!*
- *It's not force because no one has ever pointed a gun in **my** face!*
- *It's not force because I'm happy to pay!* – etc.

Culture is nothing more – or less – than a series of moral lies told to children, the purpose of which is to get them to happily lick the boots of their oppressors.

If slaves perceive themselves as the equals of their masters, the relationship becomes simply one of physical dominance – which the masters can never win, since by definition they must be greatly outnumbered by their slaves (otherwise, being a master would scarcely be economically productive!).

Since the masters are so outnumbered by the slaves, they cannot rule by force alone – this was even truer in the past, before weapons of mass destruction, when a knight could never stand against ten determined peasants, and a slave-owner had to sleep at some point.

Thus physical dominance alone cannot be used to create and maintain a slave population. Certainly, the threat of physical violence is always *required*, but it must be *approved of by the slaves* in order to remain economically efficient and effective.

Culture is an economically-convenient set of ethical fictions that lower the total cost of ownership for using force against innocent individuals. It is, fundamentally, what *creates and enables* hegemonic and hierarchical power structures.

Thus you must get the slaves to *believe amongst themselves* that slavery is:

1. Not in fact slavery.
2. For their own good.
3. A moral ideal.
4. And that all possibilities *other than slavery* would result in endless evil and destruction.

Such is the power of morality that if you can program children to revere slavery as a moral ideal, they will never even *think* of becoming free.

Define freedom as "slavery," and slavery as "freedom," and not only will your slaves never even think of becoming free, but they *will in fact attack any other slave for even **talking** about freedom*.

It is the base tragedy of our species that the power of morality is only truly understood by those who use it in the service of evil.

Slave-on-Slave Violence

Owning slaves only works if you do not have to bother yourself too much about controlling your slaves – since that is time-consuming, expensive, and threatens the profits.

No, slavery is far more profitable – in fact, it only *can* be profitable – if, instead of having to expend time and energy attacking your slaves, *you can program the slaves to attack each other.*

And *this* is the purpose of "culture."

Culture and Objectivity

Before looking into how we slaves are programmed to attack each other, rather than question our masters, let us compare "culture" to truly objective disciplines.

Culture and Science

One of the reasons that biologists chose Latin to describe species was that Latin was an international language, at least in the 17th and 18th centuries. Because the scientific method – post-Bacon – took as its most fundamental methodology the validation of human reasoning according to measurable and empirical reality, it was fundamentally cross-cultural in nature.

What is considered "good" and "proper" is very different in India than in America. The nature of a carbon atom, however, remains identical – as do the properties of gravity, magnetism, light, sound and so on.

The only thing that separates an Indian physicist from an American physicist is *form* – i.e. language – not *content*, i.e. science.

This is distinct from their separate cultures, in which both *form* and *content* wildly diverge.

The same is true for mathematicians – the only thing that separates Chinese and British mathematicians is the form of notation they use. The underlying principles and logic remain identical.

Musicians, too, through their manipulation of objective sound waves, also use an objective framework and produce exactly the same notes when reading the same notation.

Farmers also very easily work over cross-cultural "boundaries," since an ear of corn does not suddenly become a *nunchuck* when crossing the border from Pakistan to Afghanistan.

Financial transactions are also cross-cultural – with the difference, of course, that they are subject to wild predations in the form of state coercion. An objective exchange rate exists between the rupee and the yen, which allows purchasing power to objectively cross cultural or geographical boundaries.

We could continue in this vein for some time, but let us at least at this point understand that there are numerous human disciplines that are rational and objective – but *culture* is not one of them.

Culture and Objectivity

Since culture is not objective, it must be subjective, at least to some degree.

To the degree that culture is subjective, it cannot make reference to any objective facts or realities. For instance, if I say, "I like vanilla ice cream," I am expressing a subjective preference – quite distinct from saying, "Objectively, vanilla is the best flavour of ice cream."

Furthermore, if I say not only that vanilla ice cream is the best flavour objectively, but also that it is *immoral* to prefer any other flavour, and *moral* to prefer vanilla, then clearly I am going far beyond the bounds of rationality.

Not only am I claiming that vanilla is objectively "best," but also that it is the *only moral ideal*, and that any preference for any other flavour is *immoral*.

The elevation of a subjective preference to an objective ideal – especially when it involves ethics – is simply called *bigotry*.

Thus *culture*, by elevating subjective preferences for local customs to objective – and often *moral* – ideals, is merely a species of petty, self-righteous, pompous, false, prejudicial and ugly *bigotry*.

Culture is the most dangerous lie in the world, because false moral ideals are always required for the execution of evil.

Now, what is *moral* must be *enforced* – thus by turning subjective preferences into "objective morality," culture opens wide the hellish gates of violent control.

In other words, by turning violence into virtue, culture not only *excuses* violence – culture *creates* violence.

What Slaves Really Fear
Culture can thus be accurately viewed as *a set of moral mythologies that are used to create, justify and extend violence against the majority of individuals.*

What is it, then, that prevents us from shrugging off these choking and enslaving falsehoods?

In other words, who are you most afraid of?

If you start to speak the truth about culture, mythology, exploitation and violence, whose response frightens you the most?

If you openly speak about the simple reality that the state is violence, are you afraid that black-suited SWAT teams will burst through your windows and drag you off to Guantanamo Bay?

If you say that religious superstition is an exploitive lie, that the New York attacks were an unjust retaliation to far more unjust American attacks upon Muslims, that soldiers are merely men paid to kill others, like any hit-men – whose response do you fear the most?

There is a reason that we do not say these things.

There is a reason that we smile and nod and wave our flags and cheer our leaders and refuse to speak the simple truths that would inevitably set us free.

That reason is not that we are afraid of our leaders, or their thugs, or their jails, or their tortures.

The reason that we bite our tongues is that we are afraid *of each other*.

Why We Are Talking About Culture...

The reason that we are talking about culture and statism and religion – rather than only your personal relationships – is this:

The moment that you begin to speak the truth – a prerequisite for any form of intimacy – you will be attacked by your fellow slaves.

The question, then, since no one likes to be attacked, is: why bother speaking the truth at all?

Well, we speak the truth because we want the future to be different from the present – our own personal future, in terms of having honor, honesty and integrity in our personal relationships – and the future of the *world*, which yearns and deserves to be free.

If you truly take on the concepts in this book – if you speak openly and honestly about the truth – you will be endlessly attacked, your life will become very difficult in countless ways, and very few of your existing relationships – if any – will survive your new honesty.

Now, I could tell you that somewhere beyond the darkness that you will be cast into, lies a golden land of beauty, intimacy, love, laughter and true and deep friendship.

However, I cannot tell you that.

I cannot tell you that, because I cannot guarantee that.

You may be for various reasons stuck in a small town full of patriotic bigots and religious cultists.

You may be 15 years old, and remain dependent upon your parents for years to come.

You may be old, and dependent upon your children.

You may be the only sane rationalist in an Islamic village.

You may find that, if the truth destroys your marriage – or rather reveals its prior destruction – that you may never get married again, or have a satisfying romantic relationship.

You may find that, when you speak the truth to your adult children, they won't want to have anything to do with you anymore.

I want to be clear about the dangers that always follow honesty.

We are not enslaved because we are cowards.

We are enslaved because we are objectively in danger.

We should take some relief in the enormous difficulties faced by those who speak the truth – because, if speaking the truth were easy, the state of the world, its bottomless and exploitive lies, would make absolutely no sense at all.

No, speaking the truth is incredibly difficult, and very dangerous – and not because of prisons, and not because of our masters, but *because of the endless attacks from our fellow slaves.*

When you sit around your family table at Christmas or Thanksgiving, it is worth taking a moment to let this basic reality seep into your very *bones*.

When you look at the ruddy, smiling faces around the table, it is essential to truly and finally understand that, in reality, *these people are your masters*.

It is not the whips of our owners that keep us down, but the frowns and snarls of our fellow slaves.

It is not the jails of our masters that keep us huddled and frozen in fear, but the disapproval of our fellow slaves.

The "state" is not in Washington, or Rome, or Madrid, or Ottawa, or Baghdad.

The "state" is not the guns of the police, the truncheons of the prison guards, the huts of the gulags, the cells of the prisons, the grenades of the troops, or the jostling darkness of the paddy wagons.

These are merely the *effects*, not the cause.

The "state" is not far away from you.

It is not distant.

It is not political.

It is not economic.

It is not military.

The "state" *is your fellow slaves.*

The Costs of the Truth

When you sit with your family at dinner, and you begin to speak the truth, no SWAT team will come through your windows. No policeman will pound down your door. No trap door will open beneath your chair and suck you into the maw of some Syrian gulag.

The *political* state will not lift a finger against you.

Yet still – you are terrified to speak.

Why?

Simply because you know what will happen.

You know that you will not be attacked by the state.

You know you will be attacked by your family.

You will not be abused by your masters.

You will be abused by those around you.

You will not be humiliated by physical torture in the future.

You will be humiliated by emotional torture in the present.

Your masters will not try to control you.

Your family will.

And that is why masters exist.

*Your family **is** the state.*

The government is merely an *effect of the family.*

So – Why Speak?

I am telling you all of this for three main reasons.

First, so that you truly understand what you are getting into.

Second, so that you have a greater appreciation of why you have not spoken the truth in the past – so that you can be more gentle with yourself.

If speaking the truth were easy, and everyone still lied, then the world could not be saved. However, because speaking the truth can be almost unbearably difficult, the world *can* be saved, because people are not just cowards, but rather are frightened for very good reasons.

Thirdly, I am telling you this so that you can understand the essential service that you are providing the world by speaking the truth.

The world will not be saved by the violent lies of culture, but by the rational light of truth.

Idealists who disregard the real danger of their ideals tend to become masochists, or nihilists.

The future will not be improved by masochists, but by idealists.

I do not want you to embark upon this amazing journey in order to feel pain.

It certainly is true that you *will* feel pain during this journey, but you need to understand – if you are to succeed – the enormous virtue and value of what you are doing.

The reasons for refraining from speaking the truth are self-evident – we feel them all the time, every single day – the reasons for *speaking* the truth, however, are far from evident and can at times seem purely imaginary.

As we move into the final section of this book – how to implement the principles of the Real-Time Relationship in your own life – your anxiety will rise precipitously. You will feel clammy, your hands will sweat, you may shake, your sleep will decrease, your stomach will flip and your tension will mount.

That is how much, deep down, we so desperately want to be free.

And how much we fear our fellow slaves.

During this process, you will feel strong urges to fling this "evil" book across the room, and get back into the comfortable little box of social conformity.

Fling away – be my guest, I can take it!

Then, take a deep breath, walk across the room, and pick this book up again.

This book is not about me, or my ideas, but you, and your freedom.

The Goal

Speaking the truth can sometimes feel like self-abuse, but I will share with you one thought, one vision that keeps me going, when the path is darkest.

In my mind's eye, I see a world where people can be honest without fear – where the desperate terror that truth tellers feel now will only be felt by a few liars and cheats.

I see a world where relaxed and benevolent intimacy is the natural state of human relations.

I see a world without masters – not without a hierarchy, since ambitions and talents vary – but without coercive, exploitive and destructive monopolies like church, state and the cult of the family.

I desperately want to live in that world, but I know that I cannot, since what we are talking about here is a multi-generational project at best.

I desperately want to live in that world, but since I cannot, the best that I can hope for is to do my part to help create that world for the future.

I cannot live in a free world. I can barely see it from where I am. I squint at it though, like a man at the bottom of a well searching for a star in the distant circle of night sky above him.

I wish with all my heart that I lived in that world – and, if I did live in that world, I would feel such enormous gratitude for the brave souls who did everything they could to bring that wonderful world into being. I would admire their courage, to sacrifice immediate personal comfort for the sake of creating this wondrous world.

I feel that gratitude flowing down the steps of time from the future.

I feel the joy of those who live in a free world that we can only begin to create.

I feel them looking back in time to we poor struggling courageous souls, and thanking us for making their world so beautiful.

It is *their* gratitude that picks me up when I fall.

It is also the near-infinite sorrow that I would feel if I knew that such a world were to never come into being.

Imagining an eternity of human experience that is little better than what we have today – where good people cower like beaten dogs, while evil braggarts strut and rule – would make the story of our species an infinite tragedy – especially given our wondrous potential for truth and beauty.

Evil *will* fade from this world, if we act with integrity now.

Evil *will* fade from this world, but we must give up many seemingly-pleasant things in order to end it.

Surely we are glad that the early pioneers of science did not bow to the difficulties of their struggle, but persevered against torture and oppression, giving us a world of technology, medicine and wonder that they did not live to see.

We do not live in their world of medieval ignorance only because they were willing to imagine our world of science and knowledge, and work to create it.

The world *we* will create will be as wondrous to those who live in it as ours would be to the medieval mind.

I just wanted to remind you of the world we are in fact creating, because the beauty of the goal – even though we shall never live to see it – makes the difficulties of the journey all worthwhile.

Real-Time Relationships: The Theory

Let us now turn to the task of putting all that we have learned and discussed in the previous pages into action.

The Real-Time Relationship (RTR) is based on two core principles, designed to liberate both you and others in your communication with each other:

1. Thoughts precede emotions.
2. Honesty requires that we communicate our *thoughts* and *feelings*, not our *conclusions*.

Thoughts Precede Emotions

The first thing to understand about emotions is that they are not objective responses to the outside world, but rather objective responses to our internal premises – i.e. standardized responses to subjective stimuli.

To picture this in reality, think of our two good friends Bob and Doug sitting on a couch watching a hockey game, where Canada is playing the United States.

Bob the Canadian cheers every time Canada scores a goal; Doug the American cheers every time the United States scores a goal.

Here we have an example of an objective event occurring – a hockey puck bouncing into a net – which causes one man elation, and the other despair.

Clearly, these emotional responses cannot be directly caused by the movement of the puck, since the same action is producing opposite emotional results.

Now, earlier I defined "love" as our involuntary response to virtue – here I would like to append a qualifier, which is that love is our involuntary response to virtue *if we are virtuous*.

Bob is a fan of Team Canada, and so he cheers on that team – if we are a fan of Team Virtue, we cheer on *that* team. If we are a fan of Team-Not-So-Much-With-The-Virtue, we will cheer on the team with darker jerseys instead.

Now, emotions are distinct from sensations, insofar as sensations are neurobiological stimuli that occur independent of our thoughts.

"Happiness" is an *emotion*; physical pain is a *sensation*. While Bob and Doug might have opposite emotional reactions to the movement of a puck, they would not have opposite sensations if that puck happened to hit them in the face at high speed – both would feel blinding agony.

Similarly, what is called "runner's high," or the euphoria that results from the release of endorphins during strenuous exercise, is a *sensation*, as is the giddy joy that results from taking heroin.

Since physical sensations do not depend upon our thoughts, philosophy can do very little to aid us in controlling or managing them. No syllogism can eliminate a toothache – the alleviation of physical pain is a medical matter; philosophy is for the soul.

Thus we shall focus in this section on the thoughts that precede emotions, so that we can better understand how to change our thoughts – and thus change our emotions.

Emotions and Control

Everyone who has absorbed even the basic principles of psychological self-awareness and self-knowledge understands that it is impossible to directly control other people. We can only control our own thoughts and our own behaviours – we cannot control other people's thoughts, behaviours or emotions.

However, it is also important to understand that we cannot control our own *emotions* either.

If we stand at the edge of a cliff and hurl a stone with all our might into the ocean below, our only choice is whether to throw the stone or not – once the stone has left our hand, it is utterly out of our control.

In the same way, once we believe certain premises within our own minds, the emotions that will result from those premises *are utterly out of our control.*

Expectations: An Example
When I am working on a book, I plan to spend a certain number of hours a day writing. On many days, however, my plans get interrupted, because something else comes up which takes a higher priority. Perhaps there is a problem with the Freedomain Radio website, or a podcast I uploaded got cut off, or is mislabelled, or a listener wants to have a conversation

about an immediate issue, or an employee calls with an urgent question and so on.

At times, I find myself getting irritated if a seemingly-endless stream of minor interruptions prevents me from getting to my "real" task. I set myself up to begin writing, get my coffee, reread what I've previously written, raise my hands to type – and then receive a message which prevents me from getting started.

If my thought is: *I must write*, then naturally every "interruption" moves me further back from achieving that goal. I then feel acute frustration, just as if I were trying to juggle and people were tossing squash balls at my head.

My temptation on these days is to externalize and trivialize the cause of these "interruptions." What I basically say to myself is: "*Jesus Christ! I've been trying to get down to writing for the past three hours, and everybody wants a piece of me, and I just can't get down to what I* **need** *to get done! If I don't get this book finished, then I won't have enough money to advertise in two to three months, because book income is more steady than donations! And why is it that everybody picks* **today** *to need something from me – can't they manage things themselves for once, just for today?*"

And so on, and so on. We all know this mantra, which is: "I am the hard-done-by victim just trying to get something *done*, while every incompetent on the planet keeps interrupting me when they could take two seconds to figure out the answer to their question!"

When I notice myself sinking into this convenient little swamp of mythology, I try to reshape my thoughts – usually with great success – along the following lines:

"You are the victim? What nonsense! You left every instant messaging program on the planet open on your desktop. You checked your e-mail. You had a look at what was happening on the Freedomain Radio Board.

You picked up the phone. Also, *you* are the one deciding what is a higher priority than writing – no one is ordering you to do that! If you decide to republish a podcast because it was cut off, that is your choice – you could very easily keep writing and simply republish the podcast later. And finally, is the fact that people need some sort of feedback from you, or are providing you with helpful information, really such an enormous problem? Would you be more content if you had five listeners, and no capacity to do this amazing job on a full-time basis? Then you would certainly have *fewer* interruptions, but your irritation at being interrupted would be replaced by despair about the planet as a whole!"

In other words, what I can do in these situations is simply to *realign my expectations* – which has everything to do with remembering that my core goal every day is to move this philosophical conversation forward in some manner – or, at least, prevent it from being moved backwards!

Thus on any given day, my purpose is not to write, or to respond to an e-mail, or to publish a podcast, but rather to do whatever it takes to move this philosophical conversation forward!

When I remember that, I no longer view interruptions as "interruptions."

I remember that every day is a kind of dance between what you can plan for, and what you cannot. I remember that it is great to have specific goals, but they must all be measured relative to the overall goal.

Obviously, having a podcast out there that ends abruptly does not move this conversation forward, but rather irritates listeners, consumes bandwidth since they have to re-download, wastes time on the part of the listeners because they have to reload the podcast and find where it was cut off, then listen through to the end, and so on.

Since my goal is to bring as positive an experience as possible to this conversation – since heaven knows philosophy is already hard enough – clearly the immediate requirement to re-upload the podcast takes precedence over writing a few more pages in a book that will not be out for several months.

Also, it is important to remember that all days are part of a generalized "bell curve" of interruptions. Some days you can sail through with barely a ripple, while on other days, messages pile up seemingly without end. At some point, I will either explode with frustration, or surrender to the reality of where a particular day is on the bell curve, laugh about it, and put aside my writing until later.

I do find that, once I realign my expectations to take into account the empirical facts of what is happening – *interruptions are piling up* – then I find another interruption funny, rather than annoying.

Recognizing the "push and pull" of life – that we must make plans, but that our plans will be interrupted – takes a great deal of stress out of every day. Clearly, we cannot control interruptions – else they would scarcely be called interruptions – but we can recognize that interruptions are inevitable, and adjust our expectations accordingly.

Certainly, we will all face a rather final "interruption" called death – and so I try my best not to be too bothered by any interruption that is less significant!

Thoughts and Frustration

In the above example, it is clear that my thoughts ("interruptions are bad, because I must write!") are clearly contradicting the reality of my situation.

If I believe both that writing is my highest priority, and also that dealing with interruptions is my highest priority, then of course I will end up feeling frustrated and paralyzed, just as I would if I truly felt that I had to go both north and south at the same time.

Practically, it is impossible for two actions that cannot be performed simultaneously to have exactly the same prioritization, because we have to choose between them.

When the rigidity of my thoughts does not keep up with the flexibility that new information requires, I am in a situation where an unstoppable force ("I must write!") is hitting an immovable object ("I must deal with these interruptions!").

When this occurs, I cannot rationally choose to raise the priority of dealing with interruptions without lowering the priority of writing.

If I attempt to maintain both priorities – despite the physical impossibility of this – then naturally I will become anxious and frustrated. If I know that it is going to take me an hour to get to a particular appointment, and I cannot find my keys, then I know that the time I spend looking for my keys is going to be added on to the time it takes me to get to the appointment. Thus, if I cannot find my keys, I must call to tell whoever I am meeting that I will be late.

If I try to maintain two opposing absolutes within my mind: "I must find my keys" and "I must be on time" then of course I will end up feeling frustrated and anxious.

The feelings follow the thoughts.

If I accept that "I must find my keys," takes a higher priority over "I must be on time," then I must give up the absolute of being on time. There is simply no other rational choice.

Choose Your Thoughts, Choose Your Feelings…

This is a relatively minor example of how our thoughts can directly influence – or create – our feelings.

Here is another.

Years ago, I had to fly to Paris, France for a business trip. Unfortunately, I could not find my passport. I looked and looked, and got progressively more anxious, tense and upset as the hours passed.

Once I realized the panic I was getting into, I took a deep breath, and said the following to myself:

"Either I will find my passport, and go to France, or I will not find my passport, and I will not go to France."

This really helped me relax, and took the ground-shaking tension out of the situation.

As long as the absolute statement was: "I *must* go to France," there really was no limit to the emotional escalation.

The moment that I gave myself a choice – or rather recognized the *true* options – my tension diminished considerably.

Either I was going to France, or I was not going to France – but I certainly did not "*have to*" go to France.

As the old saying goes, the only thing we gotta do is die.

Attempting to sustain two opposing thoughts – "doublethink," in Orwellian terms – creates an enormous stress and tension within our minds, and tends to crank up our "fight or flight" mechanism to the boiling point.

The Impossibility of Control…

This is a continual problem in our relationships. In our own minds, we so often set up an absolute called: "*My spouse **must** do X*" – which we have absolutely no capacity to control or achieve!

This combination of an absolute requirement for a behavioural change in another person – along with a complete inability to effect that change – creates enormous tension, anxiety and hostility in our relationships.

When I was stressed out about finding my passport, it was because I had an absolute goal, *but no direct control over my capacity to achieve that goal*.

Flying to France required that I find my passport – but I had no direct control over my capacity to find my passport. I could do my best, of course, but in the end, either I would find it, or I would not. (I did find it, if you're curious, and had a great trip!)

My Best Friend and My New Girlfriend

Let us imagine that I am dating someone new, and I really want to introduce her to my best friend.

Obviously, I would prefer it if my best friend really liked my new girlfriend, since it would be far easier for me if I were able to spend stress-free time with both of them.

What options do I have to bring about this result?

I can certainly introduce my new girlfriend in the most positive light, and sing her praises, and show my friend that I am happier for having her in my life – which will all doubtless have some influence over the outcome – *but I cannot control directly whether or not my friend likes my new girlfriend.*

If I have in my mind an absolute: "He **must** like my new girlfriend!" then I will have a very stressful time of it when they meet.

(It is certainly true that my stress will *lower* the likelihood that my friend will like my new girlfriend, but we shall come back to that in a little while.)

If we understand how we can most rationally and honestly deal with this meeting, we can begin to approach the question of the Real-Time Relationship.

What is the most rational and honest statement that I can make to myself about this upcoming meeting between my best friend and my girlfriend?

Clearly, it is: "I would really like it if my friend liked my girlfriend, but I have no control over that outcome whatsoever."

Can we all feel the sweet relief inherent in this statement?

Control versus Curiosity

When I stopped frantically hunting for my passport, took a breath, and reminded myself of the reality of my situation, something very interesting occurred for me emotionally.

I actually wondered if I would end up going to France.

In other words, instead of being desperate to get to France, I became curious about whether or not I would end up going to France.

The opposite of control is – *curiosity*.

When we give up false control, we open ourselves up to true curiosity.

This is the transition from religion (false control) to science (true curiosity).

When I honestly say: "I would really like it if my friend liked my girlfriend, but I have no control over that outcome whatsoever," the wonderful thing that happens is that I can now become *curious* about the outcome of the meeting.

Instead of saying: "I must control what will happen!" I can say: "*I wonder what will happen?*"

This is a very different state of mind.

This is rational empiricism at its finest. Instead of saying: "Sacrificing this goat will control the rains!" we can say: "*I wonder why it rains?*"

Abandoning our illusions of control opens us up to the magnificent wonder of curiosity.

In my mind, when I say to my friend: "You *must* like my new girlfriend," I am treating him as an object to be manipulated for the sake of *my* desires, rather than an independent conscious being.

When I say: "I will control my friend," the greatest lie is not that I think I can control him, but that I think I am treating him as a friend.

Using Others

Catastrophes

Why do I care so much about whether or not my friend likes my new girlfriend?

Clearly, I enjoy spending time with my friend – and I also enjoy spending time with my girlfriend. It certainly would be convenient for me if they also enjoyed spending time with each other, so I would not end up torn between a complicated and antipathetic social situation.

That is the story that I tell myself.

But that is not the truth.

In this book – as in every book I write, every article I publish, and every podcast I record – I will consistently and continually tell you that deep down, you always already know the truth about everything.

The *truth* is that good people always like other good people. Good people do not like bad people, and bad people do not like good people.

With bad people, it is more unstable. They will really "like" each other, then really dislike each other, and so on.

If my best friend is a good person, and my new girlfriend is also a good person, I will feel no more stress in introducing them to each other than I would in introducing cream to my coffee.

It is not that I dislike the social awkwardness that will result if they do not like each other. Oh no, it is far worse than that!

What I am really afraid of is discovering the true nature of my relationships – and thus of *myself*.

The Truth I Am Avoiding…
If my best friend dislikes my new girlfriend, it is either because my best friend is corrupt and my new girlfriend is virtuous – or vice versa – or because they are both corrupt, in ways that do not serve each other's immediate needs, but rather remind each other of their respective corruption.

Thus if my new girlfriend and my best friend do not get along, that says something rather terrible about – who?

My new girlfriend? My best friend?

No, of course not.

About *me*.

This next part may sound very strange – but give me a paragraph or two, and perhaps it will make some sense. ☺

By introducing my new girlfriend to my best friend with the anxious hope that they will somehow "get along," I am asking them to cover up the corruption that we are all enmeshed in.

I am asking everyone to pretend that we are all good – and there is only one reason why I would do that, or why they would agree to participate in such a corrupt fraud.

Because we are not good.

We will do almost anything to avoid that knowledge – not because we *fear* our own corruption, *but because we desire to continue our own corruption.*

If my best friend is corrupt and my new girlfriend is not corrupt, then she will judge – not my best friend, but rather *me.*

If my best friend is not corrupt, but my new girlfriend is, then they will dislike each other, of course – but some rather grim fallout will result from their meeting.

If I introduce a false, insecure and manipulative girlfriend to my best friend, obviously I am doing so in the hopes that they will "get along."

If my best friend is a good man, then he will be highly insulted by this, and will say:

"Why would you introduce this woman to me and express a desire that we 'get along'? Are you not aware that she is false and manipulative? Are you not aware that she is vain and shallow? Are you not aware that she talked about herself for over an hour, not asking me a single question? Are you not aware that she told me everything about her childhood – which was not pleasant – on our very first meeting? Do you not see that she lacks any rational sense of boundaries? Do you not see how self-involved and narcissistic she is?"

If I reply that I noticed none of these things, then my friend is going to be even more insulted, and say:

"But you value *me* as your best friend, and I exhibit none of these traits – in fact, I would consider it personally dishonourable to act in such a manner! I assumed that you valued my integrity, consideration, courage and so on *because you could tell them apart from their respective opposites.* If you tell me that I am the best singer in the world, and then it turns out that you are completely deaf, then clearly I cannot take your praise seriously at all – in fact, your former 'praise' of me would be revealed as false and manipulative, since you have no ability whatsoever to judge the quality of my singing! Thus if you cannot tell the difference between this woman and myself, then clearly you have no right to call me your 'best friend,' but have rather used that term to manipulate me."

In response, I might protest that I *did* notice these troublesome habits in this woman, but it slipped my mind for a moment.

"Very well," my friend will reply, "now I am even more insulted, because you introduced this woman to me in the hopes that I would *like* her! You recognize that she is shallow, false and manipulative; you also recognize that I am virtuous, honest and direct, and yet you genuinely and honestly believed that I would *like* her? Yet you claim that I am your best friend – and that you love me – because of my virtues. How is it, then, that you expect me to like this woman because of her *vices*? Why are we subjected to such opposite standards? No, it cannot be possible that you expected me to like her – the best that you could have hoped for was that I would *pretend* to like her – for your benefit, and hers of course. In other words, you wanted me to sacrifice *my* integrity for the sake of your shallow lusts!"

Now, when faced with such a stern and inescapable accusation, what would my response be?

I could get mad at my friend – thus confirming his diagnosis and effectively ending the friendship – or I could apologize profusely, promise to get help with my dangerous and slippery "dark side," and immediately break it off with this corrupt woman.

If I were capable of this kind of integrity, though, I would never have tried to manipulate my virtuous friend into pretending to "like" my new girlfriend in the first place.

In fact, we can very reasonably go one step further and say that *since I was the kind of man who had no problem whatsoever with manipulating a* virtuous friend for my own selfish and corrupt ends, there is **no possibility whatsoever** that I would have a virtuous friend to begin with!

And *that*, my friends, is the knowledge that I am striving desperately to avoid – not my fear that my friends are immoral, but *my desire to keep my immoral friends.*

The moment that our own corruption becomes genuinely clear to us, we are immediately propelled into wrenching change.

We avoid the truth about our own corruption because we prefer our own corruption to the dreadful alternative…

To the endless attacks from our fellow slaves.

The alcoholic keeps drinking because he is enmeshed in a social network of mutual destruction.

Deep down, the alcoholic is not afraid of sobriety; he is afraid of being attacked by his fellow alcoholics and enablers.

Introducing Myself to Myself…
Thus, when I attempt to control the results of the first meeting between my best friend and my new girlfriend, I am really attempting to control my own anxiety by manipulating others.

This much we understand – but let us go one step further.

Why do I feel anxiety in the first place?

Well, I feel anxiety because I *know* the truth, and I am *rejecting* the truth.

In my real life, I do not feel anxiety when my wife comes home, because I am always overjoyed to see her. I rush down the stairs into her arms, and smother her with kisses.

I do not feel anxiety when I receive an e-mail from a trusted friend.

I *do* feel anxiety whenever I receive an e-mail from an embittered enemy – for the simple reason that these e-mails often contain unpleasant attacks which upset me.

In other words, *I feel anxiety when I instinctively feel the signs of an impending attack.*

Anxiety is a form of beneficial alertness, essential for survival throughout the history of our species. Anxiety is the crack of a stick in a thick bush on a dark night. Anxiety alerts us to impending danger.

Anxiety is part of our "fight or flight" neurological mechanism, designed to make the presence of danger uncomfortable – and so aid us in avoiding or escaping it.

Anxiety and Control

Imagine that you are the first man who ever tried to tame a horse.

You approach a horse in the wilds with great trepidation – and great desire. You know that if you can tame this beast, you can ride it and harness it to a plough. You overcome your fear by keeping your eye on the prize.

Imagine that you do catch this horse and tame it, at least to some degree. After harnessing the power of the animal, you begin to change your farming practices – you buy more land, hire more farmhands, invest in heavier ploughs, and fall deeply into debt.

Taming the horse, in other words, causes you to make decisions that depend on the horse remaining tame.

As the months pass, however, you begin to notice that the horse does not seem to appreciate being controlled. Initially, it tries to escape, but you catch it every time and bring it back. After a while, it no longer tries to escape – except perhaps on occasion – but it continually struggles to cast off its harness, throw its riders, veer to the left or right, and sometimes refuses to eat.

Here, you become stuck in a truly impossible situation.

If you had never seen the horse – or tried to tame it – you would never have changed all of your farming habits based on your expectation of being able to harness the horse's power.

If, even months after being "domesticated," the horse had simply bolted off and vanished into the wilderness, you would have shrugged your shoulders, sold your excess land, fired your extra workers, and resumed your former way of farming.

However, since the horse is at times obedient, and at times recalcitrant, you become truly stuck. Since you have invested so much time, energy and resources on the assumption that the horse can be controlled, you cannot now stomach the idea of simply turning the horse loose and resuming your former life.

The Subtle Tyranny of Inconsistency
As the weeks and months pass, the horse's inconsistent obedience continues to drain more and more of your time and resources. On any given day, you can never be quite sure that the horse is going to do what you need it to do. In the morning, the horse pulls the plough beautifully – in the afternoon, it kicks a worker and cannot be restrained.

As you sink even more time and energy into trying to control the horse, your stress and anxiety continue to escalate.

After a few months, you begin to feel truly trapped – by this time, you have invested too much to turn the horse loose, but as every day goes by, it becomes more and more wasteful and frustrating to use the horse at all. (This is also known as the "waiting for the bus" syndrome – when you have waited an hour for a bus, you are far less likely to walk. We have all been there with computers as well!)

When you initially started off, you wanted to control the horse – as time goes by, however, it becomes more and more apparent that *the horse is in fact controlling you.*

You initially tried to tame the horse in order to reduce your workload – however, it becomes increasingly clear that having the horse around makes your job harder and more stressful.

The Vengeance of the Slave

If we recast the "horse story" above in terms of human slavery, a very similar pattern emerges.

If the slave cannot escape, and is beaten if he does not work hard, then his vengeance will always take on a more subtle form.

The slave will perform his work slightly more slowly – not enough to be punished, but enough to irritate his master.

The slave will pretend to be less intelligent than he really is, so that when he loses or breaks things, he will be more likely to escape punishment, since he is pretending in effect to be a child.

As mentioned above, the slave will also do what he can to promote any negative habits his master may have. If his master likes to drink, the slave will always be on hand to refill his cup. If his master has a tendency towards jealousy, the slave will innocently "mention" that he saw his master's wife chatting with another man.

If the slave is particularly cunning, he will also do everything that he can to inflate his master's ego. He will sing his master's praises, claim joy in "knowing his place," thank the master for everything he does, and remain fanatically "loyal."

This hyperinflation of the master's ego inevitably creates pettiness, vanity, hyper-irritability, and unbearable pomposity.

In other words, the slave will always turn his master into an unhappy man – who is constantly annoyed, who cannot experience love, and who engenders no respect from those around him – particularly his children. (One of the worst aspects of being a slave-owner is that it turns you into a terrible and abusive father.)

As a result of the slave's passive-aggressive manipulations, the master becomes prone to violence – verbal and physical – self-abusive habits, crippling self-blindness, and sinks into a bottomless pit of discontent and misery.

This is the vengeance of the slave.

All slaves are Iago.

And, for the most part, all children are slaves.

As you were.

The Dangers of Vengeance
As we discussed above in the parable of the boxer, the great danger for the slave is his capacity to become addicted to the dark "satisfactions" of passive-aggressive vengeance.

By enslaving his master, the slave gains a sense of control – *and also re-creates in his master his own experience of enslavement.*

It is a subtle cry of hatred – and plea for empathy.

The horse above that cannot be free ends up enslaving its master.

A slave can only hope for freedom by *making owning slaves unbearable for his master.*

Not only might the slave's endless passive-aggressive noncompliance and provocation provoke suicide on the part of his master – but his master's miserable existence might also serve as a warning for others who might wish to own slaves.

In other words, the horse that makes its "owner" miserable *is performing an enormous service to the freedom of other horses*, since anyone else who is thinking of enslaving a horse will look at the stress experienced by existing horse owners and do pretty much anything to avoid that fate – thus leaving other horses free to roam.

However, as mentioned above, the greatest danger for the slave is that he becomes addicted to the sense of control that comes from manipulating his master.

In other words, the great danger for the slave is that he becomes addicted to his slavery.

If a slave begins to believe his own master-destroying propaganda, *then in the absence of masters, he will create them.*

The Slavery of Childhood

Most of us are raised as slaves. Our opinions are rarely sought, rules are rarely explained – and moral rules never are – we are shipped off to schools where we are treated disrespectfully; our subservience is bought with rewards, and our independence is punished with detentions. Scepticism and curiosity are scorned and belittled, while empty abilities like throwing balls, learning dates, sitting still and "being pretty" are praised and elevated.

Lies about our history become cages for our futures. Lies about our own intelligence and originality lead us to the petty enslavement of "good citizenship" – and horrifying fairy tales about life in the absence of coercive or religious control scare us back into our slave pens the moment we even *think* of glancing outside to the green and beautiful hills beyond our bars.

Collective punishments turn us against each other; the "kibbles and whips" of the classroom reward us for laughing at each other to gain the favor of the teacher; terrifying and brutal "morality" is inflicted upon us. We are punished for not treating those in authority with "respect" (do they treat *us* with respect?) – and we are bred for a life of subservience, fear, productivity and dependence as surely as fattened calves are bred for veal.

Where in the past we were not taught to fear the priests, but rather the imaginary devils the priests warned us of, now we are not taught to fear our politicians, who can debase our currency, throw us in prison and send us to war – but rather we are taught to fear *each other*. We are taught to imagine that the real predators in this world are not those who control prison cells, national debts and nuclear weapons, but rather our fellow citizens, who in the absence of brutal control would surely tear us apart!

The entire purpose of state education is to make sure that we never truly "leave" our childhoods: that we spend our lives trembling in fear of imaginary predators, begging for "protection" from those who threaten us with the most harm.

As sure as sunrise, we will grow and mature, leave the control of our parents, and strive to make our way in the world.

As children, we are slaves who will inevitably be "set free."

How, then, can we *remain* enslaved?

Why through *false virtue*, of course.

But you'll have to read my book "On Truth: The Tyranny of Illusion" for that! ☺

Holding Our Own Chains…
Because our lives are so controlled by our political, familial and religious masters, we always and inevitably attempt to regain a sense of control by controlling *each other*.

We cannot control our politicians; we cannot control the church; we cannot control our parents – and we are bullied and controlled by all these people – and so we turn in panic and fear to controlling *each other*, which makes the institutional control of all of us both possible and profitable.

To return to the incident outlined earlier, wherein I try to make my best friend like my new girlfriend, it is clear that I am really attempting to control my *own* anxiety – my knowledge of my own corruption and the corruption of those around me – rather than either my friend or my girlfriend.

What will the likely result of my "control" be?

Well, if my girlfriend says something unpleasant or awkward, I will feel great anxiety, and flash her look of anger or "concern." If my best friend sighs or rolls his eyes in response to something my new girlfriend says, then I will rush in to "explain" what she "really" meant.

Basically, I will sprint back and forth throughout the conversation, trying to eliminate or explain away any symptoms of disapproval or negativity.

What will the experience of my friend and girlfriend be?

Will they feel *free*? Will they feel that they can express themselves openly?

Of course not.

They will feel a rising irritation towards me – since no one likes to be manipulated and controlled for the sake of someone else's anxiety.

My girlfriend will look at my frantic efforts to "explain" her weird or awkward statements as insulting to her. My friend will see my actions as guilty and panic-stricken – and a foolish attempt to make him "respect" a woman *that I clearly do not respect.*

My girlfriend will also see that I am terribly and painfully vulnerable to any negative opinion that my "best friend" might have of her.

Deep down, she very well understands that this is because *I share that negative opinion.*

In other words, I am only afraid of having my bag searched in a store if I have actually stolen something. In the same way, I am only afraid of a negative opinion of my girlfriend if at some level I share that opinion.

Seeing me strive to control my friend's perception of her, she also clearly understands that I am very willing to sacrifice her own sense of self-esteem and social competency *if someone else disapproves of what she is doing.*

It becomes blindingly clear that I will sacrifice her happiness – in other words, my good opinion of her – on the off chance that someone else might react negatively to her.

In other words, I will side with others against her.

Does this make her feel treasured? Does this make her respect my loyalty? Does this help her respect my integrity?

Of *course* not.

By elevating the power that my friend has in this situation, I automatically devalue my girlfriend – and thus myself.

However, the only reason that I wish to control the power that my friend has *is because I have given him that power in the first place.*

This is what I mean when I say that *all manipulation is self-manipulation.*

Trying to control my friend's reaction to my girlfriend is as deranged as giving a gun to a madman, and then trying to talk him into giving me the gun back.

Power and Liberty

In any intimate relationship, we inevitably surrender power to others.

When you fall in love, you hand your heart to your lover on a platter.

Since love, as discussed earlier, involves integrity, and thus reduces insecurity, to refuse to be vulnerable with a lover is to openly state that you *do not love her*.

Thus there is no possibility that love does *not* involve a surrender of power.

When we try to control those who have power over us, we are clearly saying that *we do not trust them to exercise that power benevolently.*

It is a basic fact of life that virtuous people will rarely submit to the manipulations of others. Virtuous people know that they use their power over others benevolently – and thus experience it as insulting when other people try to control them.

A surgeon finds it equally insulting if someone attempts to wrestle his knife away from him, as if he were a common criminal.

The reality of trust and vulnerability is that *if you do not trust someone, you should not be vulnerable towards her.*

The solution to this, of course, is not to refrain from being vulnerable – otherwise how would you know who is trustworthy? – or to attempt to control those who exploit your vulnerability.

Remaining Vulnerable
The answer is to remain vulnerable to those around you, and systematically get rid of those who abuse your trust.

This is what I mean by the value of curiosity.

Most people take the approach that: *others must treat me well, and if they do not treat me well, I am allowed to punish them.*

This is pure nonsense, and a highly dangerous approach to relationships.

The simple fact of the matter is that *no one has to treat you well.*

We certainly *prefer* to be treated well – but that does not mean that we have a *right* to be treated well.

I *prefer* not to get colds – that does not mean I have a *right* to not get colds.

Controlling and insecure people always say: *This person had **better** treat me well!*

Curious and confident people always ask: *I **wonder** if this person will treat me well?*

In the same way, controlling and insecure people say: "There *must* be a God!" – while curious and competent people ask: "I wonder if there is a God?"

And… controlling and insecure people say: "There *must* be a government!" – while curious and competent people ask: "I wonder if there must be a government?"

Controlling and insecure people, if they receive bad service at a restaurant, feel abused and insulted, complain to everyone they know, launch lawsuits, and perform all other sorts of silly and enslaving actions.

Curious and confident people, if they receive bad service at a restaurant, simply pay their bill, leave, *and never come back.*

Now, if they have been coming to the same restaurant for many years and have always received excellent service, they will let the actions of one rude waiter slide. If they continue to receive bad service, they will speak to the waiter, and then to the manager, in order to try to help or save the relationship.

However, if their expressions of concern are met with indifference or contempt, then they simply stop returning to that restaurant.

They do not need to fight, they do not need to yell, they do not need to complain endlessly and they do not need to get engaged in all sorts of drama and nonsense, because they respect their own ability and right to choose their relationships voluntarily.

If they feel that they can only ever eat at that one restaurant – and can get food nowhere else – then of course they will get hysterical and aggressive, because they will be trapped in a situation of constant frustration and bad service!

This is, of course, our situation with regards to our government. Since we cannot choose how it interacts with us – or choose to avoid interacting with it – we remain in a constant state of frustration and hysterical or greedy control.

I would submit, though, that all of our relationships that are non-coercive in nature are subject to the same possibilities of choice.

Power and Family

uality as a concept, as a measure, can only exist as a result of *choice*.

Where we have no options, there can be no quality. We know that this is true with regards to public schools, the Department of Motor Vehicles, the IRS, the Postal Service, and all other forms of coercive and controlled "interactions."

We generally fail to remember, however, that when we were very young, we did not have *any choice whatsoever*.

We do not choose our parents, our schools, our siblings, our extended family, or our neighbourhood.

We also do not choose our country or our religion, but rather these things are inflicted on us by circumstances and propaganda.

There does come a time, however, when we *do* slowly begin to gain the capacity to choose with regards to our family.

After puberty and throughout our teenage years, we begin to experience a growing sense of choice. What we were born into no longer dominates us through natural biology or through our physical dependence upon our parents and utter subjugation to their whims and preferences.

Unfortunately, families – and society as a whole – inflict an enormous amount of propaganda upon us about the innate "value" of family and the endless virtue of "loving" your family.

However, as we can immediately see, propaganda about the value of something is scarcely required *if that thing does in fact have value*. Brad Pitt or George Clooney would never benefit from a system of "arranged" (i.e. enforced) marriage, since they have their pick of women anyway.

No, it is the man that no reasonable woman would want to marry who devoutly wishes to have marriage forced upon women.

Institutionalized coercion is all about attacking someone for noncompliance with an "ethical" absolute.

The IRS does not say: "Pay your taxes, or we will shoot you!" No, it is always presented as a virtuous obligation, insofar as you consume government services, love your country, care for the poor, the sick, the old, and so on. In other words, taxes are presented as payment for a *voluntary* interaction – like the bill that arrives with the plasma television – and thus refraining from paying your bill is portrayed as "dishonourable." Don't "cheat" on your taxes; pay your "fair share."

In the same way, parents present themselves as devoted and loving servants of your well-being as a child and thus "demand" – whether actively or passively – your love and obedience as an adult.

Yet you no more "choose" to consume government services such as public education, roads, water and electricity than you "chose" to be born into your family.

Neither of these situations are voluntary or contractual – and thus by definition cannot contain any virtue or quality in and of themselves.

This does not mean that it is logically impossible to love your parents. They may have been virtuous, considerate, solicitous, kind and firm – and thus naturally you will love them.

However, it is *essential* to understand that if this is the case, you do not love your *parents* – *you love the* **virtue** *of your parents*.

What you love is not the category "parents," but rather the action "virtue."

"Virtue" is a choice, and thus involves quality – "parent" is not a choice – at least from the standpoint of the child – and thus in no way involves quality, but rather is a rejection of quality.

Choice and Quality

In a stateless society, we will doubtless need roads, and so we will enter into contracts with those who provide our roads, based on our evaluation of their efficiency, price and competence. It is these criteria of "evaluation" that drives the criterion – and thus the possibility – of *quality*.

Those who do not bring *quality* to the table never want the possibility of voluntary evaluation to exist.

In this way, we know that those parents who demand respect and love *because they are parents* are morally corrupt.

When your government demands "payment" at the point of a gun, it is because *it is not providing value*, in the same way that a mugger does not provide value, and so must extract your money through force.

Family and History

When we interact with our families – particularly as adult children – there is an essential aspect of curiosity that we constantly strive to avoid.

The unhappy and insecure man says: "She *must* treat me well!"

The happy and confident man says: "I *wonder* if she will treat me well?"

The adult child, with regards to his parents, *knows the answer already* – in his very *bones*.

The simple question that the adult child must ask is: "**Did** they treat me well?"

If this question seems too hard to answer, because of a blankness in your history, or an excess of propaganda from your family, then you can answer it even more simply.

"When I see their phone number on my call display, how do I *feel*?"

There is nothing that we need to be taught about how our parents treated us when we were children. There is no possibility of knowledge about another human being that you do not already possess in relation to your parents (and your siblings, of course, but we shall focus on your parents for the moment).

It is a fundamental fact of human physiology that our deepest emotions are immune to propaganda, just as physical pain is immune to propaganda.

You can be told over and over again as a child that jamming a knitting needle through your hand will not hurt, but rather will feel wonderful. You may even believe this in your conscious mind, but your hand knows better. When you do stick that knitting needle through your hand, no amount of propaganda or mythology can prevent the agony you will experience.

This is why we use anaesthetic in surgery, not storytelling.

This is why Novocain is a drug, not a mythology.

Most of our emotions result from our thoughts – but our deepest and truest feelings accumulate from years of *experience*. These feelings cannot be eradicated or changed, any more than our experience can be eradicated or changed. Learning another language as an adult is a conscious decision – learning language as a toddler is an unconscious accumulation of experience and innate ability.

These deepest emotions occur in the *body* – and the body is immune to propaganda. This is why control and rejection of the body is so essential to all exploitive power structures – think of the hostility that most religions have towards the flesh.

Since our deepest emotions cannot be eradicated through propaganda, propaganda must instead focus on the creation and maintenance of *psychological defenses*.

Think of what happens when your phone rings, you look at the call display, and you see:

YOUR PARENTS!

What probably happens is that you experience an initial sinking sensation, followed by a strong desire to avoid picking up the phone. You roll your eyes, check your watch, figure out how much time you can waste talking to them, and generally feel the exact opposite of enthusiasm.

Then, of course, you feel guilt, and chastise yourself for your ingratitude and lack of consideration for their feelings.

They did so much for me, they ask for so little, they're always concerned about me, it costs me so little to make them happy, etc. etc.

The picture of your mother's long-suffering face will rise in your mind, and you imagine her sadness as she slowly puts down the phone, feeling rejected. You imagine your father's irritation when your mother complains that, "She never seems to pick up the phone any more when I call – I'm sure she's just busy, but…"

You feel – projected into the future – a growing unease about the ever-increasing emotional cost you will incur if you continue to avoid their calls. "Might as well get it over with now," you say to yourself, reaching for the receiver – and then, to avoid the guilt of *that* feeling, you pump some enthusiastic shine into your voice as you answer.

After the initial exchange of pleasantries, you feel a rising tension and boredom, because you have nothing to say to your mother. She talks about this or that, asks you some questions which only elicit monosyllabic responses from you…

Then, the awkward silence descends…

You begin to tell a story; she murmurs some noncommittal responses. She begins telling a story about someone that you barely know, and you attempt to show interest. She asks you questions which are annoying, because they're manipulative ("Have you met anyone *nice* recently?") or unanswerable ("What will you buy your nephew for his baptism?").

You realize how little of your life you can actually share with your mother, and for the millionth time you wonder how someone could have become so old and remained so uninteresting. You also wonder what pleasure she could possibly derive from these forced and empty interactions.

She must be taking some pleasure in calling you – otherwise why would she? – but you can't imagine what that pleasure could possibly be.

You sigh, listening to her tinny voice, and wonder when the last time was that you had a problem in your life, and really *wanted* to call your mother for advice.

Never, comes back the immediate answer…

Then, your mother says she is going to put your father on the phone, and you scrabble to find an excuse that will not offend him too much – and then you remember that you have used up all your excuses over the last month or two, and that if you try to make up another one, he surely *will* get offended. And so you swallow, roll your eyes, and say: "Hi, Dad!"

And you know, deep in your bones, that this crushingly dull and awkward ritual will be repeated many more hundreds of times in your lifetime – and that the outcome will be *exactly the same* each time.

After you are finally able to get off the phone, you feel empty and a little depressed – but also relieved, because you know that you have bought a certain amount of guilt-free time away from your parents.

Then, you remember that Christmas is coming up, and your depression yawns to swallow you whole…

The Empiricism of Emotions

As we can see from the above example, it is clear that the debate you are really having is not with your parents, but *with your own emotions*.

Everything that you ever need to know about any of your relationships is available to you in that split second of emotional *authenticity* that occurs when the phone rings, and you look at the call display.

Whatever your emotions tell you in that split second before your defenses can react is the natural and basic truth about that relationship.

And – believe it or not – your emotions are in fact trying to *help you* by telling you the truth about your relationships!

The Propaganda of Regret
(I will use the word "emotions" in this section to describe our deepest feelings that accumulate from experience, rather than the more conscious emotions described in the previous section.)

Your emotions are in fact telling you that you will not live forever, that there are no unchosen positive obligations, that the hours, days, weeks, months and years that you waste in negative, dull, abusive or unproductive relationships are never "refunded" to you – and that in particular, with your family, the endless "propaganda of regret" is nothing more than a corrupt and exploitive lie – a secular "hell" that was invented to enslave you.

When we are taught to fight ourselves, we always end up enslaved. The priest who hates and fears his own sexual impulses remains utterly enslaved. The citizen who hates and fears his own desire for freedom remains utterly enslaved. The child who hates and fears his own dislike of his parents remains utterly enslaved.

Emotions are the empiricism of values – defenses are the religion of subjugation.

To become authentic – to become who you *truly are* – requires *slowing down*.

When the phone rings, and you see the call display, invoking guilt-ridden or self-recriminatory defenses is the most fundamental self-rejection that you are capable of.

The insecure and enslaved man says: "*I **must not** feel this way!*"

The man who has at least a chance for freedom asks: "*I **wonder** why I feel this way?*"

In religious terms, the enslaved man says: "*I **must not** doubt there is a God!*"

The man who can be free asks: "*I **wonder** why I feel there is no God?*"

The Facts of Your Feelings

All I am talking about – like any competent empiricist – is working with the *facts*.

The *facts* of your *feelings*.

Working with the facts of your feelings does not mean treating them as epistemological absolutes. Emotions do not equal knowledge any more than our senses equal the scientific method.

Propaganda will always seek to inflict *negative moral judgments* on your authentic emotional responses.

Remember, earlier in this book, we talked about how *false answers* are the exact opposite of *true curiosity* – and so knowledge.

When faced with the reality of our feelings: "*I do not want to talk to my parents*" – it is an utterly false answer to "explain" those feelings away by saying: "*Because I am a bad person.*" It makes about as much sense as saying, "*I want to masturbate because I am tempted by the devil.*" It is a mad fiction designed to set you at war against yourself and so have you remain enslaved to those who define such false "morality."

In any science – in any rational philosophy – the real, honest, productive and true response to any new information is *curiosity*.

If you stand at the port in Lisbon in the 15th century, watching the Santa Maria sailing off across the Atlantic Ocean, and see the hull slowly disappear "into" the ocean – and then the lower masts, and then the "crow's nest" – you can either make up an "explanation" – "*OMG Poseidon, like, totally ate that ship!*" - or you can admit a lack of knowledge, and remain curious.

"I wonder what happened to the ship?"

Making up an answer will keep you mired in a stupid, exploitive and destructive state of piggish ignorance.

Retaining your curiosity may lead you to the truth: *that the world is round*.

Your eyes provide you an objective experience of what is happening – that the ship appears to be slowly "descending" into the water.

REAL-TIME RELATIONSHIPS

Based on this empirical information – what do you do? Do you make up an answer, or do you explore the question?

When the phone rings and you look at the call display, your emotions provide you clear and empirical information about your relationships.

Based on this empirical information – what do you do? Do you make up an answer ("*I am a selfish child!*") or do you explore the question ("*I wonder why I dislike it when my parents call…*")?

Propaganda and Motivation

Whenever we are conflicted, it is almost always because we have a genuine desire that does not serve the needs of others – *and we have been trained to believe that our genuine desires are always "wrong."*

Our genuine desire – *"I do not want to talk to my parents"* – does not serve the needs of our parents.

In other words, we must have a desire to satisfy the needs of our parents – by attacking our own genuine desire as "wrong."

This creates a truly terrible contradiction within us. Our genuine desires are "wrong" – but our artificial "desires" (to please our parents) are "right." Thus our desires are both "right" and "wrong" simultaneously.

Are we supposed to value our desires? Are we supposed to reject them? Who knows? All that is known is that we can waste our entire lives attempting to unravel these mad contradictions.

Power Versus Pleasure
If you do not want to talk to me, but I want to talk to you, then I have two basic options.

I can either ask you openly and with curiosity *why* you do not want to talk to me – with the goal of making our relationship more positive, enjoyable and productive for you – or, I can attack you for not wanting to talk to me.

In other words, I can either be the "free market," or I can be the government.

If I genuinely want to create real value for you in our relationship, ask you how our relationship can better serve your needs, remain open to self-correction and improvement, and thank you for bringing up any criticisms of me – and in addition make genuine and successful efforts to change – then clearly I am a valuable person to have around.

In other words, if I care about your feelings, then we do genuinely have a relationship, and so it can be improved.

On the other hand, if I do not care about your feelings, but rather only care about managing my own anxieties, then it would be very unlikely that you would ever want to talk to me in the first place, since no one really enjoys being a Band-Aid for rampant narcissism.

If I am only really bothered by my own feelings of being rejected, rather than your feelings of dissatisfaction, then it is all about me, of course.

If, then, I keep calling you and keep getting your answering machine, I am going to feel a steady escalation of anxiety, because you are clearly communicating your lack of desire to talk to me.

You are implicitly communicating to me your dissatisfaction with your side of our relationship. You are openly "saying" to me: "I am not taking pleasure in your company."

If I believe – as most people do – that you "owe" me a relationship – or even just an explanation – then any hesitancy, reticence or avoidance on your part will make me angry, just as if you were refusing to repay a legitimate debt.

You cannot reasonably call up your bank manager and say that you are feeling "resentment" towards the mortgage and so you are just not going to pay it – but that you are also going to keep the house.

Your parents very likely have the same approach to you – they have given you "the house" (life and your childhood), and now you owe them the "mortgage payments" of time, love and resources until the day they die.

Since you cannot give back "the house," avoiding your parents is the same as stealing from them – and will be met with the same passive or aggressive hostility that anyone would express if you refused to repay a legitimate debt.

I myself experience this from time to time with listeners who criticize me on various grounds. I offer to have a conversation with them over the Internet – or by phone, if they want – and yet they often come up with endless streams of excuses as to why this cannot happen. Their parents will hear, they don't have a microphone, they don't have time, their cell phone is too expensive, etc.

I do smile when I hear all of this nonsense, and imagine whether they would have the same set of excuses if returning a phone call were to net them $1 million, or whether if a cute girl or guy wanted their number, they would say the same things.

Of course not! ☺

I do not get particularly angry with these people, because they certainly do not "owe" me a phone call. I would prefer it if they told me the truth – but of course they do not "owe" me the truth either!

I simply take note of their behaviour and come to my conclusion, which is that I will not bother talking to them if they do not want to talk to me.

Follow the Benefit...

When you are conflicted, your genuine emotional response is at war with the propaganda that has been inflicted upon you for the benefit of others.

But – how can you tell your genuine feelings from your propagandized defenses?

Ah, that's easy!

The *first thing* that you feel is your always genuine emotion – the *reaction* is always the propaganda.

In the example above, when the phone rings, you experience a sinking sensation, followed by a dull litany of self-recrimination.

The sinking sensation is your genuine emotion – the negative self-judgment that follows is the propaganda.

Secondly, all you have to do is play the game called "Follow the Benefit."

Whenever forensic accountants are examining a fraud or embezzlement, they always "follow the money."

In the same way, when you are attempting to untangle your healthy flesh from your scar tissue – your true feelings from your propaganda – all you need to do is "Follow the Benefit."

If your initial emotion is that you do not want to talk to your parents, then clearly *you* will benefit from not picking up the phone.

However, when we begin to understand this process, it becomes clear that the phone call has actually begun long before we pick up the receiver.

Since we do not want to pick up the phone, it must be someone *else* who wants us to pick it up, if we end up answering the call.

In this example, clearly there are only two parties in the interaction. Since *you* will not benefit from picking up the phone – since you don't want to – clearly, the guilt and negative self-talk that you experience on the heels of your initial desire to avoid your mother – *must come from your mother*.

Follow the benefit…

In the same way, if you ever dream of a life free from income tax, the guilt and negative self-talk that you experience on the heels of your desire for freedom clearly does not benefit you – thus it must benefit *others*. (For a hint, glance at any ballot.)

Win/lose. You win, your mother loses. Your mother wins, you lose.

In positive and mature relationships – in other words, in *voluntary* relationships – win/lose interactions are utterly unsustainable.

In relationships that are either objectively or subjectively *involuntary* (state, religion and family), *win/lose interactions are the norm*.

Culture, Propaganda and Exploitation

Propaganda – *culture*, as we understand it – is entirely designed to create and sustain win/lose interactions.

Honesty is the most essential virtue, because without lies exploitation is impossible.

Slaves, as we have discussed, express their hostility to their masters through an excess of grudging obedience.

In the same way, you will answer the phone when your parents call, *but you will do a bad job of even pretending to enjoy the conversation.*

This is how you attempt to "explain" your enslavement to them.

This, however, keeps you in chains.

And now we will talk about how to become free.

Becoming Free:
Real-Time Relationships In Action

The Alternative to Grudging Compliance...

If you are a slave and you want to become free, the solution is actually quite simple – assuming that you are not subject to direct coercion.

If you are a slave and you want to become free, the solution is not to try and talk your owners into setting you free.

If you are a slave and you want to become free, the solution is not to try and talk your fellow slaves into joining your rebellion.

If you are a slave and you want to become free, the solution is very simple.

Very terrifying, but very simple.

If you are a slave, and you want to become free, the solution is simply this:

Stop *acting* like a slave!

What does this look like?

Slaves are not allowed to tell the truth. Slaves are not allowed to offend their masters. Slaves are not allowed to express preferences. Slaves must always manage their masters. Slaves must always be on guard. Slaves must always shy away from punishment.

Slaves must always fear their fellow slaves.

Slaves are not allowed to feel curiosity.

Slaves are not allowed to feel genuine emotion.

Slaves can only react to propaganda.

So if you don't want to *be* a slave, stop *acting* like a slave.

This is the core of the Real-Time Relationship (RTR).

The Real-Time Relationship (RTR)

The reason that I call it the RTR is because it is all about telling other people *in the moment* how you feel.

Slaves are not allowed to tell the truth.

So – you start off by telling the truth.

If you don't want to be a slave, when the dreaded name lights up the call display, you pick up the phone and say to your mother:

"Hi, mom. Do you know – the most interesting thing just happened – your name showed up on my call display and I felt a sinking sensation in my stomach, a kind of dread, or nervousness, and a desire to avoid picking up the phone."

And then, you say nothing.

Nothing at all.

You must be free to say what you truly think and feel – and your mother must be free to respond as she sees fit.

Just as it is essential for your mother to know your true thoughts and feelings, so it is essential that you know your mother's genuine response to your true thoughts and feelings.

Picture speaking this honestly to your mother – picture being *that* honest.

What does that make you feel?

Dread? Fear? Terror?

Hopelessness? Despair?

Like walking off a cliff?

That is your enslavement weeping.

That is your propaganda shrieking.

That is your *mother* speaking.

But if you want to stop being a slave, stop acting like a slave.

You feel terror – but really, what are you so afraid of?

Can your mother beat you now? Does she have total control over you, now that you are an adult?

Can she lock you in your room and deny you dinner?

Of course not.

So – I ask you again: *what are you so afraid of?*

The Core of Fear

I can tell you, if you like – but you already know the answer of course.

You are afraid of being revealed as a slave – not to your mother, who already knows – but to **yourself**.

The worst and most terrifying aspect of slavery is that you have to pretend that you are *not* a slave.

When you look at the history of genuine slavery, it was never justified in terms of force, but rather in terms of Christian benevolence, the mental retardation of the slaves, the "white man's burden," the need to save the souls of the savages and so on.

In other words, the people called "slaves" were not really slaves, any more than a baby is a "slave."

The mythology went something like this:

These "slaves" are only owned because they lack the capacity for self-ownership. They are controlled for the same reason that a child wandering into traffic must be controlled. These savage fools are terrible dangers to themselves – they cannot handle freedom. If given their liberty, they would act out a terrible orgy of self-destruction, sexual abandon and brute violence.

And the same is considered true of us, in our "democracies."

A terrible trap was thus set up for those who were subjugated…

If they obeyed the will of their masters, they were "good" – and "liberated" from their own tendency toward self-destruction. If they disobeyed the will of their masters, they were "evil," "irresponsible," "willful," etc.

Thus: "slavery equals freedom," and "freedom equals slavery."

Slavery and Freedom

The moment that slaves see themselves *as slaves*, they immediately begin to become free.

The true equation for freedom – the thunderous power that shatters the chains of the slaves – is the simple statement: *slavery equals slavery*.

Thus the greatest danger for slave-owners is that they will lose control of the moral definitions of "slavery" and "freedom."

However, they are in constant danger of losing control of these definitions, because of the rank hypocrisy involved in any form of human ownership or control, and because, deep down, the slaves yearn and burn to be *free!*

Reason, empiricism, science and simple experience are always dissolving the chains of mankind.

Chains must be constantly re-forged, strengthened, reinforced – they rust by the *minute*.

We can see this in the world of "democracy," insofar as people are considered to be violent, greedy, evil, short-sighted and so on – yet somehow magically possess the wisdom and foresight to elect people who will force them to be "good."

Without a government, so the mythology goes, we would all tear each other to pieces.

Human beings are by nature evil and violent – thus we should give a small monopoly of people who want to use violence to achieve their ends (the state) a monopoly over the use of force, and an endless ability to escape the consequences of their actions.

However, the truth that we all experience *in reality*, on a daily basis, is fear not of our fellow drivers, but of the police car. The violence that we are threatened with is not mugging, raping or home invasion, but rather jail for non-payment of taxes or disobeying the whims of our masters. What is more likely – that we will be robbed by a criminal, or that our money will lose its value through political inflation?

The supposed predations of our fellow citizens are almost nowhere to be seen – it is the *state* that controls the money supply, the army, the police, the guns, the bombs, the attack helicopters, the long-range bombers, the nuclear weapons – and the prisons.

True freedom would be a disaster, we are told – nature red in tooth and claw – and thus enslavement to our masters is real "freedom."

In the same way, parents define slavery as "virtue" – despite the endless hypocrisies of this mad reversal.

The Hypocrisy of "Consideration"...

To understand why we are so blind to our own enslavement as adults, we need to understand how we are first enslaved as children.

As always, our enslavement begins with moral hypocrisies inflicted upon us by those in authority.

Parents will always call us "selfish" if we fail to act on the basis of *their* emotional preferences.

If your mother wants to talk to you, and you do not want to talk to her, then you are "selfish" if you choose not to talk to her.

This is a mad moral mythology which is utterly unraveled by a moment's thought.

We are taught "consideration" not as a mere *personal* preference on the part of our parents, but rather as an objective and absolute moral principle.

If "consideration for the feelings of others" is thus such an axiomatic and universal moral value, then clearly it *must* at least apply equally to both parents and their adult children.

"It is *good* to be sensitive to the feelings of others," sayeth our parents. "It is *bad* to perform actions which cause unhappiness in others."

We swallow this as a moral absolute – and thus feel guilt whenever we violate this principle.

The Key to the Cell
Ah, but if "consideration" is in fact a universal principle, a moral absolute, *then it binds our parents as surely as it binds us.*

So…

If it is *bad* to cause discomfort in other people, and you feel discomfort when your mother calls, surely, when you tell her about your discomfort, *she should feel bad, and want to change her behaviour.*

If your mother apologizes for her lack of consideration, asks you what would make you feel better, then you can rest assured that she did not inflict the moral principle of "consideration" in order to control and bully you, but rather because she genuinely wanted you to be good – and that she knew all about goodness, because she practised moral behaviour *herself.*

When you report your discomfort to your mother, what do you think she will *really* do?

You already know the answer, because you have not told her the truth.

If your brother constantly lectures you about the need for financial responsibility – and mocks and berates you whenever you use a credit card or spend "too much" – how do you feel when he borrows money from you, and then avoids you when the time comes for repayment?

What is thus revealed about your brother's use of the term "responsibility"?

Did he inflict negative judgments on you because he genuinely understands the value of responsibility through his own personal practice of it?

Or – did he inflict negative judgments on you because he is a self-righteous hypocrite who uses the word "responsibility" to control and demean other people?

You know everything you need to know – *if you want to stop being a slave, you just need to stop avoiding your knowledge.*

Testable Hypocrisy?
Perhaps you disagree with me, though, and say that you do not know the answers to these questions.

No problem!

I think we can certainly agree that it is important to know the answer to the question, "Was 'morality' used to control and demean me?"

If you genuinely believe that you lack answers to these questions, the test is embarrassingly simple – and reveals everything we need to know about what we already in fact know.

If your mother tells you that you should pick up the phone because you are supposed to be "considerate," and not create negative feelings in her, how do you think she will react when you tell her the truth about the negative feelings that *she* is creating in *you*?

When you tell your mother that you feel a strong desire to avoid her phone calls, will she apologize for her own lack of sensitivity towards your feelings?

Will she ask you to tell her more about how you feel, so that you can get to the root of the issue, so that you can end up with a better experience of your relationship?

Will she ask you when you first experienced these emotions towards her?

Will she patiently support you as you peel back layer after layer of negative experience, which resulted in your desire to avoid her calls?

There is absolutely no possibility that she will do that.

None whatsoever.

Not a shred of a chance.

It will never, ever happen.

It is functionally, logically and emotionally completely and totally impossible.

How can I be so confident?

Do I know your mother?

No, but I know *philosophy*.

This is why it is impossible.

The Impossibility of Adult Reciprocity

If your mother were to take this course of action when you admitted your desire to avoid her calls – if she were to be truly curious about the root causes of your negative feelings – she would have a great challenge on her hands.

She would have an impossible time explaining one simple thing.

Why has she never known how you feel?

Since the roots of your desire to avoid your mother go back many, many years, how is it possible that your mother has *no idea* that she was inflicting any kind of negative experience upon you?

There are really only two ways that this could have come about.

Your mother *knew* that you were not having any fun in the relationship – and utterly ignored that reality for the sake of her own needs – which scarcely supports the theory that she values "consideration for the feelings of others" as any sort of objective or universal value.

Alternatively, she can claim that she had *no idea* that you had not been enjoying your relationship with her for many, many years – which means that she took no real interest in your true feelings, or rejected you if and when you honestly told her how you felt in the past.

Naturally, since we do prefer to tell the truth to each other, she must also be able to explain why you felt it necessary to hide your negative experiences from her.

Now, if your mother took no interest in your true feelings throughout the history of your relationship, it becomes very hard for her to argue that "consideration for the feelings of others" is a great virtue, since we generally do not enjoy it when other people who claim to love us take no interest in our feelings – in fact, that is a *horrible* experience.

Furthermore, I can completely guarantee that if you take no interest in your mother's feelings, she will be very hurt and upset – and possibly attack you to boot!

Thus, if she claims that she had no idea that you were having any kind of negative experiences in relation to her, then clearly she was taking no interest in your feelings. Since that is behaviour that both angers and upsets *her*, she is openly revealed as a multi-decade complete and total hypocrite who used moral arguments to control, manipulate and subjugate you to satisfy her own narcissistic needs.

In other words, she was a total bitch and a contemptible hypocrite.

Sort of a deal-breaker for anyone with any self-esteem.

Now, if you did genuinely end up hiding your feelings from your mother – which allows her to claim that she did not know what they were – there is only one reason *why* you would have done that.

You did that because your mother rejected what you truly felt – and attacked you for your feelings as well.

It is very hard for someone to argue that you should be considerate towards other people's feelings, while rejecting and attacking the feelings that you have if they are inconvenient or negative to that person.

It would be the same as me arguing that you should always pay back your debts, no matter what the hardship – and then, after borrowing money from you, criticizing you for being "cheap" when you had the temerity to ask me to repay the loan.

It would be a sickening, stomach-turning display of bottomless and manipulative hypocrisy.

If your mother were to admit any of these things, she would be revealed as a horrendous and destructive person who plied you with "moral" lies in order to exploit you for her own narcissistic needs *based on your very desire to be a good child and please her.*

Using false moral arguments to exploit children based on their desire to be good is the very core of corruption and evil.

Following the Maternal Benefit
Let us "follow the benefit" in this case as well.

If your mother is this type of person, then remaining obedient to her wishes is to be enslaved to corruption.

Clearly, identifying your mother as corrupt and manipulative – if that is what she is – benefits *you* enormously.

Who, though, does it *not* benefit?

Why, your *mother* of course!

This is what I mean when I say that slavery is defined as *the avoidance of the knowledge that you are a slave.*

Slavery is also defined as the desire for passive revenge upon your masters.

And this is why we lie to them, and pretend to feel what we do not feel, and refuse to be honest about what we do feel.

Self-delusion is the lie that is always inflicted upon masters by their slaves.

Freedom from slavery is nothing more – or less – then a commitment to honesty, which is also a letting go of the desire for vengeance.

RTR and Empiricism

The Real-Time Relationship is about empiricism and curiosity – fundamentally, it is the scientific method applied to our relationships.

Diagnosis

If your back hurts, you go to a physiotherapist. The physiotherapist will gently press upon your spine in order to localize and identify the problem. She will ask you, over and over, "Does it hurt here?"

She presses upon nerves to find out if they hurt.

That is how she identifies where the problem exists.

You can of course avoid going to a physiotherapist – or any other health practitioner – and simply take painkillers to alleviate the symptoms. This is a clear example of preferring immediate avoidance over long-term solutions – scarcely the mark of a mature or responsible person.

In the same way, the reason that you pick up the phone with your mother and pretend to "enjoy" the conversation is that you prefer the short-term relief of empty compliance over actually pressing a nerve ending to see if it hurts, so that you can identify the source of the problem and work towards a practical and permanent cure.

Our nerve endings signal discomfort – just as your "sinking sensation" signals discomfort – but by picking up the phone and avoiding the truth, you are simply masking the symptom, rather than dealing with the problem.

Again, this approach is fundamentally *religious*, in that you are making up instant "answers" rather than examining the empirical evidence with curiosity and rationality.

Naturally, if we are not allowed to tell the truth in a relationship, and we are consistently bullied into pretending to be something other than who we are, we will not enjoy that relationship – because in fact, it is not a relationship at all, but rather a mutual exploitation based on immediate anxiety avoidance.

Thus our sinking sensation is clearly communicating to us that we do not enjoy this interaction.

We are perfectly aware of why we do not enjoy our relationship with our mother, which is that we are not allowed to tell her the truth – primarily, we are not allowed to tell her that we do not enjoy our relationship with her.

Thus our emotions are putting forward a theory – that our mother will attack us if we are honest with her – and if we wish to establish the validity or invalidity of this theory, all we need to do *is be honest with her.*

If we are honest with our mother – if we say: "I do not want to talk to you, and I do not know exactly why, and I have been feeling this for many years," and our mother responds with genuine concern and curiosity, then our "sinking sensation" was more paranoia than accuracy.

If, on the other hand, she reacts with irritation, dismissal, avoidance, redirection, attack, or an over solicitous and cloying "concern for what's wrong," *then our emotional thesis is amply confirmed.*

The simple fact of the matter, of course, is that if our mother *did* have a habit of genuinely responding to our distress with curiosity and concern, we would never have any kind of "sinking sensation" when she called.

In the case of long-term relationships, *the feeling is the proof.*

There is *no possibility whatsoever* that a positive long-term relationship can exist if one or both parties is regularly feeling bad about talking to the other party.

Paranoia?
If your mother says or implies that you are "paranoid" for feeling anything negative about her calls, then not only is she rejecting and attacking your feelings (hence their negativity) but also she is the kind of person who is perfectly happy to continue for years talking to a paranoid person *without once productively addressing that paranoia.*

That is, sadly, in no way the mark of a healthy person.

Why is it, then, that we avoid putting our emotional theory to the test?

Well, if we avoid putting a theory to the test it is because we know the answer to that test, and we do not like it. This is one reason why religious people always avoid a rational examination of the existence of God, and always fall back on "faith," which is defined in reality as a willed bigotry in what is known to be false.

If our emotions tell us that we will be attacked for telling the truth – and we have not been telling the truth – it is because we wish to avoid *confirmation* – i.e. *certainty.*

If we wish to "avoid" certainty, it is because we are *already certain*.

Thus it is not really "certainty" that we wish to avoid, *but the results of accepting what we already know to be true.*

The superstitious cultist who goes to church does not avoid rationally examining the question of the existence of God because he is certain that God exists, but rather because he is certain that God does not exist at all. What he truly wishes to avoid is not the knowledge of God's nonexistence, but rather the inevitable *results* of that knowledge, which is the end of his association with his cult, and the inevitable attacks that will descend upon him from his fellow cult members. He also fears the contempt and hostility in his children's eyes that will inevitably result from his recognition of the truth, since he inflicted his superstition upon them with pious self-righteousness when they were young, helpless and utterly dependent. He is also afraid to put his wife's love to the test, because he knows *exactly* what will happen if he says to her: "Will you love me and the truth, or will you reject me out of fear and enslavement to our fellow cultists, if I reject falsehood?"

He already knows what her answer will be.

He already knows *exactly* where he sits on her hierarchy of "values."

He already knows that his wife will kick him to the curb the moment he speaks the truth.

Thus it is not the absence of God that he fears and avoids, but the consequences of speaking the truth – and the knowledge that he has wasted his life in a squalid, corrupt cult of liars and bullies – and even worse, that he has sacrificed his children's intelligence and integrity on the altar of his own cowardice.

Truly, to look into the mirror with such accuracy, and to see what he had truly become, would be more than his soul could possibly bear.

And so he struggles on, avoiding the truth, at war with himself, murdering his honest instincts every single day, proselytizing to helpless children and credulous fools that which he knows to be false, until nature finally takes pity upon him and puts him out of his agony with an empty and prayed-for death.

Of course for the religious, death leads to paradise, because their life is a living hell – compared to which the mere nonexistence that we all know awaits us in the grave seems like a blissful heaven.

Exploring the Facts
The simple fact is that God does not exist.

The simple fact is that "the government" is just a bunch of pompous goons with guns ordering you around, filling your children's heads with lies, and stealing from you.

The simple fact is that you do not want to talk to your mother on the telephone.

And the simple fact is that we know exactly what will happen when we speak the truth.

We will be attacked by our fellow slaves.

We will not be invited to become a master.

And thus we shall be alone.

This is the deepest horror of living among the slaves – that the very communal power that could overturn our masters is not turned against our masters, but rather against any slave who dares to say: "We are slaves."

We *have* a State because we *are* the State.

The shock and loathsomeness of this understanding – *that we have no masters but each other* – is the real horror that we avoid with our blank, smiling conformity.

This is the real reason that we make up "answers,' and believe our own lies, crush our natural hunger for truth and freedom, attack anyone who makes us uncomfortable, attack the "enemies" that we are told to hate, and lick the boots of our owners in happy, cringing abandon.

We are not ruled by masters.

We are ruled by each other.

The "masters" simply pick up the pieces.

These are the simple facts that we know deep down. These are the simple facts that are carved into our very *bones*.

These are the simple facts that we will waste our lives evading if we do not find the courage to speak the truth.

Barriers to the Truth

Before you implement what we will talk about below, I think it only fair to remind you that if any of your relationships survive your honesty, you will be in a tiny minority.

Before exposing yourself to this light, it is essential to be aware of the simple fact that when your eyes have adjusted to the brightness of this new world, almost everyone around you will have vanished.

Our theory – our instinctual *knowledge* – is that we will be attacked and reviled for speaking the truth.

If our theory is true, then this is exactly what will happen.

Let me be more specific.

If this theory – and my experience, and the experience of thousands of other people in this philosophical conversation – is true, then you will be attacked and reviled for speaking the truth.

You will be snarled at, dismissed, waved off, condescendingly lectured to, called a fool, a cultist, a traitor, a disinformation agent – angry, paranoid, selfish, ungrateful, deluded, psychotic, insane – and fat, believe it or not!

There will be no end to the vituperation and invective that will be hurled at you.

People live in the darkness, scurrying and biting and gnawing at scraps, and each other – but they have an amazing sensitivity to light – probably because it will reveal their highly unflattering reflections.

When people sense the light of truth approaching, they snarl and growl and attack. They shed all self-restraint, all pretense of dignity, any vestige of "self-respect." They attack with lies, with anger, with misrepresentation, with "confusion," with scorn, with contempt, with eye-rolling – and thankfully, in the end, with ostracism.

They attack with the ferocity of cornered rats because they imagine that the threat comes from you, not from their own hearts.

I must confess to being quite fascinated by the term "neocheater," which I have never heard before! I certainly do agree, of course, that I am no use to "society," since it is an exploitive lie.

Working with the Facts…
Of course, I am not telling you anything about the people around you that you do not already know.

The truth is such a beautiful, wonderful and liberating thing that if people surrender it to lies, we know that it must be because they are subjected to the greatest possible duress, the most extreme threats.

We also know that people in societies that are generally more free (i.e. where they are not jailed or killed for criticizing the system) believe almost as many exploitive lies as those in societies that are less free.

Thus political freedom is not the primary factor in gauging how many lies people will believe.

Since direct threats of physical destruction or enslavement are not required for people to believe all sorts of horrible moral lies – indeed, such lies would be impossible if they *required* such threats – there must be another factor that drives the conformity of mankind.

Criminal Slaves
It is a tried and true principle of homicide investigations that when a husband or wife goes missing, the first suspect is always the spouse.

Whenever a crime is committed, look first to those closest to the victim.

To unravel the riddle of the enslavement of the many by the few, our first suspects cannot be the masters, but must be the slaves.

This we all know deep down.

We know that the truth is a beautiful and liberating thing – a trophy that we hunger for, yearn for, love hopelessly, desperately, at a distance, secretly – *and that we cannot ever speak the truth at all.*

I am here to tell you that what you fear is all true.

You cannot speak the truth to those around you.

You know *exactly* what they will do to you.

But you do not really *know* this yet – not where it counts, not in the place that will propel you into real action, into real escape, towards *real* freedom!

Dare I say – towards the future? ☺

There is only one way to find out whether our fears about speaking the truth are a valid assessment of imminent danger, or rampant and self-indulgent paranoia.

I'm sure you know where I'm going with this…

Speak the Truth

Yes, it really is that simple.

That simple, and that *hard*.

If you think that I am full of nonsense, or that I am wildly overstating the case, or that I am writing more of a self-indulgent manifesto than a rational call to action, I am perfectly fine with that!

I actually think that is a very healthy approach to take to what I am saying.

Scepticism is enormously healthy because scepticism requires both logic and empirical validation to be transformed into acceptance.

Fortunately, you have access to all the logic and empirical validation you could ever desire – today, right now, this minute!

For the logic, you can turn to my two previous books, and my podcasts.

For empirical validation, things are much easier.

You do not need to buy and study any books. Thank heavens, you do not need to listen to a near-infinite series of podcasts. You do not need to learn ancient Aramaic, how to juggle, ride a unicycle, or breathe water.

You only need to open your mouth.

Integrity in Honesty
If you really *do* dislike it when your mother's name shows up on your call display, you may well be tempted to yank the phone off its handle and yell at her that she is a fellow slave who is keeping you down, that she bullies you like a cornered rat, and she serves the masters who rule us all!

Not only would this be unwise, it would also be dishonest.

The fact of the matter is that you *do not know for certain the validity of these theories.*

I am not asking you to believe beyond a shadow of a doubt that these theories are true.

I think that would be a very bad idea.

The truth of the matter – as it stands for you, right now – is that you *genuinely do not know why you cannot speak the truth with your mother.*

Earlier, we talked about a 15th century man watching a ship on an ocean descend slowly over the horizon. That observation is the *fact* that he is working with – he does not as yet have a theory as to why that phenomenon is occurring.

If this man simply started yelling at people that the world was round, whizzing around the sun at 30 km a second, that the sun was the center of the solar system, and is also whizzing along at terrifying speeds – for a combined planetary motion of 900 km/s – everyone would think that he was just mad! They would be right in that evaluation too, since he would have no theoretical or empirical proof for what could only be considered entirely wild propositions!

You have a fact to work with in your relationship with your mother, which is that you do not like it when her name lights up your call display.

You do not know exactly *why* that "sinking sensation" is occurring.

I have put forward a theory as to why that sensation is occurring – and the likely events that will unfold if you speak the truth.

However, it remains as yet only a theory.

It is a theory, of course, that should give you some great comfort – despite the anxiety it provokes.

If the theory is true, then you have *damn good reasons for staying silent*, for conforming, for refraining from speaking the truth – and for lying to yourself about why.

It makes little sense to hide if you are not being hunted.

I am telling you that you hide because you are being hunted – but this has not been proven, and therefore must be put to the test.

Your test.

So – call your mother.

Tell her that you feel unease – or a sinking sensation, or anxiety, or whatever it is – when her name lights up your call display.

That's pretty terrifying, isn't it?

Good.

Feel the burn!

I mean – you don't want to go through the rest of your short life utterly deluded about the content and quality of your "relationships," do you?

Since you yearn and *burn* for the truth – as we all do – don't you want to find out if your relationships can support it?

Since you yearn and burn for love – which requires the truth, as we have discussed – don't you want to find out if your relationships can support it?

Since you yearn and burn for intimacy, integrity, trust and devotion – all of which require the truth – don't you want to find out if your relationships can support them?

If your existing relationships will not only *never* give you what you want, but exist only to rob you blind, don't you want to stop wasting your life?

Now you can.

So – all you have to do is tell your mother *how you feel*.

When you are talking to her – particularly for the first time – you cannot with certainty tell her that you know exactly why you are feeling what you are feeling. Yes, she might frighten you with unconscious or subtle threats of attack or abandonment – but you have no real evidence of that as yet! Thus it would be entirely unjust – and abusive – to attack her with *conclusions* when you have as yet only *facts*.

Conclusions and Facts

The *fact* is that you feel anxiety when your mother calls you. The Real-Time Relationship concept demands that we are honest with each other by speaking the facts of our experience.

Not the mythologies, not the stories, not the blame, not the conclusions – just the *facts*.

The fact is that you feel anxiety – and you do not know *why* you feel this anxiety.

So what do you say to your mother?

You tell her the truth.

Nothing more, nothing less.

You say: "Mom, I feel a strange anxiety when you call – I don't know why, I'm not saying it's anything that you are doing, but I have felt it for quite some time – many years, actually as far back as I can remember. I'm not saying that this is your fault, because I don't know where it comes from – I'm just telling you what I feel."

And that's all that you say, because that's all that you know for sure.

Avoiding "Story Time"

You will be greatly tempted – and your mother will doubtless tempt you with this as well – to blame your mother, so that you can both take a mutual dive off the cliff of "story time."

The way that we do this is to inflict a *conclusion* on someone else.

Thus we are sorely tempted to say: "Mom, I feel a strange anxiety when you call, because you are always so critical!"

Do you see the difference? Do you catch the difference between the first speech, and the second?

The first speech is an honest expression of your emotional state – feedback *in real-time* to the person that you are talking to about your immediate experience.

The second sentence is a *conclusion* – easily recognizable by the terrible use of the word "**because**."

"Because" is a word that indicates a shift from *experience* to *thesis*.

Our historical friend in Lisbon, who watches the ship disappearing over the horizon, can honestly turn to someone and say: "Hey, I see that ship disappearing slowly over the horizon, hull first!" That is a true statement of his direct experience in the moment – no one can reasonably tell him that he is wrong.

The moment that he provides an explanation, however, he is open to criticism.

If he says: "The ship is disappearing slowly into the ocean *because* it is being swallowed up by Poseidon," now he is in the realm of story time, since he has just made up an "explanation" for which he has no direct evidence.

Thus when you say to your mother: "I feel anxiety *because* you are so critical," you are stating knowledge and certainty of a causal relationship for which you have no direct evidence.

It may be true that your mother is hypercritical – it may be true that she has attacked you for years, every single time that she calls – your thesis may be entirely true, *but the problem is that you have absolutely no evidence* **in the moment**.

This is how we so often shoot ourselves in the foot when we attempt to be honest with others.

If you say to your mother that your anxiety is caused by her critical nature, what is she going to say?

Come on, you know it exactly.

She is going to say, of course: "I am not critical."

And what do you say in return?

You say: "You are *too* so critical! Like – every time we talk, you say that I sound *tired*…"

And so on.

And what happens with that conversation?

You argue and debate and provide evidence and deny and attack – *and never talk about your true feelings at all*.

Do you see how presenting *conclusions* is simply a massive avoidance mechanism which allows you to debate endlessly about inconsequential details that cannot be proved, rather than talk about your actual experience of your mother?

Stories can be debated endlessly – witness the endless idiocy of medieval scholasticism, or modern theological or political debates – because *stories are not real.*

You say that your mother is critical, and she replies that she is not – that she just has your best interests at heart, that you can be careless or irresponsible, that she never *said* that, or that if she did you misinterpreted it, that you have always been so sensitive, that you must be tired now, that she has always tried to do her best, that motherhood is not easy, that she doesn't understand why the younger generation behaves the way it does, that things weren't like that when she was your age, that you're not a parent, you'll understand when you are a parent – and so on and so on and so on.

Round and round and round…

A massive, cumbersome, convoluted, baffling, frustrating, empty bag of Gordian knots that no sane human being could ever unravel.

How many times has this happened in your relationship with your mother? How about your girlfriend? Boyfriend? Siblings? Friends?

When we experience a negative emotion, we are unbelievably and inevitably tempted to place the blame for that emotion on someone else, by creating an untestable mythology that defines *their actions as causing our response.*

And it never, ever gets us anywhere at all.

Post Hoc Ergo Propter Hoc

The *post hoc ergo propter hoc* (*after* this, therefore *because* of this) fallacy is based upon the notion that simply because "B" happens after "A," "A" *caused* "B."

If I kill a goat, and then it starts to rain, it is completely irrational to say that the death of the goat *caused* the rain.

If I get angry when my wife says something, I cannot immediately prove that I got angry *because* my wife said something – all that I know for sure is that I felt anger *after* she spoke.

However, we are endlessly drawn to the fallacy of blaming others for our own feelings, because it is far easier than actually discussing our feelings in an open and vulnerable way.

Forever and a day, if you take the "blame" approach, you will be mired in dysfunctional, frustrating, empty, wasteful, negative "relationships."

How many times do we feel that we are silently and invisibly "fencing" with someone else, where we are trying to pin the blame for our emotions on him, while he is struggling to evade our blame, and trying to turn it around and blame us?

We are priests arguing about dead gods.

We are wasting our lives fencing with ourselves.

And we deserve so much better.

But first we have to *earn* it.

Avoiding Mythology

When you take the RTR approach, you simply *state the facts of your experience.*

You do not make up reasons as to *why* you feel what you feel. You simply say: "I feel X."

You can honestly say: "I felt X after you did Y. I am not saying that Y *caused* my feeling, I am simply saying that my feeling followed Y."

This is the truth. It could be that your feeling was triggered by a situation that just happened to be similar to a traumatic or difficult situation in your childhood. This does not make you paranoid, just a sensitive person with a memory. A soldier who has returned from violent combat, and who ducks when a car backfires, is not paranoid, just painfully conditioned. He felt fear *after* the car backfired, but not *because* the car backfired – and we know this because other people *did not feel fear* when the car backfired.

The backfire was thus merely a catalyst, not a cause.

If it were an objective cause, then everyone would feel fear, not just him.

An objective cause of pain is "being stabbed" – a subjective cause of pain is "being embarrassed." The first is based upon our objective physiology;

the second upon our subjective interpretation. The first is a fact; the second is a *story*.

In the same way, you can legitimately say: "When you *did* X, I *felt* Y" – it is important, however, to continually remind the person that you are talking to that you are not saying that she *caused* your feeling.

Not only has that not been established logically or empirically, but even if it *were* established, it would still not be true, because unless someone is sticking a pin in your arm, they do not have the power to *make* you feel anything.

"Inflicting" Emotions

If you and I go on a first date and I spend the first five minutes yelling at you, you will of course be frightened, anxious and upset. There is no way to avoid this reaction, since your autonomous nervous system will react to my potential attack with a healthy dose of "fight or flight."

Naturally, then, you will make your excuses, leave, and never see me again.

If you *do* choose to see me again, and I continue to yell at you, *I* am not making you feel bad, *you* are making you feel bad.

The first time that you put your hand in an open flame, it is the *flame* that burns you. If you voluntarily put your hand *back* into that open flame, it is now *you* who are burning *yourself*.

The way that we always end up in abusive relationships is that we simply ignore, reject, minimize or mythologize *how those relationships make us feel initially*.

As children, we are always taught to obey external rules rather than express our honest feelings.

Feelings destroy hierarchies – particularly unjust hierarchies.

Feelings instantly tell us whether a situation or interaction is good, bad, or indifferent for us.

When you were sitting in your classroom as a child, did you feel happy, bored, frustrated, angry or indifferent to be there?

When the teacher called on you, did you feel eager or nervous?

Did the teacher ever sit you down and ask you if there was any way that you could enjoy your learning experience more?

Private companies do this all the time – they are continually polling their customers to find out if there's any conceivable way that their needs can be better served.

Did your teachers ever ask you how they could serve you better?

Did your *parents*?

This may sound odd, but it is very important to understand.

Quality of Service

I regularly ask my wife if there is anything that I can do to improve her experience of being married to me.

I can't automatically tell if she is dissatisfied or unhappy about something – and I would far rather change my behaviour *before* those feelings arise – and so it is important to check in with her and make sure that everything is running smoothly.

Even if I am doing pretty much the same thing that I did a month ago, her needs or preferences might have changed in the interim. Sometimes, just asking the question can help uncover a new preference that she is not even fully aware that she has.

The reason that I want to talk about this aspect of a relationship is so that you understand that, as a child, *you were almost never consulted about what you wanted.*

When I say this, I'm not talking about things like "What do you want for Christmas?" or "What would you like for dinner?" – which you might have been asked, and which is all fine and dandy.

No, what I mean is not whether your preferences were solicited with regards to *material objects*, but rather with regards to *the people around you*.

As children, we are generally raised to conform to the preferences of those around us – though, as I talked about in my book "On Truth," those preferences are almost always portrayed as moral absolutes – but we are not allowed to have any particular preferences *of our own with regards to those around us*.

Consultation
For instance, did your mother ever sit you down and say:

Is there any way that I could make your experience of being my child even more enjoyable? Is there anything that I am doing that you dislike, or that you don't understand, or that you do not see the purpose of? Although I know that you disagree with me about certain decisions that I make for you in the moment – like "don't eat that third candy bar" – do you understand those decisions later on, or do they remain confusing for you? Do you think that I am teaching you to follow sensible principles, for your own good, or do you find that you are merely obeying me in the moment? Overall, are you enjoying being my child? Would I be the mother that you would choose out of all the women in the world, if you could choose who was your mother? If not, why not?

Can you identify the emotion that wells up in your heart from even *considering* this kind of interview from one or both of your parents?

I'm telling you – this is what you need to feel to be safe, loved and happy now, and in the future.

Why is it so incomprehensible that our parents would ever ask us these sorts of questions, and ask us for honest feedback about their success as parents?

Why is it that our local pizza parlour will interview us to find out what kind of pizza we like – but our parents will never ask us what kind of *parenting* we like?

Do you see everything that is *not* being talked about in the world?

Do you see why people grow up to be so compliant, so fearful, so frustrated, so angry, so lonely – and so fundamentally cut off from their emotional experience of the world – and thus so sad in their very souls?

Muscles that we do not use inevitably atrophy.

Feelings that are never consulted inevitably go underground.

If your opinion is never sought – or if it is "sought," but never acted on – you will simply cease experiencing opinions.

If your preferences are constantly rejected – which is always hypocritical, since to *reject* a preference is to *express* a preference – then you will simply cease experiencing preferences.

(Notice that I do not say that you will cease to *have* opinions or preferences – merely that you will cease to *experience* them.)

Whatever we accept as a general principle we inevitably end up implementing ourselves – thus if you grow up rejecting your own preferences and opinions, you will inevitably end up attacking, crushing and rejecting the preferences and opinions of others.

Particularly those who depend on you the most, such as your children, and your lover.

Identification and Self-Expression

It takes an enormous amount of work to first identify what we feel, and then learn how to express those feelings honestly.

Then it takes additional effort to truly understand the source of our feelings – the complex interaction of our ideas and our experiences of the world, and of others – and then it takes even *more* effort to accept the information and conclusions that our feelings provide us, *and act upon them*.

This complex dance is one of the greatest and most amazing experiences that life has to offer. Learning how to productively match the complexity of our inner experiences with the subtlety of our outer experiences is a truly magical journey.

Depth Right at the Surface

We so often feel that what is occurring for us emotionally in the very depths of our souls is somehow radically disconnected from the daily world that we live in.

When I first started going to therapy – I went for three hours a week for almost 2 years – I had a dream that I was being attacked by a hostile woman. I brought the dream in for analysis, spouting all this Jungian nonsense about how this angry woman was my *animus*, my female side and so on.

My therapist held up her hand and said: "Perhaps, but let's start with something a little more simple. Did you talk to your mother yesterday?"

Of course I had – and of course my mother had attacked me.

This simple idea – an astounding revelation to me – that the depths of my unconscious was perfectly attuned to the realities of my daily experiences – completely changed how I viewed the value and purpose of my inner life.

As I continued in therapy, it became increasingly clear that my senses did not lie, and my unconscious did not lie – it was only my *conscious* mind, and my psychological defenses, that were consistently and constantly misleading me through the endless invention of false narratives and imaginary cause-and-effect.

I was in fact a kind of "truth sandwich." My senses told the truth; my dreams told the truth – but in the middle was my conscious ego, which lied and evaded constantly.

Your dreams, your instinctual emotions, your deepest and – as you think – most private experiences – are the greatest source of truth available to you, after your physical senses (and your greatest source of *moral* truth!).

Thus, learning to trust our instincts – rather than just "follow the rules" (even philosophical rules) is essential for living a happy, safe, loving and productive life.

However, due to the fact that as children our feelings and instincts are stifled, mocked and abused, it can take quite some time to become comfortable *feeling* them, let alone expressing them, understanding them and acting on them.

Feeling Your Feelings

Since the first challenge is learning how to feel your feelings, how can we approach that most productively?

First of all, you are *already feeling your feelings*.

Your initial impulse – the "stab" or "sinking feeling" – may be subtle, brief and fleeting, but I guarantee you that it is there.

The moment after you feel your feelings, your defenses summon mythologies to label those feelings "bad," and thus prevent you from communicating, understanding, or acting upon them.

This we all learned from the sick fantasies of religion – the mythology that certain impulses come from "the devil" and so are labeled "bad," and so you must keep them to yourself – or perhaps confess them as a guilty secret – and thus never accept those feelings or act upon them.

Do you see the evil genius of religion?

Doubt in the truth of the fantasy of God comes from "the devil," and thus is labeled "bad," and so should never be communicated or acted upon.

Brilliant – simply brilliant!

Authenticity is evil; empty submission is virtue.

This is how the greatest predators feed!

Your First Feeling...

When I was 19, I worked as a gold-panner and prospector in northern Canada for about 18 months, saving money to go to university.

Every couple of weeks, I would go into town, have a nice dinner and perhaps go to a disco.

One night, I started chatting up the prettiest woman at the bar. I found it rather difficult to talk to her, though, because she kept glancing around. We chatted for about 15 minutes – though her responses were mostly monosyllabic – and then she excused herself, because she wanted to go and talk to a friend.

I sat at the table for about 20 more minutes, not knowing if she was going to come back, feeling increasingly baffled and irritated. When she finally did return, she said she had to go. I asked her for her number – she sighed, and told me that she would prefer it if I gave her my number.

I did, and then spent the next day hoping that she would call.

Two nights later, after working out, I was sitting in a sauna, and realized that she hadn't called me. I felt a stab of disappointment – which I immediately smothered by taking a deep, sudden breath and forcing myself to think of something else.

I had recently read my first book on psychology, and so, catching myself, I decided to relax, slow down my breathing, and actually *feel* my disappointment.

Shocking, I know! ☺

This began a lifelong process for me of re-learning how to trust my emotions.

It's no fun to live life as if you are inhabited by some malevolent demon that is constantly "shooting you up" with random high-stimuli emotions that will inevitably mess you up in some manner.

Setting us at variance against ourselves is a prerequisite for exploitation.

A man at peace with himself cannot be exploited, except through direct violence, which the ruling classes quite sensibly shy away from.

A man at war with himself remains jittery, insecure, consumed with self-management, overeager for approval, unable to set boundaries, always available to work overtime. He feels generally unworthy of keeping his property, unable to challenge any of the moral rules that enslave him…

He lives a life of fear and self-subjugation.

It is this self-subjugation that breeds political, religious and tribal subjugation.

It is self-slavery that creates our masters.

We sell ourselves *before* we are bought by others.

Slowing Down…
Our defenses work by creating a "rush to react," which smothers our genuine instinctual and emotional responses.

Sitting in the sauna all those years ago, when I felt my stab of disappointment that the girl had not called me, I immediately began to make up excuses as to why my disappointment was invalid:

- Ahhh, it's her loss.
- She wasn't that pretty anyway.
- Maybe she lost my number.
- She might call.

Etc.

We all know these endless litanies of excuses that we invent to smother our genuine emotional reactions. We live life so frightened, so unstable, so consumed with self-management, that we become cheap lawyers, petty sophists – ready, willing and able to talk ourselves in and out of *anything*.

Self-manipulation is our medication.

Mythology is our drug.

The only cure is honesty.

When I made up "answers" in a "rush of reaction" to my genuine emotion, I was engaged in a fundamentally religious approach to reality.

I was not exhibiting any kind of curiosity about myself, about my emotional reaction to the girl not calling. I experienced a stimulus that I considered "negative" – and so just made up an "answer" to make the stimulus go away.

This is exactly the religious approach – when religious people experience "negative" stimuli, such as doubt, they make up answers to make the stimuli go away.

When we do not know where life came from, or how old the planet is, or what makes the lightning, we can either ask questions in all humility according to the scientific method - or we can just make up "answers" to wish our doubts away.

In the latter case, clearly we are not interested in establishing the truth, but rather in magically turning our ignorance into "truth."

This habit is the eternal curse of our species.

When we are faced with the question "How are the children to be educated?" or "Who will build the roads?" saying, "Just give a bunch of guys a bunch of guns to make it happen," is a complete and total non-answer.

When we are faced with the question, "Do my parents really love me?" saying, "Yes, because they tell me so," is also a complete and total non-answer.

The Truth We Repress
Once I began to explore my feelings of disappointment about the girl not calling, some fascinating insights began to arise.

First of all, it became clear to me over time that I was not disappointed in the fact that the girl had not called me, but rather I was frightened by my desire for a girl who would not call me.

I chose her in that bar because she was very pretty. I ignored the fact that she was quite rude, and was constantly looking around the disco while I was talking to her. I ignored the fact that she abruptly got up and talked to a friend of hers for 20 minutes, leaving me sitting in the booth, twiddling my thumbs and wondering whether I should stay or go. I ignored the fact that she gave me a very scant smile when I ask her for her number, and said, "Why don't you just give me your number instead?"

In other words, the reality was that I was disappointed in *myself*, not in the girl.

And I was afraid.

Why was I afraid?

Well, I was afraid because I was putting my heart in danger.

I was afraid because, by choosing women who were obviously not very nice based entirely on their looks, I was putting myself in considerable danger. Not just in terms of disappointment, but in terms of getting into a relationship with a cold, selfish and manipulative woman – and, God forbid, having children with her – which could truly ruin my entire life.

By attempting to repress and ignore my disappointment, I was placing myself in considerable danger of ruining my life – and the lives of my potential children, which is even worse.

"Negative" feelings are designed to protect you, in the same way that physical pain is designed to protect you.

My feelings were telling me that my approach to women was going to put me in grave danger throughout my life. The value that I placed upon a woman's looks – in complete opposition to the definition of love we have talked about in this book – left me wide open to disastrous exploitation.

As it turns out, that was not the end of the story either…

Emotions and Exploitation

By placing value on women for their looks alone, it is certainly true that I left myself open to the worst kinds of exploitation – but the reality was that I only left myself open to being exploited *because I wanted to exploit the pretty women.*

I wanted certain types of women because of my own vanity. We all know that looks alone are not indicators of spiritual quality – in fact, quite the opposite appears so often to be true, except for my wife.

I wanted these women to go out with me because having them on my arm would make me "look good." In other words, I wanted to use them to dominate others, to evoke envy and establish my own superiority.

Can you see why there are considerable secondary gains in repressing these "negative" emotions?

Can you also see how far away from the truth my original "explanations" were? By providing me with instant and comforting "answers," they could not have been more opposed to the truth than if they had been direct lies, which at least can be seen and examined.

Even Deeper

Furthermore, my father chose my mother – a thoroughly nasty and corrupt woman – largely for her looks, since she was very attractive.

Thus, I have seen the results of this kind of mutual exploitation up close, and have lived through all the disasters of a nasty, brutish and short marriage.

However, if I were to cast aside my own shallow addiction to physical appearance, what would be the long-term result?

Having lived it now for over 20 years, I can tell you quite definitively.

When we begin to realign our standards of evaluation from inconsequential things such as appearance, status, money and prestige, towards moral standards such as courage, integrity and virtue…

Well, as I said earlier, almost none of your relationships will survive this transition – because, as you will very quickly discover, if you pursue this course, you think you have a relationship with others, but you really only have a relationship with your own illusions.

My particular illusion was that physical beauty – and the envy it produces in others – creates value.

Sadly, this was like putting a Band-Aid over a sprained ankle, which only made that sprain worse over time.

If I say that I need a beautiful woman in order to have real value, then clearly I am saying that without that beautiful woman, I do not have value – or I have negative value.

If I want to wear platform shoes, it is because I feel that I am short.

Buying and wearing platform shoes does not get rid of my belief that I am short, any more than buying and wearing a wig gets rid of my belief that I am bald.

Acting in "opposition" to an underlying belief only reinforces that belief.

Thus I pursued beautiful women because I felt that I lacked value, which arm-candy would somehow alleviate.

However, this pursuit only *reinforced* my belief that I lacked value – which is why it could never succeed.

As we talked about earlier, using other people to manage your own anxiety is selfish and corrupt.

For me, using the physical attractiveness of women to avoid the anxiety of my own low self-regard was selfish and corrupt.

Now – although this is of course a very painful experience to go through – and is also enormously humbling – is this not a far better approach to building a happy life than pretending to yourself that the girl just somehow "lost your number"?

Even Deeper!

Ahhh, but it went even *deeper* than that!

Like just about everyone else on the planet who was not raised by wolves, I was taught that my family had value in and of itself.

I was "taught" that my father, my mother, my brother, my half-sister – my extended relations of every kind – were valuable and deserved my love simply because they were members of my family.

Of course, as a criterion for love, this is in fact as inconsequential as height, hair, or high cheekbones.

We tend to mock and ridicule the old man who dates the busty bimbo, since he is clearly communicating his shallowness, insecurity and silly vanity.

However, we tend to "cherish" and "respect" those who value family members for no reason other than similar DNA.

Beauty is accidental.

Family is also accidental.

When I began to challenge my own vanity and greedy desire to exploit others – both the pretty women and those who would envy me for being with them – I began to understand that *virtue* was in fact required for love.

This is a strange, terrifying and disorienting realization.

If virtue is required for love, then *I cannot reasonably judge the value of my family by any standard other than virtue.*

How does *that* sit with you?

Your family has no value.

Your country has no value.

Your religion has no value.

Your gods, governments, teachers and friends have no value.

Only *virtue* has value.

Is it becoming clear to you just what an enormous minefield lay underneath my stab of disappointment in that long-ago sauna?

Can you begin to understand exactly why I felt such fear and trepidation about the very idea of *not* repressing my feelings anymore?

Deep, deep down, of course, I totally understood the road that I was taking my first step upon. I knew where it would lead, and I knew just how few people would be willing to follow me there. I knew exactly what kind of ugly and hellish confrontations awaited me down that road, how many subtle and vicious attacks I would endure, how many sleepless nights would torture me – and to what end?

Who knew?

And all this came to pass. That fateful night in that sauna, when I made the decision to stop repressing my feelings, every fear I had came true.

When I began to view and evaluate my family members, friends, girlfriends, dates and business associates by reasonable moral standards – nothing fancy, just honesty and integrity really – the whole magnificently empty house of cards that was my social world came fluttering and crashing down.

The world is well-armed against virtue.

The world is so corrupt because being good so often totally *sucks*.

None of this occurred overnight, of course. It was years before I began to really apply these values to those around me – and it was another few years after that that I broke with my mother. Two years later, I broke with my brother – and the year after that, I broke with my father, which was less important, since I had never lived with him.

But it really does all come back to that first, fateful decision, to simply *start listening to what we already know to be true*.

The Truth Within

Deep within our bodies, from the moment of our conception, lie all of the amazing biochemical functionality and potentiality of growth, puberty and maturity.

In the same way, within our unconscious minds, lies all the wisdom we could ever consume in a single lifetime.

We do not defend ourselves against our emotions; we do not defend ourselves against the pain of the past; we do not even defend ourselves against the discomfort of the present.

We always and only ever defend ourselves against the *actions of the future*.

If we have been hurt by a dentist and we fear returning, we do not fear the past, since that pain has come and gone.

We do not fear the pain of the past.

We fear the pain of the *future*.

Psychological defenses do not exist to prevent us from feeling pain in the past; they exist to prevent us from acting with integrity in the future.

Psychological defenses do not prevent us from being exploited in the past – since that has already happened. Psychological defenses ensure that we shall be exploited in the *future* – and that we shall exploit others, which is even worse.

An addict does not take his drug in order to feel bliss in the past, but in order to feel bliss in the present – and, as the addiction develops, in order to avoid the agony of withdrawal in the future.

In the same way, we avoid our feelings in the present because we wish to avoid ugly confrontations in the future.

We ignore our "sinking feeling" when our mother calls because we wish to avoid the confrontation that will inevitably occur if we accept our feelings.

I desperately wanted to avoid my feelings of rejection, because once I felt my own feelings of rejection, it turned out that I was going to have to reject others in the future – the corrupt, the false, the evil.

It was not this particular girl's rejection of *me* that I was avoiding – but rather, the inevitable rejection of *others* that would occur in the future, if I began to in fact judge people according to virtuous principles rather than shallow inconsequentialities.

Do you see *why* we avoid our feelings?

Do you see why thinking that our avoidance has anything to do with the *past* is so fundamentally counterproductive and erroneous?

Do you see how terrifying our true feelings are for those who exploit us?

Do you see how impossible it would be to exploit us if we truly *felt* our own emotions?

Do you see why I say that we must *be* slaves in order to *facilitate slavery*?

Do you understand why I say that we must first reject *ourselves* before we can be controlled by others?

We can do nothing about our enslavement in the past. We were children, we were forced to go to school and church, we were surrounded by people that we never chose to have in our lives – our parents, siblings, our extended family, our teachers…

The slavery of the *past* is unalterable.

The slavery of the future can be changed.

We cannot be free in the past, or from the past.

We *can* be free in the future.

And our souls are constantly whispering in our ears the combination to the lock that will set us free.

Feel, communicate, understand, **act!**

Dodging Defenses

When we decide to finally start telling those around us the truth of our experience of them, it is a near-certainty that they will oppose us with every fibre of their beings.

This is not because they are evil or because they are corrupt or because we are doing something "wrong."

This is because they are frightened.

People oppose us when we speak the truth because they like to hide in shadows – because when we bring the light of truth into their dark and fearful worlds, they actually see their own darkness, which is invisible to them when there is no light.

People live in the dark because they pretend that there is no such thing as light.

When the light appears, it reminds them that darkness is a *choice*, not an absolute.

Flying from Flight…
If it turned out that gravity was an illusion, and that you could fly simply by picturing it, wouldn't you feel rather foolish for all the time you spent walking or waiting for the bus?

And – more importantly – how would you feel about all those who taught you that flying was impossible?

If, for your whole life, you could have experienced the joy and freedom of flight at will, how would you feel about those who had told you that flight was not only impossible, but *evil*?

What would that do to your image and picture of the world, if with your new understanding you saw the natural and beautiful wings of children being torn out at the roots in the name of virtue and goodness?

Would you begin to understand what type of people really run the world?

Would the wars, famines, religious conflicts, dictatorships, prisons, gulags, genocides, murders, kidnappings and child abuse all begin to make sense?

It is a simple logical correlation that we are in hot pursuit of in these pages.

The world is full of evil, and no one is allowed to speak the truth.

Throughout history, men have striven to rid the world of evil by creating institutions capable of doing evil – religions, governments, and the absolute authority of parents.

They have continued to do this despite the fact that not only do these institutions not rid the world of evil, but the evils in the world continue to increase.

Thus we can only surmise that the alternative to speaking the truth is even worse. The alternative to all the evils described above is even worse.

The alternative is, of course, discovering that we are turned towards evil through our love of goodness. That we are lied to about virtue in order to lead us to vice.

Let me put forward a simple proposition to illustrate what I mean.

Evil and Lying

Pretend that you are a child again. If a vase lies broken, your mother will command you to tell her who broke it. If you evade or lie, you will be morally attacked, because *lying is wrong!*

However, when her friends are over, if you tell them that sometimes she drinks in the morning, you are attacked for being "rude" and "inappropriate" and "airing our dirty laundry in public."

This is the simple principle. It has nothing to do with morality:

If you are in possession of information that those in power want you to reveal, it is "immoral" to lie.

If you are in possession of information that those in power **don't** *want you to reveal, it is "immoral" to tell the truth.*

You are led to serve those in power – the foundational root of all institutionalized evils – by your very desire to be good – to not be called "immoral."

In other words, the devils destroy you with angels. The devils of this world destroy you with the angels of your nature.

The world is evil because we want to be good.

We are enslaved because we want to be free – of vice.

Every evil man in the world knows how desperately we want to be good. That is why Hitler had his soldiers swear an oath of loyalty to him before turning them on the rest of Europe. He knew that they would want to keep their word, and so would not need to be ruled by force.

World War II would have been impossible without this "integrity."

"Virtue" created a Holocaust; it created Soviet gulags, Chinese starvation, American prisons and African famines.

Whoever owns the definition of virtue owns mankind.

This we all know. This, deep down, does not surprise us at all. It is our desire to be good – according to the terms of evil men – that turns us to the service of evil.

False virtue makes true vice.

The reason that I wanted to talk about all of this before we get into how you can recognize the defenses of others is so that you understand the stakes involved in what you are about to do.

Really, it's not about exposing the lies of your mother.

It's about saving lives in the future.

Honesty and Proof
If we lie to evade an unjust punishment, we are called "bad."

If, by telling the truth, we inflict a just punishment, we are called "bad."

This is the simple evil of the world.

However in this – as in all things I write – there is absolutely no reason to take my word for it in any way at all.

If your mother ever told you not to lie, how do you think she should logically react when you tell her the truth about how you feel?

Because telling the truth is *good*, right?

Will she praise you for your honesty?

Try it and see.

Typical Defenses

When you begin to tell your mother the truth about how you feel, she will instinctively and inevitably begin to deploy a series of psychological defenses designed to disorient and punish you for telling the truth.

Let us have a look at the likely obstacles that will be thrown in your path when you dare to be honest.

If you tell your mother that you are afraid of answering the phone when she calls, she will immediately ask – usually in a wide-eyed, innocent voice – *but... why?*

The purpose of this maneuver is to have you provide a reason that she can reject – usually initially through the defense of minimization.

If you say: "I do not feel that you listen to me," then she will immediately say something along the lines of...

Minimization

Script	Translation
Mother: "What do you mean – I'm listening to you *now*, aren't I?"	*You're actually the bad listener, because you don't even notice that I **always** listen to you!*
Mother: "Are you trying to tell me that I have never – not once in your entire life – *ever* listened to you?"	*You're insane and exaggerating – I am going to create an impossible standard of proof, wherein a single exception to a complaint dismisses the entire complaint. ("Hey, remember that one Sunday when I **didn't** beat you?")*
Father: "Yeah, yeah, you had it sooo tough, didn't you? Why, when I was your age… [Followed by cavalcades of desperate parental childhood stories.]*	*You're a pussy.*
Mother: "Sweetie! What on *earth* could have put that thought into your head?"	*There is absolutely no evidence for your complaint. We must look for external sources for your insanity.*

Self-Pity

Script	Translation
Mother: [Bursts into tears!]	*If you ask me to have sympathy for you, I will forcibly extract sympathy from you. If you think this is a two-way street, I will run you over.*
Mother: "I'm sorry, I know that happened, I was so distraught, your father was never home, I was overwhelmed, I did the best I could in a difficult situation…"	*Only an unbelievably cold and selfish child could fail to dissolve into tears when considering **my** plight…*
Mother: "I've done everything for you! I've devoted my whole life to my kids – how can you *accuse* me of these things?"	*You owe me an endless debt of allegiance and obedience – it would be utterly evil to refuse to repay it, let alone criticize me!*
Mother/Father: "How many times do we have to apologize for this before you're satisfied?"	*You are using criticism as an unjust weapon to hold power over us and make us feel bad. You bastard.*

Denial

Script	Translation
Mother: "What nonsense – of *course* I listen to you!"	Your experience is utterly incorrect. You are attacking me unjustly. You're crushing my illusions! Dear god, whyyyyy?!?!
Mother: "You don't really mean that, do you? You can't possibly believe that!" [Tears.]	Your experience is utterly incorrect. You are attacking me unjustly!
Mother: "Nothing like that ever happened. I never did that."	Your experience is utterly incorrect. You are attacking me unjustly! I'm an eyewitness, too, and my testimony should at least balance yours!
Mother/Father: "No one else has a problem – only you. What does that tell you about the reality of the situation?"	You are attacking them unjustly. We are claiming to have no problems so that you will start doubting your own experiences and shut the hell up. Because no one else who was there will support your claims, you must have been seeing things.

Counter Attack

Script	Translation
Mother: "You kids were just so difficult. I know I lost my temper, and I'm sorry about that – but you kids just pushed me and pushed me, and never listened."	You were a bad kid, and forced me act "badly" on occasion. But it was still all your fault. I get so frustrated when people explicitly tell me to punish them and then complain when I do what they ask for.
Mother: "I never did that! Why are you saying this? Why are you making up these stories? Why are you trying to hurt me?"	I am completely insensitive to your real pain, but you'd better be totally sensitive to my imaginary pain!
Siblings: "Yes, bad things happened for sure, those were difficult times for all of us – but it was a long time ago, it's time for all of us to forgive, forget and move on."	I feel really anxious when you bring up the past, so I'm going to pretend that you're irrationally resentful, and that you're bringing up the past as a weapon in order to control us in the present.
Siblings: "Yeah, you've always had a hard time forgiving people. You can nurse a grudge until it grows a beard."	It is irrational to feel resentment about being badly treated in the past. You are just imagining all the pain that you suffered. Our parents were fine; **you** are the bad one.
Siblings: "Tell me – who is it in your life that you feel listens to you just the right amount – not too much, and not too little? What? No one does it exactly right? Well then, the only common denominator in all the problems you have with everyone is, well, you!"	The only reason that you could ever feel pain about the past is because you have impossible standards and can't ever be satisfied. Mom and dad were the victims of your irrational standards.
Father: "How many times do we have to apologize for this before you're satisfied, you selfish little…?"	I am going to get angry every time you bring this up, because since I have apologized angrily before, you should be satisfied now.

Genial Blankness

Script	Translation
Mother/Father: "I don't remember anything like that ever happening, but I can understand that it would be frustrating for you. Any time you ever want to talk about it, I'm here for you." [Followed by blanket denials if you ever bring the subject up again.]	We're very sorry that you had bad parents in the alternate universe that you inhabited as a child. We understand that you're insane, but we get understandably weary of it.
Mother/Father: "Your memory of that is different from mine. That's not how it was for me, but everyone is entitled to his opinion."	Your experience of your childhood is just an opinion, not reality. You are delusional, but we support you, because we are good parents.
Father: "I don't remember that ever happening. Are you sure you didn't dream that?"	It's a shame that you find it so hard to process reality. I am more than happy to sacrifice your sanity for the sake of retaining my own illusions.

Framing

Script	Translation
Siblings: [Rolls eyes.] "Oh, that's just how [your name] is – don't mind him. He's always got a bee in his bonnet about *something*."	Only an irrationally angry person could ever complain about our parents. Don't mind him. He's always upset and angry about unimportant things.
Mother/Father: "Oh we already know how you feel about *this* topic – don't start *that* again, we got it, you have a problem with the family…"	No matter how much we try to appease you, you always want us to grovel a little bit more, because you are addicted to shaming us.
Father: "What exactly do you want me to do with all your complaints?"	I will do my best to satisfy your insane little requirements, just to keep the peace. I have absolutely no idea what it is you're asking for, so you might want to get to the point.
Mother: "Is there anything I can do differently?" [When you give a list, you are attacked.]	I have always been very happy to accommodate your requirements – unless you actually give me your requirements, at which point I will attack you.

Aggressive Appeals to "Compassion"

Script	Translation
Father: "You should not bring this stuff up with your mother, because she is fragile."	We should be very gentle with fragile people – unless they are children, in which case we are allowed to attack them at will.
Mother: "Don't you know how much these topics hurt me? Don't you have any compassion for my feelings?"	Only *my* feelings are important in our relationship – your "feelings" only exist to serve my convenience.
Siblings: "Mom did the best she could. She had the best intentions, she just didn't have the knowledge. Things were different back then – there was no 'Oprah.'"	You are completely intolerant for criticizing mom – it's like getting mad at a houseplant for not knowing how to program a computer. The fact that she had irrational standards for us when we were children is completely irrelevant.
Siblings: "Mom and Dad are getting old now. We know they didn't always do the right thing, but they're not about to change now, so we have to make the best of things."	It requires real maturity – which you apparently do not possess – to accept people's inevitable limitations. We must forgive those who do wrong – especially those who never forgave *us* for doing wrong!

Aggressive Appeal to "Self-Respect"

Script	Translation
Siblings: "You have to give up your anger about the past, otherwise it just ends up controlling you forever."	Now that our parents no longer have total control over your environment, I'm going to try to convince you that they have total control over your happiness.
	Your feelings will overrun you if you continue to feel them. If you're strong, you'll crush them.
Siblings: "We could dwell on all this for the rest of our lives, but what good would it do? You've just got to accept things for how they were, and move on from there."	I am going to reject the pain that you feel, while preaching that it is moral to accept things for what they are.
Siblings: "Someone's got to be the bigger person in this relationship – clearly it's not going to be mom, so I guess it's up to you then, isn't it?"	The bigger person must always bow down to the smaller person – that's how we know how big he really is!
	Mom is a horribly weak person, so she can't treat family members as they hope to be treated. Surely you won't be as weak as she is!

The Conversation

Now, we are ready to put RTR into practice.

When you pick up the phone to call your mother and tell her the truth about your experience of her, an odd but insistent undertow will attempt to pull the conversation away from your real experience and towards endlessly-debatable "conclusions."

There is only one way to avoid this tendency, and that is *to continually talk about how you feel in the moment.*

Here is an example:

- Mom, I want to tell you something… [deep breath] I know that this will sound strange, because I've never talked about it before, but it's very important to me. For some time now – certainly months, and probably years – I have felt a kind of sinking sensation in my stomach when I see your name on the call display. I'm not saying that you're *causing* this feeling – I am just telling you what happens for me, and what triggers it. It might be my fault entirely, and I may be misinterpreting everything about our relationship, but I wanted to be honest about how I feel.

- Dear! I had no idea, I'm so sorry that this is happening for you – how strange! Why do you think you are feeling this way?
- I don't know. I do know that I haven't been enjoying our conversations as much as I would like to – for quite some time – but I'm not sure why that is.
- Well this is terrible! I had no idea you felt this way – why didn't you tell me something before?
- I didn't tell you before because I felt frightened to tell you – again, I don't know why, and I'm not blaming you – I'm just telling you what I felt.
- Afraid to tell me? Good heavens – why on earth would you feel that? [laughter] Am I really such an ogre?
- Again, I don't know *why* I feel what I feel – I just wanted to tell you the truth.
- Well! What do you think we should do about this?
- I don't really know – mostly because I don't know why I am feeling what I am feeling. [deep breath] I can tell you this, though – I do feel sadness now, when I hear you tell me that you had no idea that I wasn't enjoying our conversations very much.
- Well it's true! I had no idea you felt this way!
- And you were enjoying our conversations?
- Of course!
- And you thought that I was enjoying our conversations?
- Yes.
- Why did you think that?
- Well, I thought that it was just pleasant mother-daughter time. You know, where we chitchat about – I guess you could call them inconsequentialities, but – girly stuff. Nothing earthshaking, I know... But I guess I truly thought you were enjoying our chats. [sniff]
- Mom, it sounds like you're getting sad.
- I am...
- I feel a sudden sense of guilt overcoming me, because you're feeling sad.
- Oh, I'm not trying to make you feel guilty or anything – am I not allowed to feel sad when my daughter tells me she doesn't enjoy our relationship?

- I'm not trying to create any rules here – I'm just telling you the truth about my experience.
- Well I have no idea what I'm supposed to do with your – revelation. You hide this from me for years, and pretend to enjoy our interactions, and then you just drop this bombshell on me without any warning!
- Now I feel a certain amount of fear, because it seems to me that you're getting angry.
- No, I'm not *angry*, sweetie. I guess I'm just… surprised.
- I can certainly understand that this would be surprising to you – but now I'm feeling a little angry, because it appears to me that all we're doing is talking about *your* feelings, and managing *your* upset.
- Well you've certainly made it very clear how *you* feel!
- Now I'm feeling a little bit more angry, and I think it's because – though I'm not saying this is right – I've felt unhappy about our phone calls for years, but we're not talking about that – we're just talking about your reactions to what I feel.
- Oh, so we're supposed to have this totally honest relationship now, but I'm not allowed to talk about what *I* feel?
- Now, I'm feeling even more frightened and angry.
- Well perhaps you could have put just a little bit more effort into figuring out what you felt before dumping it all on me!
- Wow – oh wow, now I feel very scared, very sad, and very angry.
- And what do you expect *me* to do about that? They're *your* feelings, after all!
- That's true, of course – but every time you tell me something, I feel more and more scared, sad and angry.
- Oh, so now you're saying it's all *my* fault!
- No, I didn't say that – I am telling you that I feel bad *after* you tell me something – I don't know for sure that I feel bad *because* of what you say.

[pause]

- Are you seeing a psychiatrist? Is that where all this psychobabble is coming from?
- Now I feel confused, and disoriented – because it seems to me that you're just kind of "jumping out" of the conversation, and trying to put it in a kind of context that has nothing to do with how I feel.
- What are you talking about? I honestly don't understand a word that you're saying! Are you taking a new course or something? Is there some new Dr. Phil book out that I'm not aware of? It sounds like you're reading from some kind of script.
- Mom, now I feel confused and disoriented, because I don't know what any of this has to do with how I feel, and how I have felt for years. [deep breath] Can you tell me how *you're* feeling at the moment?
- Oh, you want to know how *I'm* feeling? Well that's nice. I am feeling that you just kind of "jumped" me with all this… psychologizing. It feels the way it has always felt with you when you get some new fad, some new idea, and just – spring it on other people without warning, with absolutely no consideration for their feelings!
- Now I am feeling frustrated, because I asked you about your feelings, and all you did was provide negative judgments.
- Well, you asked me how I felt, and so I told you! If you want us to have this fabulous, new, open relationship, I should be allowed to express my feelings too, right?
- It doesn't seem to me that when you say "I feel that you are inconsiderate," that you are really expressing a true emotion, but rather just an angry judgment.
- Oh, so now you are telling me what I *feel*? Is that where all this is going?
- Mom, I am feeling increasingly frustrated and upset as a result of this conversation – I'm not saying that it's all your fault, or that you're making me feel anything…
- Oh will you stop saying that! You sound like a robot! Stop trying to treat me like a child!

- I'm not trying to treat you like a child – I'm just telling you how I'm feeling.
- Oh, right – because it's all about how *you* feel! How your feelings affect other people – I'm sure that hasn't entered your mind *one little bit*!
- Mom, I'm going to stop talking to you right now, because I'm feeling overwhelmingly sad and upset. You might be right in everything that you're saying, that I'm inconsiderate and condescending and so on, but I can't evaluate that objectively right now, because I am feeling so upset.

[pause]

- Sweetie! I'm sorry that you feel judged – perhaps I was too hasty. I'm sorry if I'm reacting too strongly or inappropriately in some way. I just thought we had a good relationship, and now I find out that the whole thing has been a lie for heaven knows how long! Can you blame me for being upset? I guess it wouldn't hurt to be more open about our feelings – I thought I was doing that, but I guess I am wrong again…
- Now I am feeling confused, and also a little bit irritated.
- Well if I am only making you feel bad by opening my mouth, it makes sense for us to stop talking, since I am obviously deviating from your script in some manner.
- OK, mom.

The Principles at Work
Can you see the overall RTR approach in the above conversation?

Intimacy is not something that occurs in the abstract, or in a contained manner, or in some sort of mythological "story time" pseudo-interaction.

Intimacy occurs in *real-time*, in the moment, when you speak honestly about your true feelings in the presence of another.

In the above conversation, you talked to your mother openly and honestly about your feelings – you recognized that she would be surprised by your "sudden" honesty, and attempted to manage that transition.

You did not attempt to blame your mother, you did not attempt to "frame" the conversation, you did not inflict any conclusions on her – you merely tried to be honest in the moment about how you felt while talking to her.

You did not fall into the temptation of attacking her with a "conclusion," but stayed vulnerable and open about what was happening for you throughout the conversation.

Just about everyone will feel confused, frustrated, disoriented and aggressive when you continue to provide them with honest feedback about how you feel while interacting with them. In a very real way, they genuinely have no idea what to do with honesty in the moment, as they speak and interact with you.

When you provide people continual feedback about your feelings – especially in relation to their actions – they will most often attempt to project their own increasing frustrations onto you by willfully misunderstanding you, misinterpreting your motives, inventing your supposed "conclusions," accusing you of hypocrisy ("Oh, I'm not supposed to be honest about *my* feelings?"), "framing" the discussion, attacking you and so on.

The truth is that it is utter agony for most people to experience a Real-Time Relationship – particularly the first few times. They will do almost anything to avoid the radioactive pain of seeing themselves *in the moment* through your eyes.

There is nothing that you can do to manage or diminish the pain that other people feel in the presence of honesty – pain that is only increased by your unwillingness to blame them for your feelings.

When you express genuine curiosity about another person, it is agonizing for them because they have most likely *never experienced that before in their life*. The only time that most people receive "attention" is when somebody wants to hurt, control or manipulate them, or needs something from them. Thus they will inevitably react to your "attention" with fear and hostility – in order to protect their delusions about the virtue of those who raised them, and those around them.

In the above conversation, you will notice that I do not suggest trying to probe your mother's feelings. You cannot control the degree of honesty that someone else is willing to bring to any interaction. You can certainly ask others how they feel, but if they respond with manipulative or bullying defenses you cannot reasonably call them dishonest – you can only tell them how you feel as a result of their responses.

What you also may not have noticed in the above conversation is that your mother never actually tells you that you are wrong. Your mother certainly implied that you were inconsiderate, hypocritical and so on – but she never told you that you were wrong about what you felt.

This is one of the greatest strengths of the RTR – if you avoid inflicting "conclusions," no one can reasonably tell you that your feelings are wrong.

This is why the RTR exposes all of the manipulations, bullying and condescension of those around you. When you tell people honestly how you feel – without inflicting story-time conclusions – it arouses all of their defenses. If you continue to stick to the truth about how you feel, you will actually see all of their defenses, parading in quick sequence. This is, of course, both horrifying and revealing.

What Next?

What happens after the above conversation?

Without a doubt, you have tossed a hand grenade into the bunker of your mother's defenses.

Initially, her defenses will be surprised, and thus will be relatively crude, openly manipulative and obviously upsetting.

After you hang up, however, she will have a chance to sit and brood, and really embellish the mythology that she feels driven to inflict upon you in order to rescue her own self-serving illusions.

Your mother may be the kind of person who just grimly or breezily ignores discomfort, and so may say nothing about the above interaction the next time you talk.

How do you respond to that?

Why, with *honesty*. "Mom, I feel baffled and hurt, and I think it might be because…"

Alternatively, you may get a call back in half an hour – or a day or two later – after your mother has had the time to prepare a truly wonderful and moving story about what "happened." Most likely, she will take on a false kind of "responsibility" for what went wrong in your interaction – still, however, you will end up being blamed for upsetting the apple cart.

What do you do?

Why, you listen to your instincts, and speak the truth of course!

When your mother's name lights up your call display again, you will undoubtedly feel a much *stronger* sinking sensation than you did before your last conversation.

If you do end up picking up the phone – which is a decision that only you can make – then you continue right where you left off, talking about your feelings in the moment.

"Mom, when I saw your name on my call display just now, I felt even *more* of a sinking sensation than I did in the past. I know that has something to do with the interaction we just had, but I'm not sure exactly how."

And then, when your mother goes off on some mythology junket about what happened, you do not argue with her storytelling – any more than you would argue with Tolkien about whether orcs live in Isengard – but simply tell her how you *feel* about what she is saying.

Then when she starts manipulating you again, you simply continue to tell her how you feel about what she is saying.

The Endgame
Continuing this process will inevitably lead to one of two outcomes.

If, in conversation after conversation, your mother continually refuses to listen to how you feel, and endlessly manipulates you in order to manage her own anxiety – at some point, you will achieve *closure*.

In other words, you will understand in your very core the simple and tragic fact that there is no point fishing in this lake anymore, because there are no fish left in the lake.

This means that your mother is simply a mythology robot, with no capacity whatsoever to interact with you in an honest and vulnerable manner.

Fundamentally, she does not exist.

Dead Souls
In the Christian mythology, every person possesses a soul, fashioned in the image of God, which cannot be corrupted.

Thus the hope always exists that even the most evil people can achieve salvation, since they possess an immortal sliver of pure virtue within them at all times.

In the real world, nothing could be further from the truth.

The idea that our personalities possess some sort of Platonic "perfect form" that can survive every kind of abuse and corruption is a deadly myth.

If I smoke for 40 years and contract virulent lung cancer, and I am on my deathbed, what would it mean to say that somewhere within my body there still exist "perfectly healthy lungs"?

No, the reality of the situation is that my lungs are irreversibly diseased. No "magical perfect healthy lungs" exist anywhere in my body, or in any sense whatsoever.

In China, when foot-binding was a common practice, the feet of little girls would be gruesomely tortured so that they ended up "curling under" themselves, the toes burrowing into the heels.

When this process was complete, there was no such thing as "perfectly healthy feet" that floated around these women like some sort of odor. Their feet had been irreversibly mutilated and would never recover or regain their original shape.

The armies and police that are supposedly designed to "protect" citizens always end up preying upon them. When a policeman ends up as a concentration camp guard, no "virtuous policeman" clings to his shadow on the ground – he has become evil and cannot recover.

The same is true of our personalities.

There does come a time when, if we continue to act in a corrupt or abusive manner, our defenses overwhelm and extinguish the very personality that they were originally designed to protect.

When this occurs, we no longer have any access to a healthy and happy "true self." It dies, as surely as our lungs die when we have lung cancer.

When we finally understand this about our mother – or whoever we are interacting with – we feel an enormous, bottomless sorrow. This sadness is called "closure," which is the feeling that a surgeon experiences when his patient flatlines beyond recovery.

It is the knowledge that salvation is no longer possible – that no real relationship will ever occur, that we will never be seen or empathized with, that the only thing at the other end of the phone is an empty dungeon of dead ghosts.

When this knowledge comes to us, we shudder in primeval horror – and we also involuntarily raise our eyes to the light and bless the fortune that can help us avoid such a living death.

On the Other Hand...

The possibility always exists, however, that through continually and honestly speaking the truth about our own experiences, we will be able to break through the defenses of those around us.

In this case, relationships can be rescued, intimacy can begin and disaster can be averted.

It is highly unlikely – dare I say impossible? – that this can ever be achieved with anyone in your immediate family who has ever been consistently cruel to you.

Your beautiful world awaits – but not forever...

During this process, you will be constantly tempted to withdraw from your new honesty. This desire will not primarily come from you, but rather from those around you who do not wish to see their own disease.

There is nothing that compels you to continue, of course, except the truth.

I strongly suggest that you avoid getting stuck in the "null zone," where you have begun the process of speaking the truth – thus shattering your empty compliance – but then give up being honest before the process is completed, and you have gained either new possibilities or final closure.

Keep speaking the truth, no matter how hard it gets, because you deserve so much better – and the beautiful new world that awaits you will not wait forever.

CONCLUSION

In many ways, this is the most ambitious work that I have ever attempted.

Philosophy is so often discussed in the abstract – in terms of metaphysics, epistemology or ethics – that at times it can seem to have as much relevance to real life as quantum physics does to hitting a baseball.

I truly believe that philosophy will liberate the world, if we humbly submit to and act upon the tenets of truth.

Politics will not free us; art will not free us; by God "culture" will not free us; literature will not free us – only a steadfast examination of and commitment to the truth can break our chains.

I have not tried to pretend that freedom can be won without cost. Realizing the true extent of what it will cost us to become free is both disheartening and encouraging.

It is encouraging because if living the truth requires a near-superhuman effort, then we can be more at peace about the world's lack of freedom.

The higher the bar, the better our chances – because if freedom were easy but had never been achieved, then it would very likely be impossible.

We do not have to be free any more than we have to eat, breathe, or exercise.

Philosophy does not command us to act with integrity, any more than nutrition commands us to eat well.

Philosophy simply reveals the truth to us – and, in combination with psychology, outlines the likely results of living a lie – but it does not command us to be honest.

Philosophy mentors; it does not bully.

Thus you should feel perfectly free to follow or reject the suggestions contained in this book.

You can lie or speak the truth. You can live with integrity, or mislead others at will. You can disbelieve in the existence of your conscience and hope against hope that your dishonest actions are not even recorded by your own soul.

I am telling you, though, that only the mad forget what they have done.

Pretending that you do not speak English does not prevent you from understanding English.

Pretending that you have told the truth does not prevent you from remembering your lies.

Pretending that you deserve love when you have not earned it does not prevent you from hating yourself.

Pretending that you "love" a woman when you merely want to have sex with her will not prevent the problems that will result.

Rejecting the research on the dangers of smoking does not make you immune to lung cancer.

Thus I urge you to really try on the suggestions in this book. It has nothing to do with obedience to me, to philosophy, to ethics – since virtue requires independent thought, which mere obedience can never generate; any more than "painting by numbers" can generate original art.

We should be honest and courageous and honourable and strong, because those actions – and those actions alone – will inevitably result in self-respect, rational pride – and the capacity to truly love, and be loved.

The joy that lies at the heart of virtue has been clouded by pious falsehoods about *what is good*.

REAL-TIME RELATIONSHIPS

The deep pleasures that arise from living with integrity must be experienced. They can barely be described to those who have yet to feel them. Real virtue brings joy to your immediate personal relationships, to be sure, but it also spreads aloft, lighting the world, like rising sunlight over a darkened plain, far beyond the mere walls of your experience.

When we light our candles, we **ignite the *sun!***

Strike this match.

For yourself, for your future…

And for the world.

Made in the USA
Columbia, SC
30 January 2025